The Gender of Breadwinners
Women, Men, and Change in
Two Industrial Towns, 1880–1950

This is a story of two Ontario towns, Hanover and Paris, that grew in many parallel ways. They were about the same size, and both were primarily one-industry towns. But Hanover was a furniture-manufacturing centre; most of its workers were men, drawn from a community of ethnic German artisans and agriculturalists. In Paris the biggest employer was the textile industry; most of its wage earners were women, assisted in emigration from England by their Canadian employer.

Joy Parr considers the impact of these fundamental differences from a feminist perspective in her study of the towns' industrial, domestic, and community life. She combines interviews of women and men of the towns with analyses of a wide range of documents: records of the firms for which their families worked, newspapers, tax records, paintings, photographs, and government documents.

Two surprising and contrasting narratives emerge. The effects of gender identities upon both women's and men's workplace experience and of economic roles upon familial relationships are starkly apparent.

Extending through seventy crucial years, these closely textured case studies challenge conventional views about the distinctiveness of gender and class roles. They reconfigure the social and economic change accompanying the rise of industry. They insistently transcend the reflexive dichotomies drawn between women and men, public and private, wage and non-wage work. They investigate industrial structure, technological change, domesticity, militance, and perceptions of personal power and worth, simultaneously as products of gender and class identities, recast through community sensibilities.

JOY PARR is Professor of History at Queen's University. Among her other books are *Childhood and Family in Canadian History*; *Labouring Children: British Child Immigrants to Canada, 1868–1924*; and, with Beth Light, *Canadian Women on the Move, 1867–1920*. She is the winner of the 1988 Berkshire Prize for the best article in women's history.

JOY PARR

The Gender of Breadwinners

Women, Men, and Change in
Two Industrial Towns
1880–1950

UNIVERSITY OF TORONTO PRESS
Toronto Buffalo London

© University of Toronto Press 1990
Toronto   Buffalo   London
Printed in Canada

ISBN 0-8020-5853-1 (cloth)
ISBN 0-8020-6760-3 (paper)

Printed on acid-free paper

Canadian Cataloguing in Publication Data

Parr, Joy, 1949–
  The gender of breadwinners

  Includes bibliographical references.
  ISBN 0-8020-5853-1 (bound). – ISBN 0-8020-6760-3 (pbk.)

  1. Sexual division of labour – Ontario – Paris –
  History. 2. Sexual division of labor – Ontario –
  Hanover – History. 3. Work and family – Ontario –
  Paris. 4. Work and family – Ontario – Hanover.
  5. Penmans (Firm) – Employees. 6. Knechtel (Firm) –
  Employees. 7. Paris (Ont.) – Social conditions.
  8. Hanover (Ont.) – Social conditions. I. Title.

  HD6060.65.C32057 1990   306.361509713   c90-093236-8

Parts of chapter 1 appeared previously in 'The Skilled Emigrant and Her Kin,'
Canadian Historical Review 68:4 (Dec. 1987) 529–51. Parts of chapter 3
appeared previously in 'Disaggregating the Sexual Division of Labour,'
Comparative Studies in Society and History 30 (July 1988) 511–33. Parts of
chapter 4 appeared previously in 'Rethinking Work and Kinship in a
Canadian Hosiery Town, 1910–1950,' *Feminist Studies* 13:1 (Spring 1987)
137–62.

This book has been published with the help of a grant from the Social Science
Federation of Canada, using funds provided by the Social Sciences and
Humanities Research Council of Canada.

To Mary Johnston of Waterloo, Ontario, and Fred Bemrose
of Paris, Ontario, with thanks

■ Contents

▪ Illustrations

MAP

FIGURES

■ Acknowledgments

In the summer of 1983, the effects of industrial change upon town life were pressing concerns in the central Canadian communities of Hanover and Paris. Knechtel, the leading furniture manufacturer in Hanover, had just been forced into bankruptcy. Penmans was beginning to transfer its knitting and garment-making operations to a new plant in nearby Cambridge, and it was clear that within the year its Paris mills would be closed. I am grateful that in this troubled time town residents welcomed me and, as they were contemplating the effects of plant closings, agreed to help investigate the origins and influences of industrialization in their communities. Frank Boone, of Penmans, allowed me to consult the historical records of the firm in Paris, and Jim Neilson and Betty Plumstead arranged work space in the mill. Mr Neilson, Gordon Parsons, and Fred Bemrose guided me through the archives and took time over many months to interpret the documents they contained. To the knitters and mechanics who gave me a beginner's competence with their machines I am especially indebted. Greg Rumble of Clarkson Gordon granted access to the Knechtel document vaults, and Harold Magwood guided me through this splendid collection. After fire and water damage threatened the records, Peter T. Knechtel consented to their removal to safer quarters and Mrs A.M. MacDermaid, Queen's University archivist, agreed to take on the considerable task of retrieving, restoring, and preserving the Knechtel papers. We are grateful to Mark Knechtel, Glen Crockford, and Mr Magwood for their help during this painful transition. The members of Local 486 of the International Woodworkers of America in Hanover and the Paris Historical Society in Paris took on my project as their own, locating additional local documents and arranging interviews with town residents. This book would not have been possible without the generous collaboration of the many women and men of Paris and Hanover who opened their homes and with patience and tolerance helped me to understand something about their lives and work.

The technological history of the knit-goods industry was researched with guidance from Ian Keill and Joyce Ellis of the University of Loughborough, the staff of the Hosiery and Allied Trades Research Association in Nottingham, Stanley Chapman of the University of Nottingham, Peta Lewis of the Ruddington Framework Knitters Trust, John Millington, publisher of *Knitwear International* in Leicester, and Patricia Young and Catherine Cooper Cole, of the Textile Resources Group, Parks Canada. The late Adrian Knechtel, Bruce McPherson of Gibbard's, Napanee, Christine Grant of the Canadian Museum of Civilization, Ottawa, John McIntyre, Elizabeth Ingolfsrud, and Carl Schaefer all shared their knowledge of the Ontario furniture industry. I am particularly grateful to Mr Schaefer for allowing his painting, 'Summer Evening in Town, Hanover,' to be reproduced here.

Elizabeth and Gerald Bloomfield, Harriet Bradley, Peter Girard, Margaret Anne Knowles, Jane Lewis, Sonya Rose, and Donald A. Smith shared their own research, and Robert Hopwood and Dan Moore directed me towards sources I would not have located without their help. I am grateful to Carol Ferguson, Brenda Hurd Gadbois, Ross Hough, George Innis, Greg Levine, Helen McEwen, and Isobel Parr for both technical and interpretive assistance with the project and to Val Bjarnason, Madeleine Parent, and Helen McMaster Paulin for their insights concerning the post-war labour movement. The study was begun while I was a visitor at the Centre for Urban and Community Studies at the University of Toronto in 1983–4 and written during my year as visiting scholar at University College, University of Toronto, in 1987–8. Larry Bourne at the centre and Bruce Kidd at University College arranged for these stimulating sojourns, and I am especially indebted to Professor Kidd for lending me both his office and his wide knowledge of the literature on the history of gender. The research was funded principally by the Social Sciences and Humanities Research Council of Canada, through its Women and Work Strategic Grants Programme, with timely supplementary assistance from Labour Canada and the Queen's University Advisory Research Council.

Pat Armstrong, Connie Backhouse, Ava Baron, Hal Benenson, Val

Bjarnason, Roberta Hamilton, Douglas Hay, Craig Heron, Elizabeth Ingolfsrud, Alice Kessler-Harris, Greg Levine, Meg Luxton, Shula Marks and her colleagues at the Institute of Commonwealth Studies, Laurel Sefton MacDowell, Ruth Milkman, Des Morton, Laurie Nisonoff, Helen McMaster Paulin, and Joan Sangster provided commentaries on parts of the script. Marjorie Griffin Cohen, Paul Craven, and Veronica Strong-Boag took considerable time from their own work to write detailed critiques of the penultimate draft. The book is much improved by their help. Gerry Hallowell, Catherine Frost, and Laura Macleod of University of Toronto Press gave me excellent and prompt advice along the path to publication.

Throughout this work I have been supported by my colleagues in women's studies at Queen's University and my head of department, Professor J.M. Stayer. Over these years Suzann Buckley, Roberta Hamilton, Jane Lewis, and Greg Levine have challenged me by their conversation and heartened me by their laughter. This book is dedicated to Mary Johnston, an unforgettable teacher, who, through the local history of the Germans of Waterloo County, skilfully introduced a generation of young people to the historian's craft, and to Fred Bemrose, the curator of the Paris Historical Society, a fitting representative of the hundreds of tireless and careful local volunteers who both enrich their own communities and, by the by, make the professional historian's work possible.

Kingston, July 1989

The Gender of Breadwinners

■ Introduction

Historically both women and men have worked for wages. In getting and spending, in the practices of the market, they have found means to sustain life and to give life meaning. Similarly both men and women have acquired goods and services their households needed and worth and well-being for themselves and their families in activities beyond the market, both inside and outside the home. Securing a subsistence and managing the complexities of social and economic existence have required deft balancing of these different kinds of activities. As the gender balance in the labour force has varied with time and place, so too have the reasons why women and men have moved between paid and unpaid work. Who would work for pay and who for love, and how many would share in the fruits of that labour, has depended upon transformations in the wider world, but also upon the age and sex, the needs and predilections of others in the household and in the community of which it was a part.

This book is a reconsideration of the social and economic change that accompanied industrialization. Its founding premise is specific: the history of the rise of industry is not comprehensible through the story of the accumulation of capital and the recruitment of labour alone. The industrial transformation must be charted as more than, less than, and also different from the conventional history of class relations. The spatial and temporal compass of this book is also specific. However, the problems, processes, and interpretive possibilities that arise here concerning gender, class, power, and community are part of a vibrant and vigorous international conversation in which many different and contending voices lately have been heard.

On one level this is a work of local history. It compares and contrasts two central Canadian manufacturing communities, Paris, a knit-goods manufacturing centre in which the majority of the labour force was female, and Hanover, a furniture manufacturing town in which most wage earners were male. Both are small towns, rising in population from roughly 1,000 to 4,000 during the seven decades 1880–1950. In the 'men's town' and the 'women's town' factory-based industry began in the mid-1860s, was most prosperous in the first three decades of this century, and by the Second World War was moving through hesitant maturity into decline. While I was working in Paris and Hanover between the summer of 1982 and the end of 1985 each lost its principal employer.

The knit-goods and furniture industries were as different in their structure as in the gender composition of their work forces. The dominant firm in Paris, Penmans Limited, was not only the largest employer in town. It was the largest knit-goods manufacturer in the country, the leader in an oligopolistic industry with impeccable ties through its Montreal shareholders to successive federal governments. By contrast, the furniture industry was composed of many small producers, who, despite attempts at co-operation, more usually practised what economists call 'perfect' and industry analysts called 'predatory' competition. The largest and oldest woodworking firm in Hanover, Knechtel Furniture Company, was only one of several furniture manufacturers in town.

The towns differed ethnically. The mill families of Paris had been recruited, largely through assisted passage schemes, in the English east midlands between 1906 and 1928. Hanover's furniture workers were typically second- or third-generation German Canadians.

Paris was surrounded by a prosperous agricultural district. Its industries did not depend upon the nearby countryside for capital, labour, or raw materials. Its mills and its mill workers were both economically and culturally separate from the rural community outside the town limits. In Hanover local stands of hardwood and the woodworking skills of rural men had provided the foundation for the furniture industry. Over time the ties of kinship between the town and its hinterland remained strong; farmers and farmers' sons took up factory work in Hanover as the agricultural prosperity of the district declined. Through the inter-war years a farm-labour alliance elected Agnes Macphail, the first female Canadian member of parliament, to represent the common purposes of agriculturalists and factory workers, first in the federal and then in the provincial house.

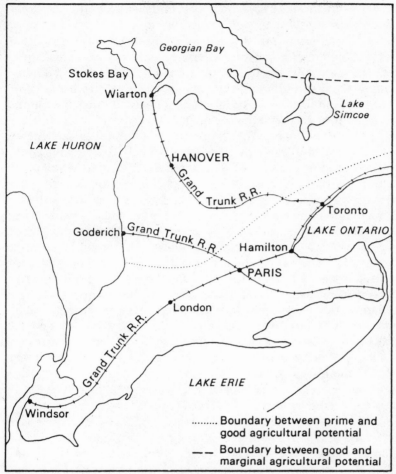

Source: Ontario Resource Atlas, Department of Lands and Forests, 1963

Location of Paris and Hanover

Hanover was laid out in a square grid on level ground. The streets were lined with substantial, well-tended family homes. The dwellings of the factory owners and the town's merchants were more ample than those of their neighbours but were intermingled with plainer residences along the straight and shaded summer streets. The town's churches were modest and soundly built, like the public buildings of Hanover, eschewing the grandiose for prudent functionality. By 1950 the municipality had both sewerage and a secure source of clean water.

Paris, by contrast, was a community of separate precincts, in their different physical locations along the heights and flats where the Grand and Nith rivers joined, a metaphor for the social hierarchy of the town. The families who had settled at the Forks of the Grand in the 1820s and 1830s had prospered as landowners and millers, building splendid mansions overlooking the river, which in their distinctive cobblestone walls and elegant pillars evoked the districts in New York and the south from whence their owners had come. The manufacturers who succeeded them as the town's elite added to the stock of grand housing in the district called Quality Hill and subscribed to the imposing churches that secured commanding corner sites just back from the commercial district. Below them on the flats, which flooded too regularly in spring, and up behind the freightyards at the junction of the two rail lines that passed through town, were the small cottages and row houses where mill families lived. With most adults from each household at work full time in the mill, there was not time for elaborate gardening, and Gordon Madden, the local night-soil collector, continued in 1950 to follow a regular route past the privies in the back lanes.

Paris and Hanover were still rural villages in 1880. By 1910 they were thriving industrial towns. Forty years later, in 1950, they were mature manufacturing communities, each having resolved in its separate way the dilemmas posed by life in and around the factory and the mill. Although by 1950 class division had become a central feature of community life in Hanover, it was in Paris where the social distinctions of industrial life were more sharply arrayed.

This book is an attempt, through two parallel narratives, to locate and understand the relationships among industry, domesticity, and community in Hanover and Paris over the seventy years following the rise of factory industry. It is a reconsideration of elements of neo-classical and Marxian analysis of this transformation, from the perspective of feminist theory, particularly the recent post-structural critiques of the categoricalism within which the study of class and gender relations in industrial society has been framed.

Writers beginning from the premises of neo-classical economic theory have given pride of place to the 'invisible hand' of the market as the instrument by which capital and labour have been brought together. The ways in which markets have differed in their characteristics, and capitalists and workers in their individual and collective qualities, have provoked sustained interest, but always central in the appraising and assigning of value has been the market's hand.

Marxian analysis also takes capital and labour as its central concepts but more explicitly and strenuously contends that the changing historical relationship between those who own and those who do not own shapes social existence generally, not through a benign weighing and directing instrument, but in the exercise of power, both lodged and contested in the ownership of the means of production and control over surplus. All historical actors in the industrial world are in these ways of seeing known by their class, sometimes rendered by proxy as race, nationality, or sex, but never fundamentally displaced.

Feminist scholars have appraised such histories of industrial change and found them wanting. They have noted the ancient and enduring patriarchal relationships that subordinate women to men, the antecedence of patriarchy to the rise of capitalism, and the salient feature of capitalism as a system run by and mainly to benefit some men. In these formulations, gender relations, the baroque and changing social elaborations that have attached to the biological difference between males and females, and the articulation of gender identities in a hierarchical sex-gender system have been accorded precedence. Power, in the radical feminist framework, is anchored in the possibility of male violence, directed by attachments and energies formed in intimate life.

Each of these ways of interpretively ordering modern life *begins* with an assumption about precedence, an implicit or explicit declaration of priority framed in our own contemporary politics. When dealing with class and gender, race and national identity, the 'tendency in social theory has been to pick one basis of interest and regard the rest as secondary.'[1] In historical cultural studies as well, 'relentlessly subordinating any combination of these factors to an ahistorical master category,' choosing the identity to be 'at all times more important than other constitutive categories'[2] has been an honourable and honoured practice.

Socialist feminists have preferred rather to think in terms of dual systems, and to analyse the history of industrial change as 'a long process of interaction between patriarchy and capitalism.'[3] From this perspective the origins and perpetuation of the sexual division of labour and the features of domestic labour have become subjects of serious study. Technological change, the labour process, the consolidation of the breadwinner wage form, and the formulation of social welfare policy have been analysed as sites where both the capitalist and patriarchal system, both class and gender relationships, were formative. But the actual workings of this interaction have remained elusive.

Often capitalism and patriarchy have been conceptualized as relatively autonomous, each system the outcome of an analytically distinct set of processes, each set built from separate constituting components. Sometimes capitalism is described as material and patriarchy as ideological in its foundation, class identity being forged at the point of production and gender relationships in the psychological processes that create cathexis and desire.[4] Any systemic approach that assumes that 'everything falls into one category or another, but cannot belong to more than one category at the same time' belies the wholeness of consciousness and experience. Life as we live it is not subdivided sequentially.[5] We exist simultaneously, rather than sequentially, in the social relations of class and gender. As Nancy Adamson, Linda Briskin, and Margaret McPhail lately have argued, considering the relations of power inherent in class, race, gender, and sexual orientation: 'The relative strength and import of these relations to groups, individuals, and political practice is determined within the context of particular historical conjunctures. This means that the prioritizing of issues, a necessity to successful political struggle, must not occur on the basis of abstract principle ..., but rather in relation to material, economic, political, and ideological conditions.'[6]

The challenge now plainly is to think beyond this history of fixed dualisms and its accompanying assertion of an ahistorical hierarchy of oppressions. We need to problematize and unmake the chain of binary oppositions – masculine/feminine, market/non-market, public/private, waged/non-waged – and rethink the categoricalism that cantonizes gender, class, race, ethnicity, and nationality, so as to see past the conceptual signage, which has illuminated the previously invisible but now threatens to obstruct our view of the living space beyond.

The two cases here are developed in rough parallelism. Each presentation begins with a chapter on labour recruitment and ethnic composition. The next chapter in each part deals with gender and policy, both the formulation of management strategies at the level of the firm, and the arguments for national policy tariff protection for the industry as a whole. The third chapter in each section is a study of the sexual division of labour in the town's industry. The fourth analyses the relationships among wage work, domestic labour divisions, and family and community values. The last chapter in each narrative treats the history of labour organization in each town.

These two ruminations – sometimes shared, sometimes solitary, sometimes diverging, sometimes converging in their relationship to a common theme – are an attempt to make space for a series of questions about the categories in which the analysis of gender and class has been lodged. The questions are like those lately raised by Mary Poovey in her research into 'the ideological work of gender in mid-Victorian England,' by Joan Scott and Denise Riley in their work on the politics of gender categories, and by R.W. Connell in his studies of social practice, gender, and power.[7] They entertain the possibility that the meanings of these galloping pairs – class/gender, male/female, market/non-market, public/ private – behind which our thinking has trailed, are moot; that these meanings are not fixed, but, as Connell suggests, are multiple and mutable.

We come from a long tradition in the west which finds meaning by specifying difference, and clarity by concentrating and amplifying presence and absence. We subordinate continuity and diversity so as to feature our world as a series of fixed oppositions, depending upon the differences between each part of each pair as our way to know the other. Thus, as Poovey suggests, 'the epistemological term *woman*' is seen to 'guarantee men's identity only if difference' is 'fixed – only if, that is, the binary opposition between the sexes' is made 'more important than any other kinds of difference.'[8] But fixed oppositions are established contrasts, which distil diversity to dualism rather than inherent antitheses.[9] By the urgency with which we seek out binary oppositions, so as to know private by what is not public, class by what is not gender, manliness by what is not womanliness, we lose sight of 'the multiple determinants'[10] that constitute any individual's social position and access to power and also of the ways in which social identities are simultaneously formed from a multiplicity of elements.

And so we must turn our attention from these categories themselves, to question their naturalness or universality, by focusing upon the processes by which their meanings have been made. We need to acknowledge that social identities and conceptions of common predicament and purpose are forged in particular spatial and temporal settings,[11] and both these understandings and the processes and elements from which they are formed are themselves changeable rather than fixed.

Gender and class relationships are considered here as part of the same social existence. It has not been possible to separate social institutions into those made by and to serve class or gender interests. In these narratives claims lodged in gender relations intrude to reorder and subvert 'the logic of the market' and reconfigure the pursuit of profit. Workplace roles reconstrue manliness and womanliness, remaking the boundaries between family and community, making contingent the authority gender might bequeath. The assumption of uniformity within the categories of gender and class proves difficult to sustain. It is not true that women are made in gender and men in the wider culture of their age. Both women and men are gendered subjects, but there are many ways of being in gender within a single time and space. The entitlements of the single fellow and the family man emerge as distinctively as those of man and woman, the behaviours of husbands and single girls as starkly different between the two communities.

The mainstream ideologies about class and gender roles are here to see, but the location from which these prescriptions were viewed begins to take on salient importance. A considerable distance might exist between what was normative and what was common practice in any particular time or place. This distance might create tension, bemusement, or pain, or a collective parodic habit of mind. For the men of Hanover in the early 1920s the ideology of the breadwinner wage as promulgated by mainstream unionists seemed a code of cowardliness and complicity. But retrospectively they used the breadwinning metaphor to encapsulate their family values and justify their domestic divisions of labour. In Paris respectable motherhood became the foundation upon which workplace militance was grounded, yet the ideology of maternal nature frequently must have seemed less a description of the lives of female mill workers in the town than a judgment or a reproach.[12]

Through time and space, the processes by which class and gender identities are formed, and the elements from which these processes are constituted, change. By time and place, the parts and proportions of the social landscape covered by class and gender relationships alter. There are conjunctures when gender identities are lodged firmly in the foreground, plainly precedent among the ways men and women understand themselves, give meaning to their experience, claim rights to goods and authority to act; when class identities are distant and shrouded elements in the composition. There are times when the relative positions of class and gender relationships are reversed, times when racial, ethnic, or national identities assume greater prominence with respect to both gender and class. The character and precedence of class and gender identities are a matter of history, not universals but specificities, which by their particularities present pressing questions for research.

This being the case, let us not apologize for looking closely and reading in detail. As Virginia Woolf urged, 'Let us not take it for granted that life exists more fully in what is commonly thought big than in what is commonly thought small.'[13]

PART ONE

■ Chapter One

Gender, culture, and labour recruitment

The notable character of Paris as a 'women's town' had begun to emerge by the 1880s. John Penman, a first-generation Scottish-American, arrived in Paris in 1868, attracted by its several fine mill sites and good rail connections and intending to expand the knitting enterprises he and his father lately had begun in nearby Woodstock. Three years later Penman was employing fifty-five women and twenty men in his mill; probably another sixty-some workers were on the payroll at Adams and Hackland, a second knitting firm in town.[1]

Although there were several other industrial employers in the community in the first years after Confederation, and in 1871 only one in twenty Paris residents worked in the knitting mills, after tariffs of 25 and 30 per cent were established on knit goods from abroad in 1879, knitting quickly came to dominate the town's industry, and John Penman became pre-eminent among local industrialists. By 1883 there were three knitting firms in Paris and 750 knit-goods employees, 440 of them women. One in four Paris residents now worked in the knitting mills. Through the next decade Penman gained control of the best mill sites and water rights in town and through additional purchases consolidated his title to the limited level land along the banks of both the Nith and the Grand rivers. By the early twentieth century Penmans employed 1,000 workers in a community whose total population numbered only 3,500.[2]

In the 1880s most of the female factory workers of Paris were single women living with their parents in town. Unlike the first generation of New England mill girls, who came to textile work from modestly prosperous farm families seeking a measure of personal autonomy and economic independence,[3] these young women went to work in the mill to help support their needy families. One in four lived with a widowed mother; half were the daughters of fathers who were out of work or employed in unskilled occupations.[4]

In the countryside around Paris the appeal of mill work was considerably more limited. The farmers of Brant County, and of South Dumfries Township in particular, prospered in the late nineteenth century. While the agricultural districts a hundred miles to the north in Grey and Bruce counties began to feel the effects of falling grain prices and western competition, the longer-settled southern tier of farm communities rose from strength to strength. Brant was close to growing urban markets and cross-cut by railway lines competing to carry food and fodder as well as manufactured goods to the cities. Between 1882 and 1888 the value of farm property per acre in the county was the second highest in the province, and the proportion of land under cultivation amply exceeded the Ontario average.[5]

The young women who came from South Dumfries into Penmans mills were not from these flourishing farms. They were the daughters of widows or rural non-farm households, increasingly under pressure as mechanization reduced the demand for seasonal farm labour. They were part of the small rural minority who in household structure or class most closely resembled the mill families already in Paris.[6] They came, not alone, but with their families, rural smallholders and the landless quitting the countryside for the towns. While daughters raised on prosperous farms left home, with their parents' blessing, to take up teaching or white-collar city jobs, mill work was a less attractive alternative, assumed by the smaller number of local girls faced with more pressing family needs.

Through the 1880s, the Penmans firm was expanding, but the population of Paris was not. In fact there were fewer people living in town in 1891 than there had been a decade before. Penman controlled and chose to leave undeveloped the remaining mill sites along the Nith and the Grand. In this way he removed the risk that other large employers might locate in town. Paradoxically, firms that might hire men, particularly the male kin of his own female mill workers, posed the greatest threat. Good jobs for men locally would remove the pressing economic incentive for town women to go into the mill. But a strategy of restricting competing employers also limited growth in the town's population generally.

To compensate, Penman began explicitly to recruit female employees further afield, a common practice among textile manufacturers. In Quebec, Japan, and the American South, mill owners depended upon daughters from impoverished agricultural districts. Whole families in Quebec and the u.s. south accepted incentives to work away from the farm in the mills in order to raise cash with which to return to the land. The fathers of Japanese textile workers, and New England mill girls themselves, agreed to construe the workrooms and factory villages as acceptable situations in which young women might pass their years before marriage.[7] Crafting a female labour force, in the presence of contemporary beliefs about the differences between women and men, entailed ideological and economic negotiations over the meaning of gender, unnecessary among employers recruiting men.

Through the 1880s and 1890s Penman's advertisements for help appeared in small-town newspapers across Canada, and increasingly he began to rely upon immigrants as hands. Significantly, between 1881 and 1891 the proportion of foreign born among the female factory operatives of Paris rose from 14 to 26 per cent.[8] The first English hosiery workers arrived in the 1870s, soon after the Penmans partnership began factory production.[9] Then as Penmans grew after a major financial reorganization in 1906, the labour shortage in Paris became acute. To overcome this problem, between 1907 and 1928 the firm assisted 700 British hosiery workers, principally women from the east midlands, to emigrate to the town.

By the early twentieth century they became the mainstay of the factory labour force in the town, the resolution to both the economic and the cultural impediments that Penman had faced when recruiting mill workers locally. Their midlands accents and confident strides and their undeferential domination of the streets in the minutes before and after the mill whistle blew gave pause to the Canadian-born residents of Paris. With their arrival the stricter parsing of the distinction between mill families and non-mill families in the town began.

These women emigrated when preference or circumstances led them to lives without men. They had come to a place where their futures in the work force were much more certain than their prospects as wives. After their arrival a different set of relationships among gender solidarities, wage work, and family forms grew increasingly apparent in town. But as women, for some years with neither political authority through the franchise nor strong unions eager to represent their interests, and always without time after a long double day or the authority accorded male household heads, their ways of living became increasingly common but always problematical in their relationship to the norms of social life generally held within the community.

During this period there was considerable British emigration to Canada. Although government advertising was directed towards agriculturalists and domestic servants, and the Canadian Manufacturers' Association more frequently sought out male industrial workers for its members, the recruitment of female factory operatives did occur. The British Women's Emigration Association sponsored a factory scheme from 1904, publicizing requests from Canadian employers, principally in textiles and garment manufacture and among girls' clubs in industrial cities, and arranging for the extension of assisted passages to young women who decided to go abroad.[10] Penmans used Canadian Manufacturers' Association representatives and hired its own recruiters to work through the commercial emigration bureaux associated with shipping offices, advertising in the local press and labour exchanges for experienced help.[11]

The knit-goods industry in Canada grew rapidly between 1907 and 1928. Labourers building two new transcontinental railways and opening mines in the Rockies and the northern shield wore Penmans underwear and sweaters. Wartime contracts followed the completion of the railways, and the post-war fashion for knit-wear prolonged strong demand until the late 1920s. Through this period Paris remained a small town in a prosperous agricultural district in which the mill's demand for female labour continued to exceed the local supply.

Raw recruits could have been found nearer to hand than Leicestershire. The Penmans emigrants were recruited because they were accomplished hosiery workers. The contradictions between being female and being financially independent did not exist for the recruiter while he was recruiting them. Rather, he assiduously searched out skilled female wage earners for the very combination of attributes that complicated their lives at home. He was looking for female wage earners simply because they were wage earners, promising steady, long-term employment; but his offer presented these emigrants with a social possibility as alluring as the expected hike in pay.

'Skilled and experienced workers, those able to earn the highest wages' were what the firm specified in British advertisements. The demand was greatest for operators with machine-specific skills on equipment traditionally run by women. Penmans purchased knitting and looping machines from midlands builders and on occasion arranged for both mechanics and operatives who knew a new technology to come

Seamers, joining cut garment pieces, using flatlock and overlock machines in the Penmans underwear mills, c. 1924. Seamers were the last group of workers to be brought from domestic workshops into the factories in the midlands. The effectiveness of these machines, skilfully run, in linking cut knit fabric allowed knitwear to become an expanding fashion industry in the 1920s. The older women in the room, by seniority, had succeeded to the machines by the windows where the light was best for working. Finished goods hang by the foreman's station at the back of the room.

to Canada with the equipment. More generally, the firm wanted that combination of judgment and dexterity that allowed a worker simultaneously to maximize volume of production and quality, to make the most efficient use of their equipment, and to generate the fewest possible seconds. The smallest flaw, of no significance in woven fabric, easily spread the length of a knitted garment. A firm selling under trademark needed both operatives who knew the machines they were running well enough to diagnose imperfections and a cadre of meticulous inspectors and menders who reliably detected and stabilized seconds. A male Penmans manager called these 'limited skills,' comparing the specific expertise of the female immigrants with the all-round knowledge of the trade he had gained in a midlands technical apprenticeship. (Might he, considering males, have said specialized?) The healthy profitability of the firm, however, depended on these limited proficiencies; depended upon them sufficiently to justify the inconvenience of offshore recruitment and the risk of extending pre-paid passages. The midlands was considered a reservoir of such skills, with a population so long engaged in the trade that 'expert hosiery production [had become] an instinct.'[12]

The east midlands hosiery industry was not experiencing the gradual sectoral extinction that had expelled earlier agricultural and mining immigrants to the Canadas and other colonies. Relative to the woven-cloth trade, in fact, the knit-goods industry fared relatively well in the first third of this century. There were, however, certain general, and gender-specific economic reasons for midlands hosiery workers to consider emigration. When Penmans began their Nottinghamshire and Leicestershire recruiting in 1907–9, times were slack in the British trade. It was in the spring of 1910, in the wake of these hard times, that Canadian agents had their greatest pre-war success in encouraging hosiery workers to consider Canada. This activity was not well regarded by midlands hosiery manufacturers, who wondered in print about the improbability of British hosiery hands departing 'old England for the land of the maple leaf – and snow' and who suggested suspiciously that 'whoever has succeeded in persuading so many workpeople to leave these shores must be given credit for a rare fund of tact, energy and persistence,' given the 'extreme briskness of the English hosiery trade.' When Penmans recruiters used the Leicester and Nottingham labour exchanges to secure a contingent of 130 female hosiery emigrants in 1910, the editor of the *Hosiery Trade Journal* protested that the exchanges 'were certainly not intended to find skilled labour for competitors even though they may be colonials.'[13] The deportation of one of the May 1910 parties, after a week's detention in Quebec, was widely publicized as a cautionary tale for 'poor knitting folk' who might be tempted to break up their homes and hazard their fortunes to colonial 'red-tapism.'[14] The warnings went largely unheeded. Penmans June and July 1910 parties proceeded to Canada without incident.

After the war there was a brief fillip in the midlands hosiery industry and then, beginning in 1921, a stretch of years in which union officials reported 'uncertainty in the trade,' 'bad trade' and finally a 'general slump.' Unemployment in the hosiery averaged 8,200 in 1923 and 6,700 in 1927. Many of these redundancies were caused by productivity-enhancing technological changes and were unlikely to be reduced even when demand recovered. Heightening external tariffs in Germany and Canada, among other jurisdictions, limited Britain's traditionally vigorous export markets for knit goods. In this sense, the emigration to Canada was part of a new international division of labour.[15]

Within the new regime women's prospects in particular were better in Canada than in Britain. As the number of jobs in British knit-goods firms was reduced, the hosiery unions moved, cautiously but deliberately, to protect men's jobs to the detriment of women's, and to redraw gender divisions in the industry so as to favour men. In Canada, partly because the hosiery industry was not unionized until the late 1940s, the jobs in knitting, countering, and shading that remained, or were becoming increasingly men's work in the midlands, were still open to women. Besides more jobs, Canadian recruiters could promise, and deliver, better-paying and steadier work. Travellers between Paris and the midlands reported women's wages to be 50 per cent higher in Canada in both 1908 and 1923.[16] Because capital in the Canadian industry was highly concentrated, Penmans and the small number of companion firms with which it colluded in the market could work to inventory rather than to order, running their plants at a reasonably steady rate year round. The promise of regular work was especially inviting to employees of small midlands firms which had always produced seasonally and which, in the 1920s, quickly assimilated the advantages of the new Unemployment Insurance Act, 'using the people whilst it was necessary and then giving them their cards.'[17]

Many midlands immigrants came to Paris independently, using their own savings or tickets sent to them by kin already established in the town. Others came with state support, having declared their intention to farm, and then reached Paris by way of Saskatchewan or Alberta. Some were directed to the town by their children, who found the picture of Penmans mills in their primary-school geography books. There were a few mill families in town headed by male spinners or mechanics who had been to Australia, New England, the American west, and back to England before they settled on Paris.[18] The core of the mill workers' community in town, however, consisted of the some 700 persons assisted by the firm to emigrate in the twenty years after 1907 and their kin.[19]

Of the assisted emigrants, at least three-quarters were female, four-fifths of them unmarried.[20] In Britain they were given tickets covering their rail fares and their transatlantic passage and, in some cases, small cash advances. They travelled in parties, accompanied by a Penmans agent. On arrival in Paris they were required to sign a contract agreeing to repay the sum advanced at a rate of 50 cents per week while earning less than $6 per week and $1 while earning more, the unpaid sum 'at all times constituting first lien' on their wages, and the whole unpaid balance becoming due immediately should they leave the company's employ. Most immigrants arrived owing Penmans about $60 in 1910 and $110 in 1928, sums that throughout the period took between twelve and eighteen months to repay.[21]

Contract labour schemes such as this were usually fine failures in both the settler dominions and the United States. Workers simply decamped, leaving their ticket stubs behind them, to find jobs anonymously away where their wages would be their own. In Paris, by contrast, most assisted immigrants faithfully repaid their loans. It was the depression of the 1930s rather than defaulting debtors that caused the firm to discontinue overseas recruitment. One in four of the 'imported help' left before the loan was entirely repaid, but in most cases the sum remaining on the firm's books was small.[22] Most of the immigrants stayed in Paris for the rest of their lives, for most of their years as employees of the mill.

It was not a keen sense of contract that kept them. As Philip Corrigan has noted from Marx, there are 'chains' in capitalism apart from the law.[23] The distinction between bound and free labour is to be found in the 'conditions of work' and in the social relations that accompany it. For migrants, as Colin Newbury has argued, the distinction lies between those 'allowed to enjoy a measure of vertical mobility and participation in the organization of a political economy, and those whose entry into such economies was partial, peripheral and without political influence.'[24]

In a sense the Penmans immigrants, as skilled female wage earners, had no place to go. Among the emigrant parties, those who began at the Paris mills as lower-paid workers were most likely to quit before their loans were repaid, partly because they were discharging the debt at a much slower rate, but also because they had much less to leave.[25] Those who found other jobs in town quickly confronted the customs of loyalty and mutual protection among local capitalists and had their wages at their new employment docked for remission to the 'masters of the mill.' Having arrived without savings, set down in a small community in a strange country, even those without ties in town and willing to take any job were likely to linger through most of the repayment schedule, accumulating the cash and information with which to make a move. For skilled workers leaving was less attractive. They were unlikely to be able to get good hosiery work and to evade their debt. The fraternity among the few Canadian knit-goods manufacturers was close, and those who, in applying for new jobs, had to explain themselves to new employers found their obligation to Penmans followed them.[26] More importantly, they would be leaving behind a range of other advantages which, as skilled female wage earners, they were less likely to secure elsewhere. In Paris they were at the centre of the local economy; community social relations were organized around wage-earning women, and they were not an anomaly.

Penmans recruiters went to the east midlands, not only because it was a reservoir of skill in the hosiery trade, but also because, particularly in Leicestershire, the tradition of lifelong female wage work, lacking in the surrounding Ontario community, was strong. In searching out women such as Miss Florrie Morris – born in 1895, emigrated to Paris in 1912, retired from Penmans in 1970 at age seventy-five – and Mrs Annie Smith – born in 1890, emigrated to Paris 1913, retired from Penmans at age seventy-nine in 1969 – managers were seeking both skill and stability in their work force. Through overseas recruitment they could overcome what Charlotte Erickson has called the 'social obstacles' that existed locally to the labour system the firm wished to sustain. In this conjuncture was a social setting that female mill workers made their own. Florrie Morris and Annie Smith were exceptional in their length of service at the mills, and exceptions to the common Canadian story about the passing of an adult woman's days and years, but they were not, as lifelong wage workers, considered oddities in Paris. This acknowledgment, if only ambiguously acceptance, opened a range of possibilities which drew several skilled female immigrants back to Paris from confinement on the margins of the mainstream economy in larger centres (and also to discharge the debts that remained unlapsed on Penmans books).[27]

Even in the midlands, the tradition of lifelong female wage work was as anxious and self-denying as it was persistent. There are enough affirmations in the record that married women's employment should not exist to convince a careful scholar that indeed it did not.[28] As female seamers and menders were brought from domestic workshops into the factories in the 1890s, industrialists railed against mothers' wage work 'on moral and humanitarian grounds' claiming that children were thereby 'persistently neglected' and 'very, very poorly cared for.' Yet they continued to employ wives during all but the first month after childbirth, 'on business grounds ... some of them are the best workers we have, and we should be sorry to lose them.' Unionists worried that married women with husbands at work would undercut the wages of single women and men.[29] Both the oral history and the wage book evidence is clear. Large numbers of married women were employed in the east midlands hosiery industry through the first half of this century.[30] In 1919 'hundreds' of these workers struck in Hinckley, 'determined their custom continue of going in at 9AM instead of 8,' presumably so as to have time for their home duties before reporting for wage work. Male union officials were both individually conflicted and organizationally divided on the issue of married women's employment. Although they recognized the question as one to be handled 'very delicately,' since 'married women had the same rights' as all others in the union, they worked steadily to shift the boundaries between men's and women's work in favour of men. There are examples of women themselves, while largely supporting their households, struggling to maintain for their children the illusion of the husband as breadwinner.[31]

A wage-earning woman existed in the thralls of an awkward and unsatisfactory negotiation, not only to retain the right to work and to be employed on schedules which made wage-earning tenable, but also to reconcile social ideology with her own experience. In other communities women were employed for a time in their teens and twenties and perhaps returned to the labour force later in life when their children were grown; so that wage work was scripted to a safe place as a contingency, to be pursued only when it would not collide with primary obligations as mother and wife.[32] Where the labour force tradition was different, where daughters followed mothers in patterns of lifelong wage work in the presence of a patriarchal culture that declared these patterns pathogenic, a safe place was more difficult to secure. The antipathies between female wage work and heterosexual conjugality called for a different resolution. There are signs of these negotiations in textile towns: the later age at marriage, the greater incidence of non-marriage, the commercial provision of food preparation and laundry services that were elsewhere labelled as wives' work, the more intense networks for labour exchanges among households.

These struggles to reconcile material sustenance and domestic satisfaction pose questions about consciousness of gender and the experience of security in same- and cross-gender connections. Like Ross and Rapp's parsing of the relationships of inheritance patterns through nuptiality to sexuality, these indications take us towards an emerging social possibility.[33] Could it not be that for some, wage work came to be understood as the continuity, and marriage the contingency, in the unfolding of an adult woman's life?

Were this the case, how would one come to acknowledge it as a social existence rather than as a personal happenstance? There must have been many routes through which this process of 'self-discovery' as a group developed and as many paths at which it was blocked. For Penmans mill households emigration was a section in one of the open routes. Midland women workers were coming *from* wage work, *to* wage work, making the decision to emigrate based on the gains they could achieve as wage workers. The emigrant group was dominated by widows with families, veterans of troubled marriages, women alone, single women with children, and pairs of women friends. For many, marriage was not an active post-emigration consideration. Emigration by congregating numbers of women who were living without men clarified this cultural alternative. They came, with common experience of wage work and the domestic dilemmas female employment engendered, to a women's town, a place where the prevailing wage form did not require a male breadwinner or give precedence to households that included men, where the numerical dominance of female wage earners offered a certain psychic and physical protection, a shelter for a woman-centred culture.

Among widows the domestic provocations for emigration were most plain. For older women whose spouses had died, especially those with several daughters, emigration was a way to keep the family solvent and together. Mary Cavan and a female cousin came to Paris in 1912 and returned to Glasgow in 1914 to fetch her widowed mother, a younger sister, and one of her two brothers. Maud Chappell, her three sisters, and her widowed mother arrived in Paris in 1913. All but Maud had worked previously in lace and box making in Nottingham. In her first week in Canada, fifteen-year-old Maud began her twenty-nine-year career in the mill. Anne Hedley and her sister were urged to emigrate by their mother when their coal-miner father died, so that they could make a home together, rather than live separately in domestic service. Each of these households became the nucleus of a spreading mill family in Paris, bound together by strong female kin ties. In each of these cases, and characteristic of midland families in town, links with male siblings were attenuated. There were brothers in the Cavan, Chappell, and Hedley emigrant groups, but all left town and lost close connection with the family circle. On several occasions it fell to daughters to assume their brothers' passage debts as family obligations when sons lost patience with their widowed mother's choice of destination overseas.

Atypically of chain migrations, males among the Paris emigrants were frequently the last rather than the first in kin groups to go abroad, reluctantly following the initiative of female family members. Betty Shaw's widowed mother, a lace maker, went to Paris alone in 1913, leaving two-year-old Betty in the care of her grandparents and returning later to persuade them to join her overseas. Betty's grandfather, a coal miner, did a youngster's work as chore-boy in the mills in Paris, but the earnings of several skilled women in the household carried them through until 1949, when, to a woman, they were fired as militants in a long local strike.[34] Their husbands' deaths made widows consider emigration to a place where they and their children might be self-supporting. The widow's initiative gave her household independence, drawing daughters together, but frequently cast sons and male kin in dependent roles.

For women in troubled marriages, as for widows, emigration to skilled work overseas offered an opportunity to overcome the wrecked promises of conjugality. Edith Elliott remembered that her grandmother summoned all her children and shepherded them to Paris; as Elliott recalled, 'the whole family came out, except the father and he stayed back because he worked in the coal mines over there and they came here.' The Elliott family became prominent in the mill community, proprietors of a large boarding house, where grandmother Elliott might supervise her daughters' courtships with lodgers and arrange for aunts to initiate their nieces into the better jobs at the mill. Hilda Sharp's mother had come to Canada at the urging of female kin already established in Paris. Her husband had been invalided after the South African War; she may have seen the move as a way to reduce the domestic tensions arising from his limited earnings. The household prospered in Paris, turning its female members' domestic and hosiery skills into accumulations of real estate, and earning the respect of the mill community as boarding-house-keepers and midwives. Mr Sharp, however, saw none of this, having early returned to his old job in Ilkeston. Ida Pelton's father stayed with her mother in Paris, but emigration consolidated a change in their household relationships. Mr Pelton's parents had come to Paris at the turn of the century from Bulwell, Notts. He stayed behind, employed by an uncle in a declining trade: 'in those days they had horses not cars, and they had funerals and weddings and they had all the outfits for them, that's what he did. My Dad had to go to war and he was in Germany a year after the war ended and when he was away my Mother had read in the paper where people like us, we could come to Canada ... so she told my Dad this when he came home and ... it was all fixed for us to come.' Ida's mother earned good money as a mender at Penmans; Ida became a looper, a job which paid high piece rates. Together the women managed, pooling their earnings and sharing domestic labour, although none of Ida's three brothers stayed in town, and neither her father nor her husband was regularly employed. For Ida and her mother, as for many others, Paris offered a certain hedged and hesitant refuge to those for whom the scripted plan of stable marriage to a male breadwinner had gone awry.[35]

Within the mill community the intertwining of emotional and economic reasons for emigration was commonly experienced and understood. Emigration offered a resolution to domestic tensions which poverty, legality, and convention made otherwise unresolvable. Among women, so long as there was no harm done to others, an accepting discretion surrounded the paternity of youngsters and the mortal and marital state or whereabouts of spouses. A line between discretion and the countenancing of deception, however, was maintained by group scrutiny. Sam Horsley, a midland knitter active in the mill community but exceptional in town as a mature unattached male, found himself vexed by 'false stories being circulated around town that I am a married man, and have left a wife and children in England'; to counter the rumours, he posted a $100 reward in the local paper in 1926 to 'be paid to anyone bringing forward the slightest evidence that these stories are true,' and he threatened action 'against any person making such false statements.' In the case of Margaret Etherington the local gossip turned out to be true. Etherington had emigrated from a textile town in Yorkshire to work in the local flannel factory. She declared herself a widow and in December 1923 married Bert Raynes, a knitter mechanic at the hosiery mill. Seven years later something made Raynes enlist the aid of the local police in Paris to inquire into her past. Word came back from the chief constable in Burnley that her husband, Frank Etherington, was alive in Earby, Yorkshire. He had commenced divorce proceedings twelve years previously, 'but being short of money was unable to go forward with the case.' Raynes chose to resolve the matter by full disclosure, declaiming in the press, 'she is still his wife and I give this notice that the public may know that I have no lawful wife.'[36]

In most early twentieth-century communities the respectability of

Immigrant women employed at Penmans, dressed in their Sunday best outside Mrs Fick's boarding-house on Walnut Street, near the sweater and under-wear mills, c. 1910. Boarding-house-keepers were women, sometimes retired mill workers; the residents were predominantly women and children dur-ing the immigration period.

young unmarried women was closely scrutinized, female factory workers with, perhaps, more public flourish than any others. The majority of the Penmans assisted emigrants were single women; few travelled abroad by themselves. Most came with friends or female kin, many to join relatives already established in Paris.

For single mothers with children the demographics in town were sheltering. In 1936 more than a quarter of Penmans female employees lived in single-headed households, the majority of which included children. Ann Wilson had been a winder in Nottingham. In a slack season she and a woman with whom she worked in the hosiery encountered a Penmans recruiter and decided to emigrate, Ann bringing with her Gordon, her pre-school-aged son. They set up housekeeping together and worked side by side in the knitting mill. In time Ann's friend's daughter joined them. Penmans and their employees developed housing forms, work schedules, and child-care arrangements that accommodated wage-earning mothers. Among others whose household form was similar, and living at a distance from past personal events, widows, deserted wives, and single mothers shared the dilemmas of wage work and child rearing outside conjugality. Frances Randall, a child born out of wedlock in Bulwell, came to Paris at age fourteen to join her maternal kin in a community where, although her early circumstances were known, they distinguished her less than they might have in the town of her birth.[37]

Emigration and the help of female kin did not resolve all the problems of being single and alone. In December 1919 Christina Addison joined her sister, Mrs Ireland, in the comfortable boarding house she ran on Elm Street near the Grand River and took a job in the mill. Her family noted her melancholy but could not assuage it. In April she rose one morning, instructed the postmaster to destroy all further correspondence, walked to the mill race, set her hat by the dam, and jumped to her death. But the community of single women was large in town; in 1936 28 per cent of Penmans women workers entered middle age unmarried, and the female society of the boarding houses smoothed the transition. The acceptance that women should live as well as work together, organizing events and convening festive gatherings in their homes, extended through the Penmans Pleasure Club and the company-owned YWCA to the churches, the Maids and Daughters of England, and the Ladies Auxiliary of the British Empire Service League. All female households composed of sisters and friends were among the most vigorous social centres in the mill community and their members unselfconsciously claimed the scrupulous and attentive acknowledgment their domestic milestones were due. When the local paper reported in May 1935 that a 'friendship of seventeen years had been severed' by the death of Miss Susan Baldwin in the house she shared with Lottie Trueman on Yeo Street, the editors were obliged to publish a correction noting that the two women 'had been friends for 35 years, and came to Canada together 23 years ago, during seventeen of which Miss Baldwin was an invalid.' Susan Baldwin was survived by five sisters in England but had remained through years of heart trouble in her Canadian home with her friend.[38]

It was rare for single immigrants to wed within their first eighteen months in Canada. Paris was probably not the easiest place in which to find a spouse, if one were looking, there being relatively few jobs to attract or keep unattached men in town. However, combining wage work with marriage was common in the community. In 1936 40 per cent of Penmans female employees were wives.[39] Among the skilled emigrant women who had come to Canada as wage earners and commanded the highest piece-rates as knitters, loopers, shaders, and finishers, continuing on at the mill after marriage was especially common. Coping with employment, marriage, and motherhood simultaneously rather than sequentially required adaptations in domestic gender divisions and household boundaries which the midland emigrants shared with couples in the mill community generally. But there were some ways of signalling symbolically the rules that must govern marriage between wage-earning spouses which were unique to the east midlands emigrants.

Most intriguing of these were the mock weddings which Sallie Westwood describes as continuing in Leicester to this day. The midlands origins of the mock wedding are unclear. Today in Leicester factories, where men's and women's occupations are strictly segregated and men command the best-paying manufacturing and mechanical jobs, mock weddings are women's rituals. Brides wear pornographic costumes designed by female co-workers and are left by their women friends tied to the factory fence in a frightening public display of bondage, as 'a celebration of their own oppression in marriage.' The rites mark changes in a woman's intimate life, acknowledging that she now will be sexually available to her husband and that, in accord with the appropriate power relationships of marriage, her sexuality will be 'crucially mediated by men.' While these bridal rituals take place on the shop floor and around the factory gate, they are not about the particular imminent dilemmas of wage-earning wives.[40]

As practised among the east midlands emigrants in Paris in the 1920s and 1930s, the mock weddings had very different functions. As pantomimes of gender roles they ridiculed conventions of patriarchal hierarchy within marriage; as celebrations among co-workers who would continue to be employed together, they warned the couple that the intense commitment they were about to make to one another must be exclusively domestic and not privilege their relationships on the shop floor.

It was in the mixed-gender knitting, spinning, and cutting rooms, and when both spouses worked in the mill, that mock weddings were most common. On these elaborately costumed occasions, sex and age roles were reversed, the bride being a senior male skilled worker or foreman, the clergyman a young girl, the groom an older married woman, the best man one of her peers. The games were raucous parodies of domestic life.

A social gathering of English mill families on the flats across the Nith River from the hosiery mill, 24 August 1913, five years after the Penmans assisted-passage scheme began. Note the predominance of women and the presence of the Union Jack. The elegant bell tower which faced onto West River Street is visible in the upper right. The steam plant was hidden from the street, behind the mill, but its smoke stack appears here, at centre through the trees.

Sam Horsley, the machinist who a decade earlier had taken to the press to refute rumours concerning his own marital state, organized a mock wedding in 1937 at the home of a male co-worker in the shadow of the hosiery mill. Horsley himself was the bride, 'charmingly dressed in black and pink velvet, carrying a bouquet of roses and sweet peas.' Mrs Crump from the finishing room 'took the part of the groom dressed in evening suit and top hat.' Mrs Alice Russell, a sixty-year-old winder, was the bridesmaid, 'dressed in pink and silver lace, carrying a spray of forget-me-nots. The flower girl was Miss Williamson and the best man Miss Raycraft. The ceremony was ably performed by Miss F. McLaughlin. After the service Mr J. Raycraft and Mr S. Horsley rendered the beautiful duet "Love's Sweet Dream" accompanied on the guitar by Miss M. Williamson ... Mr C. Wiliams executed an old fashioned clog dance to "Bye Bye Blues."' The workplace parity between male and female co-workers in mixed departments (the bride in this case, Violet Jones, was a skilled burson knitter) carried over into sociability. The ritual affirmed that these conventions must influence marital politics as well if the bride were to continue effectively in her job. The inversion of the mock wedding played upon the suppleness of gender boundaries. The common laughter affirmed that equality among co-workers did not imply sameness in marital partners.

Because most women from midlands immigrant families worked in the mills after they were married and for many years after they had children as well, the politics of mill and domestic life were interdependent and intertwined. When Jean Elliott, the grand-daughter of a woman who had brought her family from Nottinghamshire, married her foreman in 1938, the mock wedding took place in their department in the hosiery mill. Here the significance of the role reversals was especially marked. Co-workers used the occasion to emphasize that nepotism must not intrude after the marriage, prejudicing the fair distribution of work in the room. The topic of mock weddings came up in this interview while we were talking about workplace tensions, rather than discussing marriage:

> JOHN: She was just another worker there; I could love her up at home but not at work. If there was a choice of a good bag for this one and a bad one for that one, she would get the bad one.
>
> EDITH: Wasn't that nice.

Then John came to the question of mock weddings:

> JOHN: You couldn't play favorites – people would be looking for that type of thing. They had a mock wedding for us – the whole mill up to the department, over a hundred people. It was something I tell you, the old po that goes under the bed, they had that all tied up in ribbons and I know I blushed too. I wish we had pictures of it but we didn't.

The mock wedding had achieved its purpose, reminding the foreman of his vulnerability before shop-floor consensus and of the limits on his authority as both husband and boss.[42]

CONCLUSION

The lives of the female skilled workers and their kin in Paris were formed by a series of common transatlantic experiences passed down as family lore and neighbourhood reminiscence to daughters and grand-daughters. The women from the east midlands were recruited for their workplace proficiencies with hosiery machinery and knitted fabric and their community traditions of lifelong female wage work. In English hosiery districts these traditions were embattled. They were fortified by manufacturers' preferences for experienced lower-waged women em-ployees and long-standing community acceptance of the jointly consti-tuted household, rather than individually garnered male-breadwinner wage. They were challenged by the male-dominated hosiery unions who claimed wage-earning wives were complicit in pay cuts and who feared long-serving female employees as competitors for the declining pool of skilled jobs in the knit-goods industry. For all parties to the convention, lifelong female wage work existed in awkward contradic-tion to the prevailing social ideology governing gender roles. For skilled women workers, emigration mitigated these conflicts by offering steady, well-paid employment and anonymous distance from the domestic tensions their English circumstances had conditioned. Emi-gration brought together women experienced in wage work, selected because of their workplace skills, and congregated them in a community where their prospects as wage earners were brighter than their likely fortunes as wives. Among the female emigrants and their kin the economic and emotional reasons for leaving Britain were recounted as of a piece. Emigration, by offering women in one generation a way to evade or escape conjugality, opened a social possibility that wage work rather than marriage would be the continuity in an adult woman's life. Where, as in Paris, women were at both a numerical and an economic advantage among wage workers, life after emigration was characterized by stronger bonds between women, weakened links with male kin, a more comfortable social acknowledgment of variously constituted female-headed households, and a greater willingness, at least within the emigrant community, to use group pressure to reinforce marital relations which would facilitate lifelong female wage work. Their differences became tenable, patterns that by their numerical force required logistical accommodation in town. The distance between observed patterns in social life and prescriptions for social life, however, remained, troubling and contentious for the town as a whole, most troubling in particular for the mill workers themselves.

■ Chapter Two

The politics of protection

John Penman was a paternalist employer by inclination and by necessity. His presbyterian sense of stewardship and his penchant for moral instruction impelled a lifelong commitment to the dominion-wide temperance movement. In Paris his roles as guardian of social respectability and arbiter of moral conduct were also pressing business obligations.

The sense in which these responsibilities were incurred because the knit-goods sector was protected behind part of the dominion tariff wall became clear in the spring of 1882, just three years after Sir John A. Macdonald's Conservative government promulgated the broad protective legislation known as the National Policy. As part of the campaign leading up to the election of 20 June, the Liberal Toronto *Globe* put the textile industry at the centre of a serialized parable about the 'wickedness' of factory life, crafted to demonstrate the social evils the Conservatives had created by stimulating the growth of secondary manufacturing. The Liberals' choice of the textile industry for polemical scrutiny was not accidental. In a sector that employed large numbers of women, many of them young and unmarried, the case against the degrading, unnatural character of industrial life was most compelling and unambiguous. In the rising textile towns of the dominion, the *Globe* reported, 'If the mill and home life of the operatives is deplorable, their moral condition is more so. There is something in the social atmosphere that ... produces a feeling of utter apathy in the hearts of most of the operatives ... Their morals are bad, very bad. The conduct of the girls is immodest in the extreme ... A good-looking girl is almost certain to fall before she has lived long in the surroundings.'[1] John Penman and his fellow textile manufacturers in Paris and Brantford came forward, quickly claiming their 'duty' to defend those 'large numbers of the mothers, wives and daughters of our townsmen ... practically defenseless in these insinuations against their reputations.' At a large meeting held at the Paris town hall the Saturday night before the vote the female employees of the mill reportedly tendered thanks 'to the proprietors of the knitting mills of Paris, who so promptly and without solicitation on our part, bore testimony to the exemplary conduct of the female employees of their establishments, and recognize in this expression of their satisfaction with our conduct, additional evidence of their kindly feelings toward us and interest in our welfare.' The town's Conservative newspaper counselled immediate action, urging 'Workingmen of Paris! [to] revenge at the polls this insult to your wives and daughters by voting down the party that hesitates not to rob them of their good name and trample their honor and chastity in the dust.'[2]

Women mill workers figured in this dispute in three ways, as the 'mothers, wives and daughters of townsmen,' as the 'wives and daughters' of male voters, and as grateful employees, thankful in the passive voice, that their exemplary conduct had been affirmed and a kind interest in their welfare taken. Through the next seventy years their role in the protecting relationship would change in the community. Once there were large numbers of prominent female-headed households in town, it became less acceptable to acknowledge female workers only through their ties to town men. From 1918 women were voters in their own right. But because textiles remained exceptional as a female-dominated manufacturing occupation, the sense that women workers owed their jobs in the mill to the good offices of their particular patrons remained strong.

In the late nineteenth century, when factories were still modelled on the familial patterns of authority and responsibility that had governed craft and agricultural production,[3] John Penman protected the good names of the women he employed by claiming common cause with their fathers and husbands. 'All gentlemen who have sisters or daughters,' A.M. Young reported about Paris in 1883, 'must rejoice at such avenues to respectable employment being opened to women,' adding more improbably, 'their duties are light, requiring more taste and delicacy of touch than of actual work.'[4] As the patriarchal presence receded in many mill families in the twentieth century while the respectability of female manufacturing employment remained obdurately in doubt, the compensating force of the company's public face – securing the good names of the employees through the good name of the firm – became ever more important.

For John Penman creating and maintaining the image of textile work as respectable womanly employment was essential. Not only were there the continuing political questions about whether the costs to the nation of the textile tariff were worth the social gain and in addition the periodic election-time harassment suggesting tariff-sheltered factories were corrupting the nation's womanhood, but there was also a proximate business concern. Working women would come forward in sufficient numbers to take jobs in the mill only if (in fact were not available from the surrounding agricultural districts even when) they were regarded as 'as worthy of respect as their more fortunate sisters who have been reared to spend their time in idleness and reading trashy novels.'[5] If he was to employ women workers, John Penman had no choice but to make the affirmation of their respectability his business.

In 1874, as the small knitting firm he and his father had established in 1868 began to grow, Penman took care to secure a respectable public image for factory textile work through close attention to the architectural facade and physical fabric of the mill itself. No. 1 mill, always the pride of the firm, was described by a nineteenth-century observer as 'a spacious and stately building, quite unlike the popular ideal of a factory; four stories high, and with lofty, well proportioned apartments.' Reporters gave the mill itself a feminine aspect, calling it 'a model of architectural neatness and beauty,' likening the machinery to domestic furnishings, emphasizing the 'wonderful discretion' with which it had been placed in the 'commodious departments,' and the safety and cleanliness which characterized all parts of the building.[6] The West River streetscape was dominated by the Penman six-storey, slate-roofed bell tower, which dwarfed the smoke stack set further back near the Nith river bank, and the mill itself was topped with an elegant, dormered slate roof.

Penman lived in the community, even after Montreal interests took over his Paris mills in 1906, in a barnacled, gothic pile called Penmarvian, located on a height, which local folk called Quality Hill, overlooking the Grand River and the town. His Christian paternalist concerns extended beyond his own work force to the community as a whole, and continued even after his own business interests were no longer located in Paris. He financed a night school, the YMCA, the YWCA, and the central public school; subsidized university students and the work of a

The Penmans hosiery mill, looking along West River Street, towards the railway junction on the heights beyond, as mill workers were leaving for lunch hour, probably in the fall of 1912. The hosiery mill, with its bell tower, slate mansard roof, and cast-iron roof decoration, was built in 1874 to contradict, by its stately and ornate facade, the dark image of factory work for women.

community nurse; and provided food hampers for needy families.[7] These interventions created a deep sense of loyalty and personal indebtedness toward Penman in the community. As Richard Thomson, president of the Board of Trade, declared when honouring Penman in 1907, the mill had become a 'civic institution,' 'interwoven with the welfare of the Town,' the places of work, education and recreation connected in the community mind through their common patronage. Though he did not have to demand that it be so, Penman's philanthropy was acknowledged as compensation for the low wages paid in the mill, in part because the amenities he installed in the community, by establishing the civic virtue of the town, secured the respectability of all those who looked to him for their livelihood.[8]

In 1906 the control and headquarters of Penmans Manufacturing Company moved from Paris to Montreal, and the name of the firm

Penmarvian, John Penman's home, on a height overlooking the Grand River, and his mills on the opposite bank. The house, when built as Riverview Hall by the founder of Paris, Hiram Capron, was a relatively plain structure, but by the time this photograph was taken, during Penman's tenure, the dwelling had acquired the full gambit of Victorian affectations, including several towers and a firmly planted ironwork perimeter fence and gate.

changed to Penmans Limited. The impetus for the change remains shrouded. John Penman had expanded his business rapidly in the 1890s, taking over small knitting firms in Thorold and Port Dover, Ontario, and Coaticook, Quebec. In 1903 he bought out the Canadian Woolen Mills in St-Hyacinthe. He may have become overextended. He may have lost the leverage he needed to retain executive control over the firm.[9] Certainly, Penman had not lost interest in owning knitting mills. Soon after his formal departure from the firm that continued to bear his name, he established the Mercury Mills in Hamilton as a vigorous competitor for both labour and a market share in the industry. It is clear that by late 1906 the group of Montreal financiers associated with the Bank of Montreal and responsible for the contemporary consolidations in both woven textiles and glass had assumed control of his firm, the largest knitting concern in the dominion. The Montreal group included two textile wholesalers, David Morrice, whose firm for many years had marketed Penmans products, and Charles Blair Gordon.

The new company faced a problem common to the larger joint stock companies of the day. As Mr Justice W.F.A. Turgeon observed in his royal commission report on the textile industry in 1938, 'as long as the factories were small and operated by owners, the relations between employer and employees were relatively close and the owner could scarcely avoid accepting direct responsibility for the welfare of his employees.' The wider diffusion of share capital characteristic of the new firms created by the mergers of the early twentieth century made the relationship between owners and wage earners indirect and impersonal. Yet corporate employers were loath to relinquish what Donald Reid has called 'the system of discretionary power embodied in paternalism' and they sought ways to maintain the impression that the paternalist owner remained present in the system of labour relations, 'whether or not he really was.'[10] In the corporate consolidations in both knitted and woven goods, advisers to the textile industry took on this question directly, emphasizing that without the 'good will' of the worker, business could not 'be conducted with propriety nor with the greatest success.' They urged executive officers to choose in their super-intendents and foremen effective 'go-betweens,' who would stand as 'proxies' for the corporate owners, demonstrating the continuity of 'the employer's personal and voluntary interest in his employees.' This perception of the need for continuity may explain why the new Montreal owners allowed John Penman to retain his office in their Paris mill for six years after he had severed his connection with the firm, even as his Hamilton Mercury Mills were recruiting labour in the area and gaining prominence in the national market.[11] Advocates of factory 'welfare work' were much more explicit about the nature of the exchange underlying their work in the community than paternalist owners, such as John Penman, had been. They called employee good will 'a prime economic factor,' and urged employers to function, in a contractual sense, as 'the party of the first part'. They also redefined the substance of the exchange, insisting that 'the secret is not in paternally doing for' the workers, but in securing a 'spirit of mutuality and cooperation.'[12]

The 'civic welfare of the town' thus remained an important concern of the company, although the forms in which the company interest was manifested changed in crucial ways. Penman had functioned as a philanthropist, using his personal wealth to build and maintain community institutions. His charitable influence upon town life was welcomed, seen as privileging the town as a whole rather than the firm in particular. Penman, himself, as an American citizen, had never been eligible for municipal office. The salaried executives of the new corporation as individuals did not endow any new community institutions but rather arrived at civic receptions bearing cheques upon which the company's name was embossed. The contributions Penmans now made to support the hospital, the community club, and the skating rink, and the scholarships they funded for local students were voted by the board of directors in Montreal.[13] Penmans officials did begin, however, to play a more conspicuous role in the political life of the municipality.

Richard Thomson, who served as general manager in both the old and the new firm, was elected regularly as councillor and reeve, headed the Public Utilities Commission for a time, and was later a justice of the peace. C.B. Robinson, who had begun his career in textiles with the Montreal wholesaler D. Morrice and Sons in 1886 and came to Paris in 1911 as secretary-treasurer of Penmans Limited, was elected twice as town mayor and several times as councillor. E.G. James, transferred from Penmans St-Hyacinthe branch to his position as supervisor of the Paris hosiery mill, served for many years on the Board of Education. Although each man stood for office as a citizen of the town, and Robinson in particular established the breadth of his community concern through volunteer work of many different kinds, all were regarded as representing Penmans Limited on the municipal bodies to which they were elected. Whereas John Penman's philanthropy had been seen as public spirited, a sign of his 'personal and voluntary interest' in the community, the business strategy underlying the concern of Thomson, Robinson, and James for the 'civic welfare' was talked about more explicitly in town.

The popular belief was that Penmans executives in elected office looked first to their employer's concerns, often to the detriment of the community welfare. Paris historian D.A. Smith reports regularly hearing allegations that Penmans members on council blocked the establishment of other industries in town. He recounts how twice in his days as a teacher salary increases were refused by the Board of Education, influenced by company representatives, who argued that their workers would demand equivalent raises in pay.[14] In the early 1980s former Penman's employees asked to characterize the community

VIEW AT PARIS   The prettiest Town in Canada

A postcard view of Paris from the height south of the Nith River where it joins the Grand, at lower right. The Grand Trunk Railway bridge is at upper right, with the towers of Penmarvian beyond. The town's merchants were concentrated along Grand River Street, which rises at the centre of the photograph towards the district called Quality Hill, where the pyramid roof of the Presbyterian church Penman endowed is clearly visible. The large buildings in the upper left are the Methodist church next to the YWCA, the Baptist church, and the King's Ward Public School.

in the inter-war years began with the affirmation that Penmans controlled the town through the town hall, 'that's how they kept other firms out,' so that 'if you didn't work for Penmans you didn't work.'[15]

There is nothing in the council minutes to substantiate these allegations. It is likely that by the time Penmans changed hands, topography and pre-existing land title had determined that industrial diversification in Paris would be slight. The valleys of both the Nith and the Grand rivers, as they meet in town, are steep sided. The flats by their banks were already built up by the turn of the century and were predominantly in Penmans hands.[16] New firms would have had to locate on the higher land outside the settled area of the town, an unattractive climb away from the community's established housing stock. The one attempt to bonus a new firm in town, an engineering works, did pass by civic referendum. To keep down their tax rates, by limiting municipal improvements (another common claim), executives of the firm did not have to act independently. As householders relying on low textile wages, their employees could be counted upon to resist civic capital expenditures.[17] Whether or not the rumours were true, that employer representatives as elected officials conspired to keep wages down by keeping other firms out, the persistence of the allegations muted the gratitude acknowledged for their public service by the women and men who worked for them in the mills. One local employer, realizing whispering campaigns had compromised his earlier candidacy for federal office, found it necessary in 1930 to deny explicitly that he had ever 'conspired to keep wages down.'[18] Conversely, as Horace Timpson, a fine knitting machine mechanic and perceptive observer of town life, recalled, whether Penmans actually did or did not have power to control who worked in Paris and for what wages was irrelevant, so long as 'that was the way it was felt, people were afraid for their lives.'[19]

The primary goal of the welfare capitalist management strategies practised at Penmans Limited was to secure an adequate and stable labour force for their knitting mills. William Davis, a respected adviser to the British hosiery industry, in a 1920 article entitled 'Present Day Factory Problems, The Real Meaning of Welfare Work,' republished in the *Canadian Textile Journal*, emphasized that 'given the considerable difficulty in obtaining operatives, and in retaining them once they have been secured,' welfare work must be 'considered, not in a philanthropic spirit, but as a business proposition ... to stabilize the labor situation.' As a retired personnel manager at Penmans recalled, 'while the manufacturing was so labour intensive, it was practically impossible to maintain a complete labour pool. With that requirement, there just wasn't the normal family growth within a town to supply the fodder required in the mills.'[20] Managers in small communities such as Paris, particularly if they preferred as employees workers who by their age or gender were unconventional participants in the labour force, took a long view in labour relations, saw themselves as installing and then regulating a labour system, and spoke of their labour problem both in terms of recruitment and reproduction. Michelle Perrot, analysing similar patterns in the French case, suggests, 'We might even speak in terms of the eugenics of industrial populations.'[21] Textile manufacturers seeking to establish a work force that was stable, female, and low waged often preferred to locate in small towns where there were few other firms, especially firms that paid men high enough wages to support their wives and daughters at home.

Two strategies for building a female textile labour force are usually distinguished, the Waltham system, which recruited women who lived in company-owned dormitories and worked in the mills for a brief time while they were young and unmarried, and the Rhode Island or Slater system, in which companies employed and provided domestic accommodation for family groups. As Gary Saxonhouse and Gavin Wright have argued, 'each system had corollary features and evolutionary tendencies which were not necessarily part of the originator's plan.' As the members of the labour force had chronological lives, so in a sense, did the labour system, particularly the pattern of recruiting family groups to take up long-term residence in the community. Managers had to consider not only the changes the years made in the age and gender composition of their mill families, but also the dynamic of deference and discontent which their initial business decision had set in play. Many textile employers made a discrete choice between the two systems; others dabbled in both, in the manner Judy Lown describes at Courtaulds early Essex mills.[22] Penmans managers in Paris used a mixed system, recruiting and securing housing for both single women and family groups.

If the participation of Penmans officials in municipal electoral politics was seen as predatory and economically grounded, even when it was not and need not have been, the firm's labour recruitment schemes became almost entirely detached in the public mind from the corporation's needs and took on a glow of helpfulness and benefaction as sunny as the corporate councilman's image was dark. In the shifting balance between conflict and co-operation in labour relations, which Patrick Joyce has recently described, this was one of those times when, 'workers, just like employers' wanted to think of the employment relationship as 'consensual in form,' 'if developing out of material interests ... inseparably linked to cultural representations' of justice and respect.[23] As Penmans wanted a stable work force, the women who came to town to take jobs in the mill wanted regular work. That mutuality of interest led both parties to the labour relationship to accommodate certain unwelcome traits in the other, or to rename those traits so that they became easier to tolerate. Women mill workers reconfigured the employers' need for their labour, as a kindly recognition of their need for a job, emphasizing the steadiness of the work as compensation for the low levels of pay. Asked to reflect upon changes in the community through the inter-war years, Ida Pelton, an assisted immigrant from the midlands, replied:

I think it is a different world. I don't think the young people, I know they wouldn't work under the conditions we worked. They just wouldn't.

Q: Was Penmans more dominant in the community in the earlier days?

I don't know. I don't think they were dominant. I think people were so glad to get a job.

Henry Kelly, whose family had returned to Paris after a failed attempt to homestead in the west, made the same point in a different way. 'I never regretted [starting work at fourteen]. I can't complain. A lot of people run Penmans down but I never lost a month and a half in 51 years.'[24]

The Young Women's Christian Association played a central role in the recruitment of single women to work in the mills of Paris. John Penman had built the YWCA; title to the property passed to Penmans Limited in 1906; during the First World War, the firm expanded the facilities at the YWCA to include club rooms and residential accommodation for forty-five.[25] The wives of Penmans senior executives figured prominently on the board of the local association.

Whereas overseas recruitment had been predicated on the assumption of lifelong female waged work, the young Canadian women to whom Penmans promotional literature was directed were assumed sceptical about factory employment and likely to remain in the mills for a limited time. 'What Penmans Offer You,' a glossy, twelve-page, illustrated pamphlet published in 1923, introduced the various manufacturing processes in the mill, emphasizing the similarity between those tasks assigned beginners and 'the ordinary sewing found in any home,' promising light work 'readily picked up by any girl' in 'the most modern and sanitary workrooms in the country.' To assuage concerns that mill work was unconventional for young Canadian women, this literature claimed that 'fully half of the girls in Town are from other places in the Province,' about 1,000 in all 'employed under the same conditions as you would be.' Newcomers were assured 'arrangements' would 'be made to meet you at the train,' and that 'comfortable board' could 'be had at reasonable rates in well equipped homes with every effort being made to make the stay in Paris a happy and profitable one.'[26]

In addition to the forty-five rooms in its residence, the YWCA, acting under Penmans auspices, provided a rooms registry of accommodation available in 'suitable' private homes. Through Sunday morning services, Sunday afternoon fireside singsongs, classes in home nursing, first aid, physical culture, dressmaking, handicrafts, and dramatics, YWCA programs reached beyond its own residents to serve and monitor the wider population of young female factory workers in the community. Staff fostered a family atmosphere within the residence, attending carefully to interior decoration and to homely celebrations of birthdays and engagements.[27] They described their industrial work generally as 'for the social, physical and mental development of girls so that they may become the heads of splendid homes.' Through this emphasis upon domestic interests, and the validation of aspirations to marriage and motherhood, the YWCA programs comforted young Canadian women away from home for the first time and encouraged them to think well of mill work as a part of prudent financial preparation for a respectable married life. The YWCA was to be both a 'refining influence' and an acknowledgment of the aspirations to 'worthy womanhood' that young rural women brought with them when they came to town.[28]

For Penmans, contracting out to the YWCA a portion of the public relations work required to secure the respectability of female textile employment was both efficient and expeditious. The YWCA had both a cadre of experienced staff in their industrial department whom they could rotate through the Paris branch and provincial facilities to run educational and industrial conferences in which Penmans workers could participate.[29] Even in the nineteenth century young women had rebelled against the discipline of company-owned boarding places in other textile towns.[30] By the 1920s offering moral guidance indirectly was surely the preferable course for employers of young women. Although forthright that the goals of the residences for industrial workers were 'to protect, to shelter and to guide,' in a ringing declaration of gender solidarity, Mrs Percival Foster of the Dominion Council at the same time described the YWCA as 'a banding together of girls of every type; girls working for girls, backed by women of the highest ideals and ambitions.'[31] In Paris the leading backers and board members of the local YWCA were the wives of Penmans executives, Mrs Isaac Bonner, wife of the general manager, Mrs Henry Barrett, wife of Bonner's successor, Mrs C.B. Robinson, wife of the secretary-treasurer, Mrs H.W. Lundy, wife of the assistant general manager. These women, like the residents of the YWCA, lived in Penmans-owned accommodation, which they opened to the public for lawn parties, teas, and fund-raising sales to benefit the work of the association.[32] Their work as women together on the board made them knowledgeable about the character of the protection and guidance being offered female mill workers through YWCA programs, by means that delicately veiled the distinction between the class and gender bases for their concern.

In 1922, when Isaac Bonner was paying $60 per month and Henry Barrett $45 per month for the large Penmans houses they rented in the King's ward district called Quality Hill, the firm also owned a score of smaller dwellings on the streets near their factories. These were let to mill employees for rates between $10 and $18 per month.[33] Most were built to accommodate single families, although Mrs Ireland ran the larger house she rented from Penmans as a boarding-house for young women who worked in the mills, and Lillian Wilson remembered that her mother always kept lodgers in their Penmans house on the river flats in South ward.[34]

Harold Watson, a Toronto architect writing for the *Canadian Textile Journal* in 1920, argued that providing industrial housing was a good way for employers 'to insure the adequacy, stability and efficiency of labor,' and that at least in small communities it was prudent to consider whether 'it is best to pay a low wage and bear a part of the employees' housing costs,' 'in order to secure good workmen and hold them.'[35] A builder with experience constructing mill housing in Sherbrooke, Quebec, contended that the provision of good-quality dwellings would also inspire 'industry and stimulate ambition,' keeping working people from dissipating their pay 'at dances, in saloons, or buying foolish amusements that meant nothing.' For firms that needed to attract and hold experienced women workers, he argued, quality company housing had much historically in its favour. The provision of good housing stock adeptly addressed the mutual interests of the male employer and female employee. 'Young women, skilled workers, with the eternal main chance always in view – which is part of a woman's heritage – learn of this community, decide they will meet a better class of young men there, and promptly seek employment with the company.' 'A handsome little cottage' by signifying 'a most promising future to look forward to,' he contended, would draw 'the very best class of working men and women' into the community.[36]

Penmans built most of the housing it owned in Paris during the years between 1907 and 1928 when it was recruiting experienced hosiery workers, among them family groups, in the British east midlands. Midlands assisted immigrants are conspicuous among the tenants of Penmans-owned dwellings in the rent lists preserved for 1922. New-comers arriving in town in the years following the First World War found accommodation extremely scarce, and especially after the bonus for the new engineering works was passed, the town council – under pressure from the Board of Trade – tried to find ways to use federal and provincial monies to increase the amount of housing being built in town.[37]

Penmans board of directors did not seem to have featured the firm as a landlord in the long term. Although workers remembered the modest rents on company-owned housing as acceptable compensation for the low wages offered at the mill, the firm seemed more interested in the creation than in the continuing control of local housing stock. In the spring of 1922 the board authorized the sale for $1,800 of one of their dwellings on Walnut Street to George Keen. Keen, his wife, son, and daughter-in-law were production workers in the mill. Yet the following year the directors agreed to the building of more houses for workers in Paris. Lillian Wilson, who began work at Penmans in 1922 and retired in 1970, remembered buying on the urging of the firm the house in which her mother-in-law, also a long-time mill worker, had lived.[38]

Facilitating house ownership in a community in which there were few other places of employment was certainly as good a means, perhaps in the long run a better means than maintaining rental accommodation, by which to secure a stable work force. Employees were loath to leave their homes to take jobs elsewhere. Housing sales freed corporate capital for other purposes, and in a community in which the supply of company-owned housing had always been limited, reduced the sense of grievance against the company among those who had not been favoured with subsidized rents. Whereas the generations of young Canadian women who worked in the mills for limited periods before marriage created a persisting need over the generations for respectable boarding places such as the YWCA, the needs of the mill families who remained in town changed. By providing houses for rent to families of newcomers and then facilitating their transition to home ownership, Penmans insured a continuing mutuality of interest between the firm and the 'old hands' in town.

Briefly, in 1919 Penmans considered implementing profit sharing. From 1910 until 1918 executives of the firm encouraged the functioning of a benefit society among the employees of the Paris mills. Upon the recommendation of her or his foreman, a woman or man might join and in return for small fees become eligible for six months' benefits in the event of illness or accident. The society's executive, which always included a senior official of the firm as well as women and men representing each department in the mills, retained the 'power to refuse membership to any whose state of health or general habits, in their opinion, made the party an undesirable member.' Those who left the employ of the firm forfeited their accumulated fees and their entitlement to benefits.[39]

Of longer duration among management strategies to ensure stability in the work force was the Penmans discretionary pension plan, begun around 1922 and continued until 1964. Unlike the benefit society, the pension was not contributory or jointly managed by employer and employee representatives, but, in the words of a former manager, it was 'purely on the part of the company.' At their pleasure, the board of directors in Montreal granted specified payments, always for indefinite terms, to selected, long-serving employees who were no longer able to continue at the mill. Most of these women and men had been with the firm more than thirty-five years when they retired, some for as long as sixty-one. Typical among them was Miss Nellie Granton, granted $26 per month for an indefinite period in 1933, when ill health forced her to leave the mill after forty-eight years. Granton's pension would have been about half a month's take-home pay for the most skilled female piece-workers in the plant in 1934, an important supplement to the small federal pensions available to Canadians at age seventy after 1926. The prospect of a pension was thus a considerable inducement for workers to stay on at the mill as long as possible. The fact that these payments were discretionary and revocable made both aging employees and their kin consider carefully before they hazarded their good relations with the firm.[40]

Workers asked to characterize labour relations in town during the years after the First World War spoke not about the Benefit Society or pensions, but about the Penmans Pleasure Club. In winter the Pleasure Club organized dances and card parties twice a month, after 1924 in a dance hall provided by the firm on a floor of the underwear mill. In summer there were Penmans-sponsored sporting tournaments, picnics, and annual excursions by train and boat to Port Dalhousie on the Lake Erie shore, with prizes for the best baby and the largest family in attendance. These entertainments were described as 'for the sole benefit of the Penmans employees, to bring them together in a social way.' Sam Howell recalled, 'It was kind of old-fashioned; I don't think it would work now but in those days Penmans was more like a family affair ... we had a lot of social things going on, everybody was involved, the money

STRIKE AT PARIS, OCT 14, 07

Strikers, wearing their blue ribbon badges, pose on the steps of the Penmans General Office on Willow Street, 14 October 1907, surrounded by young supporters. In the foreground are the tracks of the street railway which ran from Paris to nearby Brantford.

wasn't there but I don't think there was too much opposition to the company.'[41]

A sense of indebtedness to Penmans was thus built into the physical and social fabric of the town. There were few other jobs available within the community for men, few comparable manufacturing jobs available in the economy generally for women. Through the extension of assisted passages to immigrant workers, the provision of boarding places for young women and subsidized housing for family groups, the patronage of valued community institutions, year-round recreational facilities, and seasonal outings for their employees, Penmans gave the firm's needs for a stable work force a public countenance of helpfulness and concern. Still, there were moments when managers misjudged the strength of their position within the community.

Before the celebrated three-month strike at Penmans in the winter of 1949, there were two earlier walk-outs of shorter duration. At the time of the transfer of control of the firm from John Penman to the Montreal interests, day shifts in the Paris mills were ten hours long, six days a week in winter, with Saturday afternoons off from mid-April to mid-October. In the fall of 1907 a group of twenty-seven women, who met regularly in the Virginia Club rooms in town, circulated a petition requesting that the Saturday half-holiday continue year round. Many began to wear blue ribbons, a symbol borrowed from contemporary temperance organizations, to signify their support of the campaign. When Penmans refused the request, 850 women and 150 men employed at the mills walked out and stayed out a week, until the firm agreed as a compromise to institute year-round Saturday half-days from the first week of 1908.[42] In February 1922 '150 girls and 25 men,' as the press consistently reported, walked out to protest the institution of an 18 per cent pay cut at the hosiery mill. The women were circular knitters; the men ran American flat-bed burson machines. For the duration of the ten-day strike the women met every afternoon in the town hall to discuss their problems. Many were recent immigrants whose diminishing pay packets were being docked constant weekly sums to repay the loans extended for their Atlantic passages. The firm settled first with the women, agreeing to rescind the latest pay cut, and three days later made a similar offer to the men. There was no union involved in either the 1907 or the 1922 strike, but the company's quick about-face early in the second week of the latter dispute may have been precipitated by rumours Penmans workers had approached a textile union to help them bargain for better wages.[43]

Why women workers should have stepped outside the dialectic of deference and undertaken collective action against the firm in 1907 and 1922 is difficult to specify clearly on the basis of the scant remaining documents. Conditions in the wider economy probably came into play. Both 1906–8 and 1920–2 were periods of recession. These economic downturns coincided with moments when the contractual basis of local labour relations pierced through the gauze of moral guardianship and mutuality. In 1907 mill workers were absorbing the implications of John Penman's departure from the firm he had built into a 'civic institution,' measuring the balance between rights and duties in their new relationship with distant and faceless financiers and shareholders. In 1922 the dark side of the transatlantic assisted-passages scheme loomed. The contracts to repay travel loans upon fixed schedules were legal and binding. Penmans promises to pay good wages had no status in law, were revocable, and were being revoked.

Times were buoyant for the knit-goods industry in the late 1920s and were especially prosperous for Penmans, which effectively diversified its product lines to met the rising demand for fashion-knitwear, swimsuits, and silk hosiery. In 1926 the firm was running its mills at 115 per cent capacity, and through the late 1920s the success of the firm was heralded in trade journals as unparalleled in the history of the Canadian industry.[44] As the depression deepened in the early 1930s employment levels in the knit-goods sector remained high. Mill activity declined from 1930 by 3 per cent in 1931, 4 per cent in 1932, and 6 per cent in 1933, but by 1934 it had regained 1930 levels. Penmans employed 724 factory workers in 1929 and only forty fewer in the worst year of the downturn. It increased its number of knitting machines by 25 per cent between 1926 and 1935 and continued through these years to run at 82–97 per cent of capacity.[45]

With rare exceptions, throughout and after the inter-war period Penmans was hard pressed to find enough women and girls locally to run the mills. Women who had proved themselves high-production piece-workers, knitters, loopers, seamers, overlockers, and cutters were particularly valuable to the firm. Although the logistics were awkward for the foremen, mothers not yet willing to return to the mill, where their earnings on belt-driven machinery would be higher, were offered motor-driven sewing, looping, and griswold knitting machines to work on at home. Yarn boys from the mill trekked about town bearing yarn and finished goods, and mechanics were on call to service the machines of homeworkers. Those who returned to the mill while their children were young, by agreement, came in late and left early. Widows who found they could not afford retirement after their husbands' deaths, were taken back to their old jobs. All these accommodations are described retrospectively by mill workers, foremen, and managers alike, in highly personalized terms, as favours, grounded in a tradition of mutual helpfulness. At the community level, both parties felt confirmed in their own worth by the mutual benefits of the exchange and marked their ability to meet one another's needs as a sign that they worked with good people in a good place.[46]

At no time, at least retrospectively, was the sense of indebtedness to the firm deeper than during the 1930s. Most mill workers remembered slack time during the depression not as a penalty inflicted upon them by the firm, but as an unbidden shared burden portioned out by regretful managers and foremen, in fairness and as a last resort. Rather than impose long lay-offs on younger employees on the basis of seniority, Penmans rotated short time. Even those witnesses before the Royal

Commission on the Textile Industry hearings in town in 1938 who were most willing to state their grievances against the firm agreed that the rates were held steady and 'efforts were made to the share the work around,' to see that 'everything was evened up.' Thomas Blaney remembered 'In the cutting room, there were seven of us there, so they tried to share it. Maybe I would be off tomorrow and the next guy would be off for a couple of days. They were pretty fair that way.' Because the federal and provincial regulations governing relief payments excluded women, on the grounds that they had husbands to support them or could return to their parental homes, these work-sharing arrangements were particularly important to female mill workers, many of whom were alone or living in female-headed households. Ida Glass, also a cutter, began at Penmans in 1936 and carried her memories of the 1930s through the whole of her thirty-four-year career at the mills. 'When you come through a depression you are pretty careful about your job. We came through the depression the hard way. They didn't get a lot of work, but they always tried to give them one or two days. They always tried to be fair and see that they were working.' Frank Boyle, a burson knitter, was clearer about the firm's interest in rotating work. With the others in his department he worked week and week about to get money to buy groceries, and in his off time he was sent over as a learner to the spinning mill: 'just to hold onto us, we never got paid for it. It was just something we could learn in the meantime if we wanted.'[47]

The practice of rotating work which allowed Penmans to keep its experienced employees in town was more effective because family incomes in the community were jointly constituted, so that week by week it was likely that someone in each household had wages to bring home. But it was the industrial organization of the knit-goods sector and the security founded on its place within the national political economy which made it possible for the firm to maintain relatively stable production through the depression. Whatever may have been the case for its workers, Penmans was never a company that lived from hand to mouth. The firm always worked to inventory rather than to order. Clarence Cobbett, a knitter who rose to superintendent of the hosiery mill, remembered: 'They were a great firm for going by their records, seeing what they produced in a similar line last year and putting in inventories. They were fortunate those times to have enough financially that they could carry stocks until things caught up.' Stocks grew so formidable in the 1930s that the firm took over part of the skating rink next to the underwear mill to store unsold goods. Charles Harrison recalled vividly his father's returning home wearily from the mill and saying, 'We had to lay off. There are 1200 dozen in the warehouse. We've got to cut back to 1000 dozen.'[48]

Penmans was well situated to weather a downturn. In 1906 the Montreal group had taken over $2.4 million in assets from the Penmans Manufacturing Company and then by increasing the appraised value of the existing assets by $0.4 million and creating a good-will account of $2.1 million recapitalized the new firm, Penmans Limited, at $5 million, more than twice the original purchase price. With a cash payment of $500,000 Charles Blair Gordon, David Morrice, and their colleagues at the Bank of Montreal had created a company with a book value in 1906 of ten times that amount. Steadily through the next ten years they directed earnings into reserves, gradually replacing with real investment the phantom good-will that had backed the watered stock. Every year through the 1920s, save 1921, earnings were transferred into reserves, to a total of $2.7 million in the period 1919 to 1925 alone. Despite the large portion of retained earnings, dividends on preferred stock were paid at the rate of 6 per cent per annum throughout the period 1907 to 1935, earnings on common shares averaged 7.5 per cent, and a 1928 split trebled the book value of common shares. In 1927 Penmans was described by financial analysts as 'one of the most consistently high earners for some years past among Canadian industrial corporations,' and even in the hard years, 1930 through 1935, Penmans net profits averaged 4.1 per cent of annual sales.[49]

Whereas the knit-goods industries in Great Britain and the United States were characterized by many small competing firms (the manufacture of full-fashioned hosiery in the United States became a classic textbook case for state regulation to curb predatory wage and price cutting in a competitive sector),[50] the highly concentrated pattern of ownership in the Canadian industry made it relatively easy for 'an association of manufacturers ... to establish control over production and prices.' In 1933 eight firms accounted for 54 per cent of knit-goods sales; in 1935 eleven firms controlled 70 per cent of the market. In both years Penmans alone produced almost 18 per cent of the knit-goods sold in Canada.[51] Penmans sales dropped from $5.9 million in 1930 to $5.2 million in 1936, but firms carefully filed advance notice of price changes with the Canadian Woollen and Knitgoods Manufacturers' Association and attended closely to the circulars sent out regularly by Major Douglas Hallam, the association's secretary, specifying his 'understanding of our lowest prices on certain merchandise.' By this means, as Penmans

TABLE 1
Index numbers of wholesale prices, (1929 = 100)

Year	All exports	Wheat No. 1 Northern	Cotton underwear	Wool hosiery and knit goods
1929	100.0	100.0	100.0	100.0
1930	83.9	70.2	97.2	86.2
1931	65.6	43.8	90.4	77.9
1932	59.5	41.1	84.7	72.2
1933	59.9	45.4	82.4	72.2
1934	65.7	55.7	86.9	80.9
1935	67.5	62.9	87.5	77.1
1936	72.5	69.8	87.2	76.9

SOURCE: Royal Commission on the Textile Industry, *Report* 1938, 94, 96, 100

general manager, H.W. Lundy, observed in 1936 testimony before the Royal Commission on the Textile Industry, it was possible 'to keep the market from going to pieces.'[52]

Far from going to pieces, Canadian manufacturers actually consolidated their control over the national market during the early years of the depression. Although Canadian consumption, for example, of socks and stockings declined from 5.7 million dozen pairs in 1930 to 5.2 in 1933, the proportion of this market met by Canadian production rose from 68.4 to 98.3 per cent.[53] The protected position of the Canadian knit-goods sector is particularly apparent when prices for its products are compared with those facing export industries in world markets.

The Canadian textile industry had always enjoyed considerable tariff protection. The tariff on hosiery and knit-goods was 35 per cent in 1896 when John Penman, as first president of the Canadian Woollen and Knitgoods Manufacturers' Association, led a delegation to Ottawa demanding a rise in current duties from the newly constituted Tariff Enquiry and Commission, headed by Liberal Finance Minister W.S. Fielding.[54] Despite grimaces and threats, succeeding Liberal governments maintained the general tariff on knit-goods at this level for the next forty-one years until 1937, when, as part of the Canada / United Kingdom Trade Agreement, the duty on non-British imports was raised a further 10 per cent. In a gesture towards imperial solidarity and to safeguard British markets for Canadian staple exports, British wares had entered Canada at preferential rates of 25 per cent on hosiery and 22.5 per cent on garments since 1898.[55] These were the only real competitors against domestically produced knit-goods in the Canadian market. The Liberal government of Mackenzie King had reduced these duties to an even 20 per cent in 1928. But in a sweeping 1930 upward revision in the tariffs, the newly elected Conservatives, led by R.B. Bennett, raised the level of protection against British goods to 30 per cent on hosiery and 25 per cent on knitted garments. Only after the worst of the depression had passed and the Liberals returned to power were the 1928 British Preferential duties re-established.[56]

Canadian knit-goods manufacturers had never argued that their claims to protection would be short term, that their industry would in time outgrow the need for tariff shelter. John Penman in 1896, Richard Thomson in 1905, and Henry Barrett in 1927 used the same defence of high duties against import competition in the sector their firm dominated. Canadian production costs would always be greater than those abroad, they contended, because Canadian workers were better paid: 'thank God that our textile wages and living conditions are higher than those of Europe'; and Canadian manufacturers could operate 'continuously throughout the year and give steady employment' only if they could count on a 'fair share' of the domestic market.[57]

The case for well-paid, steady employment in the textile industry entailed an embattled corollary proposition. Against the public consensus, growing more unanimous in the 1930s, that women's place was in the home, textile manufacturers as the largest employers of female industrial workers in the dominion, argued that 'the health and success of our women workers is just as essential, if not more so, than that of male workers.' To mitigate the contemporary anomaly of their claim, employers cited historical precedent as entitlement. 'In the past women performed in the home a great deal of work ... spinning, weaving and making clothing, carpets and hangings. This work is now done in factories, and it is an economic necessity that they follow their work to the factory.' Attempting to make common cause with rural Canadians (primary producers were the most vociferous opponents of the tariff which offered them no apparent direct benefit yet raised their costs as consumers), industry spokesmen tried to address rural fears, emphasizing that the majority of woollen and knitting mills were located in small towns 'where they provide congenial work for the bright young men and women who would otherwise drift to the larger centres of population or to the United States, to the impoverishment of the life of the rural towns.' Addressing female audiences, the secretary of the Canadian Woollen and Knitgoods Manufacturers' Association discounted the fashion appeal of imported labels and, stressing the sorry working conditions in overseas mills, argued that buying Canadian goods made by Canadian women added 'to the comfort and freedom of women generally.'

No claim for the tariff was more at odds with the times than the defence by the textile lobby of the jointly earned family income. The polemic was frequently repeated and bears rendition in full.

> If women who desire to work, because of necessity or to supplement the family income, are unable to find suitable employment they are consumers and not producers. They must be fed, clothed and housed. The cost of their maintenance falls on the wages paid men and must either lower the standard of living or increase the prices of goods produced in industries which employ men only, such as lumbering and papermaking, mining, steelworking, building etc. 'Light' industries employing women are necessary for the economic operation of 'heavy' industries.

Here was the political and economic bedrock upon which the high textile tariff was firmly grounded. Dissonant as it was with the male-breadwinner ideology gaining currency among social reformers and organized labour, industrial jobs for women justified lower wage bills, made more 'economic' the operation of those key sectors of the economy where men alone might be employed, and in the bargain spared wage-earning fathers the keep of their daughters 'between the time of leaving school and marrying.'[58] In most Canadian manufacturing communities men predominated in the labour force. In these municipalities, local councils, on the urging of local boards of trade, actively recruited firms that would create complementary female payrolls in town, increasing family incomes and reducing the upward pressure on wages for established businesses employing men. As we shall see, Hanover was one such community. Firms such as Penmans, with large female payrolls, located in towns such as Paris where there were few jobs for men, reaped a twofold benefit from the winning contention that light industries and heavy industries thrived in happy symbiosis. They gained both tariff protection and – as Harold Wilson, the British-born textile adviser to the Advisory Board on Tariff and Taxation in 1927, observed, puzzling over the peculiar circumstances of the Canadian industry – 'cheap labour and labour which would not be tempted to other occupations, as would be the case in proximity to a larger centre.'[59]

Many textile communities were essentially, as Paris was, single-industry towns, whose collective fortunes rose and fell with the changing circumstances of one large employer. Early in 1936 in the midst of bargaining for protection against Japanese imports, Dominion Textiles closed its artificial-silk mill in Sherbrooke, Quebec, dumping 1,000 employees from its payroll onto the municipal welfare roll. The newly re-elected Liberal government of William Lyon Mackenzie King, wishing both to resist this industrial blackmail and to buy time, called the question which had so long lurked beneath the surface in the tariff debate. King chose Mr Justice W.F.A. Turgeon, a Liberal from the wheat-producing province of Saskatchewan where anti-tariff sentiment ran deep, to head a royal commission on the textile industry, directed to appraise the extent to which an employer that had accepted tariff shelter 'can reasonably and properly be expected to maintain employment over periods of temporary difficulty.' Once 'the community has accepted to tax itself for the industry's benefit,' what duties did the industry owe the community in return? Turgeon acknowledged the asymmetry between the explicit and implicit obligations historically entailed in the tariff bargain, and yet he concluded: 'In the case of a manufacturer operating under a protective tariff there is no express contract between parties, but there is surely an implied understanding on the part of the manufacturer, so long as he continues to enjoy the advantage of the tariff, to refrain from throwing workmen out of employment especially in times of distress, without reasonable justification or excuse.'[60] In 1931 section 17 had been added to the customs tariff, allowing the cabinet to reduce the customs duties or impose equivalent excise taxes upon producers who abused the protection of the tariff by raising prices. Drawing largely upon the advice of two leading members of the recently founded Canadian social democratic party (the Co-operative Commonwealth Federation), sociologist Leonard Marsh and lawyer and law professor Frank R. Scott, who argued that the obligations of tariff-sheltered industries towards workers should have the same status in law as their obligations towards consumers,[61] Turgeon recommended an extension to section 17 which

> would make it clear to shareholders that in such questions as that of giving or withholding employment (as in that of fixing the selling price of the company's products, already provided for), the management must be mindful of the interests of the community as well as those of the shareholders; that the shareholders' interests may have to give way, on

occasions, to those of the community; and that arbitrary action by the management detrimental to the community will result in the withdrawal from the company of the advantage which it enjoys by law in common with other Canadian companies selling in the home market.[62]

With this recommendation and the parallel advice that collective bargaining be recognized within the textile industry,[63] Turgeon envisioned the closing of the circle in the duties of protection, establishing a statutory symmetry between the obligations of the protector and the protected, both at the level of national policy and in industrial relations within the firm.

The commissioner's advice went unheeded. By the time his report was published in 1938, both the political and the economic conjuncture that had spawned the investigation had passed. As Riane Mahon has convincingly argued, the tariff bargain always had been contested in a nation that relied primarily on primary export production to generate its wealth. After the Second World War the political and economic forces governing world trade changed radically, and with them the place of the textile industry within the national political economy.[64]

In small textile communities such as Paris the duties of protection arose from a mutuality between gendered identities and class interests. The factory paternalist by his fatherly concern seemed to assuage the anomaly of female industrial employment, by his authority securing both factory discipline and respectability for factory work. The welfare capitalist functioned more indirectly in his relations with female employees, directing their aspirations for marriage, their opportunities for courtship and play, their fears of unemployment and penurious old age, leveraging these hopes and fears through company concerns. Within the town the recognition that the mainstream culture regarded female factory work as unfitting, strengthened employers' hand, and employees' gratitude for the gift of mill work. In the wider political economy, the complementarity of female mill work with male employment in heavy industry tied the textile interest in protection to the interests of major employers of men in the crucial debate over the tariff.

■ Chapter Three

When is knitting women's work?

When immigrant families compared their experiences on two sides of the Atlantic, women said they preferred Ontario; men thought the midlands a better place to work. Several households actually divided after a few years in Canada, the men returning to the Old Country, the women remaining in Paris with their children. There is a deceptively simple, essentially economic explanation for why, among families long employed in the hosiery and knit-goods industry, husbands and brothers should differ from sisters and wives as they compared Canada with Britain. Despite the fact that the technology employed and the products produced in the English midlands and southwestern Ontario were much alike, men were far more likely to find work in English knitting mills than in similar Canadian firms. Relatively there were more jobs for men in English than Canadian plants. Conversely, many positions considered suitable for men alone in England were routinely filled by women in Canada and relatively there were more jobs for women in Canadian than English knitting mills. Charles Harrison's wife, a war bride from the midlands, remembered her English uncle's astonishment that customarily she and other women in Canada shaded stockings, matching fine hosiery for pairs, a task open in Britain only to men who had served a lengthy apprenticeship. There were more women employed in all aspects of the finishing process in Canada than in England and more women involved in yarn preparation as well. There were other jobs which did not differ in their gender ascriptions across the Atlantic. In both England and Canada all factory seamers, the most numerous employees in the industry, were female as they had been when hosiery and knitted garments were pieced together in homes and small workshops. All the fixers who set up and restarted machines and the mechanics who repaired them were male in both Ontario and the midlands because mechanical aptitude was considered, whether in the Mother Country or the new dominion, to be a masculine rather than a feminine attribute.

Among all the jobs in a knitting mill, the most contested and intriguing in its gender ascription is knitting itself. At the turn of the century in the English east midlands and in southwestern Ontario knitting was both women's and men's work and exceptional in the hosiery industry as a mixed gender occupation. Simultaneously, in the 1850s and 1860s, on both sides of the Atlantic, knitting had moved from the workshop to the factory and become steam rather than hand powered.[1] In the technological and organizational changes that followed knitting rooms became disputed terrain. As the sexual division of labour in the hosiery was reformulated with increasing automation, the knitter was the worker whose appropriate gender was most in question, most frequently seen to require explanation and defence. In the midlands and in Ontario knitting was made men's or women's work through a complex interaction which combined tradition from the workshop and the early factory with social prescriptions about who was entitled to work for wages at all and characteristics of the local labour market and labour organization and of both the product market and the prevailing technology. In Canada and in England the process arrayed managers against workers and men against women but also forged alliances across class and gender differences. The result was descriptions of what knitting was and who knitters were which differed markedly between the English districts from which the Paris emigrants came and the Canadian mills where they – the women at least – were employed for the rest of their working lives.

THE EAST MIDLANDS

The east midlands was the centre of the English hosiery industry. Traditions from the workshops that were being replaced remained strong in the hosiery factories of Nottinghamshire and Leicestershire in 1900, and customary gender divisions in knitting persisted, as theorists have suggested, 'regardless of the reason women or men were initially used' in certain jobs.[2] The most common workshop knitting machines were the fully fashioned frames said to have been invented by William

A Canadian stockinger knitting on a hand frame, Port Hope, Ontario, c. 1870.
Note the two women finishing stockings behind the frame in this domestic
or workshop setting.

Lee in the sixteenth century. From the establishment of the industry in
England there were women knitters, as the membership lists of the
Worshipful Company of Framework Knitters for the early eighteenth
century clearly show. In a small number of cases, for example, Unwin of
Sutton-in-Ashfield in the eighteenth century and Wolsey in Leicester in
the nineteenth, women are known to have run important merchant
hosier enterprises.[3] In domestic production gender divisions needed to
be relatively flexible, because at any given time the number of males and
females available for work in a family was fixed. Women knitters were
not oddities in the framework villages. Still, men more often knit while
women seamed, and the struggling stockinger portrayed in poems and
royal commission testimony was usually male.[4]

From the mid-nineteenth century, however, another kind of knitting
machine was used by some domestic knitters. The circular machine,

attributed to the engineer Marc Isambard Brunel, was manufactured for women, 'small and compact enough to be screwed to a lady's work-table.' The rotary motion of the circulars was adapted to steam power sooner and more successfully than was the alternating clatter of the stockinger's frame, and the circular machines, inconspicuous in domestic industry, achieved early and continuing dominance in the factory stage. The circulars, small, physically undemanding, and well adapted for domestic use, were thought of as 'ladies' machines' and run by women 'from the first years of factory production.'[5]

Both male capitalists and male knitters had reviled circular knit goods, what Felkin called 'stockings in the form of bags,' from their inception as threats to traditional craftsmanship and wages in the industry, but by the 1890s, with the numerical dominance of more productive circular knitting technology firmly established, male knitters began to reconstrue tradition. When A.J. Mundella, a Nottingham manufacturer with long experience in the industry, reminded a hosiery union official appearing before the 1892 Labour Commission that 'Women always did the circular trade very largely,' Samuel Bower, secretary of the Midlands Federation of Hosiery Workers, disagreed and answered by talking instead about men's traditional work on full-fashioned frames. A workman wrote to the journal of the trade decrying the 'supplanting' of male by female labour in the circular branch and both hosiery manufacturers and technical experts fretted that with women knitters 'a divided interest entered the trade' challenging the honoured male stockinger tradition of the industry.[6] By 1900 men with diverse and often conflicting interests in the industry shared a sense that the status of knitting had been devalued, not by the factory transition but by the greater dependence in the factory stage upon women's circular machines. Using the tradition of male knitters on the flat-bed frames (the most numerous steam-powered version of which was the Cotton's Patent), they were arguing that all knitters were historically and preferably male. Making the claim stick was another matter.

Among east-midlands communities, gender divisions in knitting varied depending upon the relative numbers of men and women

A modern, Canadian-made, hand-powered circular knitting machine similar to that patented by Brunel, for use in domestic production. Such machines, about fourteen inches high and ten inches in diameter, were driven by an egg-beater-like crank affixed to the side.

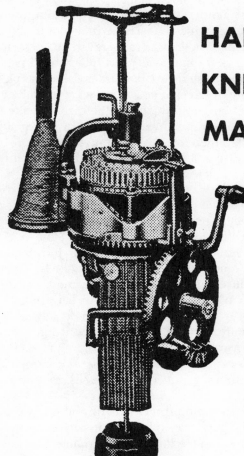

available to work. Jobs were not reassigned between men and women in seaming or fixing where customary female and male ascriptions had not been challenged. But once the gender of knitters was contested, these tasks became the rudders through which imbalances in the local labour market could be adjusted and turned to advantage. In colliery and agricultural districts where work for men was plentiful and well paid, hosiery firms employed surplus local female labourers as knitters as well as seamers and menders. Only overseeing and fixing were unambiguously male occupations in the hosiery industry in the early twentieth century. Expert observers, for example, William Davis of University College, Nottingham, suggested therefore that 'the one-sided nature of the labour conditions which arise when the knitting industry develops on a large scale' made it 'an essential condition of success ... that engineering or mining industries exist side by side so as to stabilise the labour position.' Alternatively when jobs for men were not available locally, for example, in Hinckley, Leicestershire, manufacturers found it in their interest to name all knitting jobs men's work, fearing 'the loss of female labour if families were not retained in the district.' In the process male capitalists seemed to be conceding male unionists' claim that men should be knitters locally because 'there was a great many more chances for a woman getting a job than a man.' By contrast, in Leicester, the rising boot and shoe industry which employed many men allowed for the smooth and steady feminization of hosiery production.[7] The advantages of complementarity with other local employers and the need to secure a stable labour force made the traditional gender divisions in knitting contingent – sometimes reducing, sometimes reinforcing customary practices.

As local labour availability and reinterpretations of tradition in the industry made the appropriate gender of circular knitters increasingly ambiguous in the years 1890–1910, the technology itself changed rapidly. Circular frames became more automatic. Through a programmable reciprocating action, hosiery machines completed a stocking from top through heel to toe, and round underwear frames made changes in dimension and splices without operator intervention. Both American and English machine builders sold these innovations in trade journals as 'light to handle,' 'easy running,' and 'comparatively easy to operate,' and following contemporary engineering conventions emphasized that such equipment lent 'itself to female and unskilled labour.'[8]

Engineers' deskilling strategies have been stressed in the literature on the degradation of work and labour segmentation. But it is misleading to

Female knitters working circular rib machines in the Nottinghamshire village of Daybrook, 1924. Two male fixers and a white-shirted foreman are also visible.

assume that machine builders' design goals were determining on the factory floor. Certainly midlands knitting experts were unwilling to concede authority in determining knitting gender divisions to engineering firms. Why automated circular machinery should 'increase the demand for female labour' was 'a question in the minds of many that [had] not yet been satisfactorily answered,' according to James Quilter, editor of the *Hosiery Trade Journal*. Neither Quilter nor John Chamberlain, his frequent collaborator in technical manuals on knitting and successor as editor of the *Journal*, welcomed the feminization in knitting which the growing pre-eminence of circular machines seemed to portend. Quilter argued that if the stockingers of the future were 'to be more of the female class ... the ever remembered and respected old type of stockinger (would) be only known in history,' and the standing of the industry inevitably would be compromised. Lecturers at midlands technical colleges did not associate deskilling technological change with the decline of the hosiery; they admired the 'near perfection' of the new machines. Their apprehensions were not about the changes in stockingers' jobs, but about the change in the gender of the stockingers. For this transformation they blamed not the machine designers but male knitters who had 'not taken to' the new equipment at its introduction or 'before giving it a good trial, made conditions which were not acceptable by employers.' That the new circulars were 'not under the control of men' was 'the fault of the men themselves,' the technical experts charged.[9]

The men Chamberlain and Quilter meant were male unionists. Unions were not an implacable force in the hosiery industry. They were segregated by locality and craft, organizing distinct firms in an industry that showed little vertical integration. In the largest knitting centres, Nottingham, Leicester, Loughborough, and Hinckley, union influence was strong, but the country districts remained difficult to organize even after the several branches of the union movement consolidated their forces. None the less the hosiery unions tried to take an 'active role' in the subsequent reformulation of gender divisions in knitting, forwarding men's interests to the detriment of female members.[10]

Women did not join the unions in as great numbers as did men, either in the country districts or in the towns in the late nineteenth or the twentieth century. Wells estimated that about 20 per cent of women employees by comparison with 40 per cent of men were unionists: women in all industries, he complained, were 'notoriously difficult to organise.' But union leaders did not serve their female members well. Neither their benefit plans nor their interventions on behalf of employees provided much incentive for women workers to join. The unions, male institutions from the pre-factory stage, were still in the 1930s 'run by the men for the men.'[11]

Fewer benefits were paid to women and in lesser amounts. In 1915 in Nottingham women victimized for organizing were voted half the compensation offered men. Many hosiery unions opted out of the early state unemployment insurance plans which offered equal benefits to men and women. The Leicester trades' alternative plan took equal subscriptions from men and women, while providing unemployed women with two shillings less per week than unemployed men. When Nottingham hosiery finishers suggested that the sick benefit be paid in maternity cases, the request was denied. Only in payment for dues collection did the unions craft a gender gap that favoured women, acknowledging that women collectors had a more meagre benefit package to sell to female members who had other grounds to be sceptical as well.[12]

Union officials intervened more frequently and firmly to defend men's jobs than they did those of women and, in disputes over entitlement by gender to jobs, consistently favoured males. The terms of settlement of a 1919 strike in Nottingham made the lines of defence

clear: 'no restrictions in the use or output on any machine by either male
or female, but it shall not be permitted to put female labour on machines
ordinarily worked by men.' Women who had worked on Cotton's
Patents, the 'men's' flat-bed machines derived from the stockinger's
frame, were treated as blacklegs.[13] But men's claims to circular machines
were treated with some delicacy. When a group of unemployed male
knitters in Hinckley demanded the right to replace women then running
a certain type of circular, officials did refuse their request for a men-only
meeting to decide the question. But they agreed that men should be
given every 'chance to learn this kind of machine' and priority when
vacancies occurred. Employers were regularly advised that 'it would
remove unrest in the trade if they could see their way clear to replace the
women with men' in the circulars, and employers frequently obliged.[14]

Although class interests regularly arrayed male unionists and male
manufacturers against one another, their common gender formed the
basis for a consensus on some matters. Both manufacturers and men
believed that gender-specific restrictions on women's night work were
appropriate. Both capitalists and union leaders saw mechanical facility
as a valuable trait possessed exclusively by men. Through the inter-war
years these shared beliefs about the essential differences between men
and women overrode any contravening considerations of profitability or
technical feasibility and became key to reforming gender divisions in the
knit-goods industry.

The convergence of male interests around shift work formed slowly.
In the 1890s when the circular technology was changing rapidly,
manufacturers argued for double shifts, 'anxious to get what they could
out of new machine' before it was 'superseded by something better.'
Male workers pressed rather for overtime in rush seasons, a strategy
that maximized their earnings and emphasized their preferability over
women knitters – whose home responsibilities conflicted with extended
hours. Equipment shortages in the wake of the First World War created
pressures to institutionalize shift work, extending the two wartime
shifts to three. At the level of policy, unions' opposition to shift work
remained firm, but a technological change in seaming, which seemed
likely to favour women's circular knitting machines over the flat-beds,
forced the men to a pre-emptive concession. The newly perfected
flat-lock seamers made so comfortable and durable a join in cut-up
circular fabric that the shaped selvedges of garment parts knit on the
flat-bed Cotton's Patents lost a crucial advantage. In the spring of 1921
'to compete better against the circular' and the women knitters who ran

Male knitters running flat-bed sweater knitting machines at Penmans, Paris
1935

them, the Cotton's Patent men agreed to run double shifts, allowing
their employers to recoup more quickly the heavier capital costs of
flat-bed equipment.[15] In the same months the unions of Nottingham,
Leicester, and Ilkeston protested vehemently against the new Employment of Women, Young Persons and Children Act, under which the
home secretary was authorizing women to work an extra shift on the
circulars, thus undermining the advantage greater access to shift work
gave men.[16]

A combination of cyclical and technological change in the 1930s
consolidated night work and a three-shift system in the midlands
hosiery. Union officials continued to condemn shift work, 'from an
idealistic viewpoint' as a 'trespass on the social rights of the people,' a
damning example of how the hosiery trade was 'failing in its duty
toward mankind.' But the new non-unionized knit-goods plants in
London and Lancashire were gaining cost advantages by running shifts,
and the new finer-guage interlock machines ran poorly or not at all
unless, to maintain constant temperatures and relative humidity, they
were worked continuously day and night. The crisis, competition, and

a more capital-intensive technology forged a consensus between masters and men. Manufacturers' costs were minimized and production workers' earnings maximized by the shift system. By law, the night shift alone was exclusively male, but men were unwilling to work permanent nights. Peter Armstrong has argued for the footwear industry that 'the firm's drive to maximize the return on capital investment combined with the constraints presented by "protective legislation" on the one hand and the unwillingness of the men to work permanent nights shifts on the other' resulted in the exclusion of women from capital-intensive processes.[17] In practice, most knitting soon became a male preserve. But how men were able to make their disinclination to work permanent nights into an accepted claim of control over all knitting, night and day, requires further explanation.

Here job composition, the tasks grouped and labelled one person's work, becomes crucial. Job composition is as dependent upon social relations in a particular setting as upon the engineering properties of a given technology. In the inter-war period in the midlands, management and union agreed that the job of the male circular knitter consisted of tending a third more machines than did the job of female circular knitter. In time men became acknowledged as more productive and then more efficient knitters, a confusion of output with entitlements which technical experts in the industry, long averse to female knitters, readily endorsed.[18] More important in the long run, however, in establishing knitting as men's work, was the inter-war renegotiation of the appropriate balance, within the job, between the functions of minders and mechanics.

Hand-frame knitters had been mechanics, but with the advent of the factory and power machinery the knitter's and the mechanic's functions had become separated in the midlands. Industry commentators linked this change to the precedence of the female circular knitter 'who could not be expected to be a mechanic.' As Millicent Fawcett noted, concerning the contemporary woven textile trade, 'It was looked upon as a law of nature that a man could set a machine and that a woman could not,' when the central distinction was rather between what men were allowed to know and women were not allowed to know.[19] But manufacturers, technical advisers, and union leaders in the hosiery industry shared the social consensus that mechanical aptitude was gendered male, and with it the implication that men appropriately controlled machines and only 'lent' them to women.[20]

The line between the knitter's 'minding' and the mechanic's 'maintaining' varied with the context (and starkly across the Atlantic). Once 'a thorough knowledge of all the mechanisms involved' was required of all knitters, the women to whom the circular frames had been 'lent' began to find the loans recalled.[21] After the Second World War machines for making both seamless hose and tubular fabric became so productive that it was no longer worth the trouble for employers to contest the union's claims that these few jobs should be men's.[22] Amid the radical changes in the technology, labour process, and relations between owners and workers, the gender balance of the stockinger's workshop had been re-established by the 1940s in midlands factory knitting rooms.

SOUTHWESTERN ONTARIO

The knitting technology used in Ontario and the midlands was essentially the same. Machines were purchased from common English and United States engineering firms and innovations were installed at roughly similar rates. Yet transatlantic differences between the two contexts in the structure of firms, the pattern of labour recruitment, and the strength of workers' organizations meant that by 1950 Ontario conventions concerning the preferred gender of knitters and the appropriate rewards due those with the mechanical knowledge to set up machines were not those current in the east midlands.

Whereas the English hosiery was characterized by many small independent firms specializing in one phase of the production process,[23] the Canadian industry was oligopolistic and vertically integrated. Penmans controlled the making of outerwear, underwear, hosiery, and socks from the opening of bales of raw cotton and the scouring of wool fleeces to the boxing and shipping of finished garments. Their facilities in Paris included a yarn mill, dye house, three knitting mills, and a box factory.

Like the midlands hosiery, the Ontario knit-goods industry employed a preponderance of female labour, and for the same reason. The most labour-intensive part of the production process – seaming – was, by unquestioned convention, women's work. Canadian managers, like English owners, saw a good community mix of men's and women's jobs as the best way to secure a stable female labour force, but the more diversified structure of Canadian firms meant that they had more flexibility in pursuing this goal.

Demand in the knit-goods industry was booming at the same time as new 'automatic' circulars were being put in place in Canada. Penmansclad construction workers built two new railways across Canada in the first decade of this century and opened many new mines in the north. Rather than designate men's jobs from among mixed-gender occupations such as knitting in order to anchor more families of female mill workers in town, Paris managers expanded their local production to include spinning, dyeing, pressing, and box-making – all processes that included many tasks conventionally assigned to men alone. By creating these separate new departments in which men predominated, the company assured the labour segmentation that kept its large seaming and finishing departments safely separate, female, and low waged. And the expansion of the spinning mill complemented the continued employment of female circular knitters. By ensuring more closely monitored, higher-quality yarn supplies, Penmans reduced the incidence of breakdowns in knitting rooms and thus the disadvantages of using women, assumed less able to deal with mechanical failures, on the circular machines.[24]

The oligopolistic structure of the Canadian knitting industry also made active labour recruitment strategies more cost-effective in small-town Ontario than they would have been among small competing firms in the midlands. Whereas midlands hosiers moved *to* pools of female labour in the countryside, Penmans recruited *from* overseas. Among the parties Penmans brought from the midlands to Paris between 1906 and 1928 there were some male family members who took 'men's jobs' in the mills, but the majority of the assisted immigrants were women, among them a number of women knitters. Confident of their command over all jobs in the small Canadian knit-goods industry, Penmans used gender-specific recruitment overseas to secure the extra women employees it needed in boom times, obviating the need to reassign jobs that formerly might have been held by either men or women to male workers alone.[25]

With the exception of a small, hand-powered circular machine used by female outworkers to manufacture argyle socks, all Penmans knitting technology was imported – before 1950 in approximately equal portions from England and the United States. The machinery brought with it certain scripted gender divisions. The accompanying engineering manuals described the characteristics of the operators for whom the machines had been designed. The factory technicians dispatched to set up the equipment reiterated these specifications. The lead knitting foremen until the Second World War were male immigrants from either the midlands or the United States. These men were hired for their experience with the knitting-room personnel practices, as well as the machines, used in their homelands. They arrived with clear preconceptions about who knitters ought to be. Together imported engineering targets and management conventions influenced gender divisions in Canadian inter-war knitting perceptibly towards those current whence the machines came. All flat-bed machines, whether the American bursons or the English full-fashioned frames, were run by men. In 1936 60 per cent of knitters on American circulars were women; only 36 per cent ran British circulars. These echoes of distant conventions about gender lingered after the Second World War.[26]

Penmans workers themselves did not have strong preferences between English and American machines. Knitters tended fewer of the English Komets and Spiers because the completed socks came from these machines attached to one another by threads of waste, which the operator had to clip, rather than dropping singly into a waiting bin. But knitters' earnings on the two technologies were indistinguishable, and knitters manoeuvred to secure the best running set to work. Mechanics noted complex and simple equipment in both the midlands and American lines and remembered the work of set-up and repair as being of similar difficulty. The firm owned both technologies because each was best suited to different products, the English excelling in ribs, the American in cables and patterns.[27]

Plant managers found one feature of American equipment especially useful in the small Canadian market. American machines were designed on the 'Universal' principle: each model could be accessorized to produce a wide range of goods. These elements made the equipment more complicated, but in the Canadian context more efficient because better adapted to shift from one short production run to another. Their implications for job composition and gender divisions in knitting were, however, ambiguous.[28] The advice foremen received on these questions was conflicting. American correspondents to the *Canadian Textile Journal* argued for a strict separation of machine operation from maintenance, 'A simple and effective means of promoting efficiency is to insist that the knitter attends to the very minimum of tasks related to the actual processes of knitting and leave such jobs as adjusting yarn tensions, correct fittings, changing pattern chains, putting in needles and sliders, to the knitting machine fixer.' While reserving all active intervention, albeit to make only minor machine adjustments, to male fixers, they provided a minder's job description which emphasized affinities with women's domestic work: 'The greatest single factor in maintaining knitting machine efficiency and at the same time preserving machine parts' being 'cleanliness ... it is the operator's duty to see that the machine is wiped off carefully many times a day.'[29] English contributors advocated merging the minding and mechanical parts of the labour process into a single job under male control, 'Other conditions being equal, male operatives can be relied upon ... to maintain a higher standard of work as regards both quality and output. Where freedom of choice exists the modern tendency seems to be to prefer men ... A competent male knitter should be capable of making fine adjustments and effecting minor repairs when necessary, thus leaving the mechanic free to devote his whole attention to serious troubles.'[30] This was the agreement about gender divisions in the knitting room which midlands manufacturers and unionists had reached by the mid-1930s after their disputes over shift work.

Penmans managers and foremen were unconstrained by union influence as they weighed this contradictory English and American advice. In Paris in the mid-1930s a textile union representative worked briefly among the male spinners and boarders at Penmans, but before 1946 when the United Textile Workers of America-AFL began a concerted card-signing drive, the knit-goods industry in small-town Ontario was entirely unorganized.[31] The province had legislation prohibiting female factory night work and Canadian managers shared the belief that mechanical aptitude was gendered male. But the absence of a union, when the firm had few competitors either for its products or for its labour supply and a small market to serve, meant that Penmans managers had different priorities as they framed job composition. Among these, the preferences of male employees, whose labour locally was in excess supply, did not rank high.

Whereas in the midlands male unionists successfully claimed all equipment run on shifts as 'men's machines' around the clock, in the inter-war period Penmans managers unilaterally drew the line between men's and women's work in knitting rooms between night and day. Girl and boy knitters started on the day shift, 7 a.m. to 6 p.m., learning from experienced female knitters, married women with work histories of fifteen years or more in the room. After six or eight months the young knitters graduated onto their own sets of machines, and the boys moved onto the men's shift, 6 p.m. to 7 a.m. with an hour's lunch break at midnight. Their piece rates were the same as those of day knitters; they worked the same number of machines; there was no shift differential. The best male knitters earned 20 per cent more than the best women in 1934, but they worked longer hours. Men hated permanent nights.

After ten or twelve years they felt the physical toll of perpetually interrupted sleep and resented the social confinement: 'You couldn't go anywhere. You were like a slave to your work.' Wives understood that management had little reason 'to be bothered' about these stresses among their male workers. Penmans controlled the local mill sites and the town council. There were few other jobs for men in town. Despite the irritations, in the inter-war years turnover among men in the knitting rooms was not high. Burdened with longer shifts and all the anti-social hours, limited to the same number of machines and rates as women were assigned by day, male night knitters were left with a fickle fantasy as compensation, the illusion that they, more than day knitters, commanded the machines.[32]

For as the gender of knitters varied between night and day, so did the composition of the knitter's job. Until after the Second World War Penmans used American knitting-room conventions on the day shift and midlands practices at night. The social meaning applied to the difference between day and night knitters' duties was that male knitters controlled the machines while female knitters only cared for them. In the 1930s, the fathers and sons of Paris had to be content with whatever psychological satisfactions they could derive from this distinction. Its economic advantages accrued entirely to the firm.

During the day the labour process in knitting was divided among three different workers. A 1923 Penmans recruiting booklet illustrating a latch-needle knitting cylinder promised that 'girls are simply required to keep these machines running and have to feed the yarn into the guides and splice any broken ends. Repair work is provided by men especially employed for that purpose.'[33] Female machine minders kept the equipment cleaned and oiled and the yarn cones filled, inspecting each sock or stocking as it came off the machine for flaws caused by developing machine faults. Day foremen said they preferred women minders because they were 'more fussy,' and day knitters claimed this trait with pride. Because management agreed that mechanical skill was gendered male, a floor fixer supported each pair of knitter-minders, intervening when the minder had shut down the machine, changing needles, setting up new patterns, retiming the cylinder before the restart. A practised and observant female knitter-minder could do much of the fixer's work on her own set, and did so when her fixer was occupied elsewhere. But having a fixer to do these tasks allowed the minder more time for the other parts of her job so that she produced higher quality work. A mechanic supported the fixers. He worked out the sequences in the jacks and chains for new patterns and conducted or guided fixers through major repairs.

At night both American and British machines were run according to midlands practice. The job was divided into two rather than three parts. Male knitter-fixers did fine adjustments, restarts, and minor repairs on the machines they were tending, the mechanics assuming responsibility for more complex diagnostics and time-consuming rebuilding of the equipment. But because Ontario knitter-fixers on the night shift worked the same number of machines as day knitter-minders, men at night were not able to produce more socks per hour than women did by day. Rather than appropriating productivity gains for themselves by demanding more equipment to work, as midlands knitters had, unorganized Ontario male knitter-fixers worked for the same rates as women while contributing more labour to the production of each sock. Male management and male knitters divided the proceeds from this arrangement unequally; Penmans took the material gain and encouraged gender pride based on mechanical proficiency among their knitter-fixers.[34]

After the Second World War an engineering innovation reinforced a change in the power relationships between management and men. The American practice that divided knitting into three jobs, distinguishing a fixer's role between the minder and the mechanic, always had a particular technical advantage on the Canadian shop floor. In a smaller market all production lines were shorter. It was necessary to stop more frequently to change yarn colours and patterns. Whether the English or the more amply accessorized American 'universal' machines were being used, someone was spending proportionately more time doing set-ups and re-starts in an Ontario knitting room than would have been the case in Britain or the United States.

In hard times in a tight job market, male knitter-fixers might, within limits, be obliged to do these tasks in addition to their other work. But technical changes in the 1940s increased the complexity of set-ups in both American and English machines. On the day shift it was necessary to decrease the ratio of machines to fixers. At night knitter-fixers were spending enough time away from minding on these other tasks that the quality differential, long suspected, between the production of 'fussy' women and 'careless' men became marked.[35]

Coincidentally, the men's predicament had changed. Ex-service men returned with more experience in the outside world and more confidence. There were jobs available in heavy industry in nearby towns, at wages that would support commuting by car. A union with a formidable record of harrying Penmans Quebec parent was organizing in town. When individual men balked at working steady nights, challenging the pre-war gender division in knitting by shift, and began to demand rotations through the day work, Penmans complied, hoping to stem the union drive. Both night and day knitters were given fixers to help them, and premiums were paid when men took the night shift.

For a time boys were given hiring priority among learners in the knitting rooms because fixers needed to know how to knit, the new knitting-room protocols required more fixers, and the belief that fixers must be male remained firm.[36] After the union was defeated in 1949, the three-part knitting-room task division remained in place, but the distinction between floor-fixer and mechanic was sternly drawn. Floor-fixers were described as sloggers. Their mechanical knowledge of the machines was limited to set-ups and restarts. As daily rated workers they frequently earned less than knitters and other women piece-workers, but young male knitters could not refuse transfers to fixing. In the absence of strong worker organization, when a small number of firms dominated a small market, male managers conceded only that male workers possessed greater mechanical skill than women, not that they were entitled to higher wages. Knitting remained a mixed-gender occupation.[37]

There were common features in the two cases considered here. The technology used was similar as was engineers' advice about who ought best to use the equipment they designed. A shared gender ideology distilled to the common propositions that women ought not to work at night and only men possessed mechanical skill. But across these commonalities class and gender interests arrayed themselves in different ways. The structure of the industry and of the labour market and the state of labour organization tipped the balance towards male managers in Ontario and male unionists in the midlands. On both sides of the Atlantic there was ground for common cause between managers and men, but alliances across class through gender were approached warily. In Ontario men's gains from this alliance were formal, not substantive; in the midlands the men's gains were residual, but real. By 1950 sexual divisions and gender hierarchies in knitting favoured women in Paris, Ontario, and men in the organized workplaces of Nottingham and Leicestershire.

■ Chapter Four

Domesticity and mill families

Paris was a good place for women who needed to earn their livelihood by wage labour, but not a good place for men, even in the early twentieth century. As the years wore on, women stayed at their jobs. They married. Their brothers and sons grew to working age. And the men in textile workers' households had increasing difficulty finding jobs. The problem was not cyclical, a short-term consequence of the post-war recession or the depression of the 1930s, but was structural, a working out of a labour recruitment system that brought to town more women than men. The wider economy, which offered few female employment opportunities, gave women incentives to stay.[1]

For men there were two kinds of jobs in the mills: entry-level work and lifelong work. In the lifelong jobs of spinning, carding, dyeing, boarding, and fixing, turnover was low. These men typically had wives and daughters working in the mills, an adequate merged family income, and few other job options in the town.[2] They were protective of their jobs and secretive about the skills they had learned as apprentices in Britain or on the shop floor. By the 1920s, younger men were finding their movement from entry-level jobs blocked by men in their forties who would stay on in the mills until their seventies. Managers were unsympathetic to these new employees' demands for better jobs and pay; supervisors had little incentive to mediate disputes between the two groups. Even the most skilled men found their bargaining power with the firm limited.[3]

The other much smaller employers in town were a flannel mill, which hired both women and men, a screen factory which employed men, principally in the winter months, a needle works and a printing plant. In 1920 the municipality guaranteed a bond issue for an expanding local engineering firm, hoping to provide 'employment right at home' for men, as in Hanover the town fathers subsidized a 'factory for girls.' In Paris, as in Hanover, the new plant, intended to even out the gender balance in the local labour force, soon folded. The building was then taken over by an American branch plant. This firm, the Adams Company of Indianapolis, has endured in the community, manufacturing heavy road grading and mining machinery, but assembling to order rather than to inventory, and employing, in the inter-war period, only a small and fluctuating work force.[4]

Some male textile workers retrained and took white-collar jobs in town. Others started their own businesses or bided their time until local federal government positions became available. Some of the men from the midlands returned to England. Most sons left town. By the 1940s, the popular impression was that there were five women for every man in Paris, that 'it was a woman's paradise, but men always had to work out of town.' This, indeed, became the most satisfactory solution for men whose wives had secure jobs in the mills – a daily commute to neighbouring centres where metal, woodworking, and electrical industries hired men.[5] In these circumstances men became the secondary wage earners in many households. The optimal solution for mill managers was that these men would remove themselves from the local labour market but not so far or to such well-paying jobs that their wives would be tempted to do the same. As in mill villages of the American south, managers in Paris offered most males little prospect of a better job or higher pay, counting on the woman's wage and the family tie to keep just enough men in the community to supply their limited need for male employees. As the secondary wage earners in many households, men showed the low levels of security and earnings and the characteristic irregularity in employment dual labour market theorists usually associate with women workers.[6]

Girls started work in the mills at an early age, much younger than boys. Most girls began at fourteen because it was the tradition in the hosiery industry, a tradition made of necessity, because no one member of the household earned a breadwinner wage. The firm sought out fourteen-year-old female employees, the supervisors sending home messages with kin when they had a job and knew there was a youngster nearing this age in the household. Many started in departments where

A young girl and her supervisor in the sewing department of the underwear mill. c. 1912. The garments are 95s, the men's long winter underwear which Penmans sold in great quantities to outdoor workers, and in black to miners. The daughters of mill families began work as young as twelve years in the pre-war period and routinely at age fourteen in the inter-war years. Boys rarely were able to secure mill jobs before they were eighteen.

kin could take responsibility for teaching them the job. Some girls had their own reasons for complying: the wish to escape school or to have 'all those things girls like to have, clothes and things.'[7] Forty per cent of those employed in 1936 got their first jobs when they were fifteen or younger; another 26 per cent began at ages sixteen to nineteen. In mill families the consensus was that 'when you were old enough you were big enough to work.'[8]

When a girl was 'old enough' to enter the mill became a matter of some dispute after 1921 when provincial legislation raised the school-leaving age to sixteen. The municipal council protested the law, noting that 'wage earners were badly needed' in the homes of Paris, and that the act penalized those who could little afford to comply. The act allowed the local police chief to exempt individual children from its terms. In the first four months the legislation was in force, the police chief in Paris issued fifty-one exemption certificates, and the council came to regard this procedure as 'an easy way to get around the act.' Sometimes the police chief resisted, particularly if the applicant was only thirteen, but girls found he could be persuaded, and the municipality successfully set its own standard on this matter.[9]

With this earlier entry into steady wage work, girls were initiated into a pattern of relations to their households, the firm, and the local housing and marriage markets, which made their work lives more secure and autonomous than those of their brothers while intensifying their perceived obligations towards kin.

Although the firm actively recruited girls, boys often had to wait about for a job in the mill. Although one-quarter of Penmans male employees in 1936 first had gone to the mill in their early teens, more commonly young men began work there in their late teens or early twenties.[10] In the interim young men worked seasonally on surrounding farms or picked up casual jobs in town. Thus from their teenage years, males of mill families were aware that in their town men's connection with the market economy was more precarious than that of women.

Patricia Hilden, noting that girls started textile work earlier than boys in the north of France, suggests that as 'girls fell under the rigid control of factory discipline at an earlier age than most boys' they became more habituated to and compliant with textile workplace regimes. No doubt long days in the mill from an early age narrowed women's horizons. A knitter in the hosiery mill, the wife of a unionist who worked out of town, remembered that 'in those days you could get a working permit when you were fourteen and go to work in the mill and that's all some people knew.'[11]

But earlier and longer careers in the mills also had other implications. Because the firm needed more female employees than male, particularly experienced workers who were quick, reliable, and accurate, women knew they had more leverage with the boss and comported themselves accordingly. Female employees started younger because the firm's demand for their labour was greater. Girls who took days off for their own good reasons, even against their supervisors' explicit orders, returned to find their places waiting. Yet men who had disputes with bosses found themselves out of work. Women may have been more pliant employees than men, although an analysis of their activism in the town's one major labour dispute in the winter and spring of 1949 suggests otherwise. But supervisors were cautious in dealing with women workers, even when they left the plant during shift, typically after disputes over the allocation of well-paying piece-work. Thomas Blaney, a master cutter, recalled 'the odd time one of them would walk out and go home, but you daren't take that work and give it to someone else, that had to be there for her to come back, or you would be in big trouble then.'[12]

The greater autonomy facilitated by their steady wage work was manifested in the housing decisions of young female migrants who came to town. In her study of nineteenth-century Halstead, Essex, Judy Lown has shown a clear connection between the employer's sponsorship of a women's residence, his construction of company housing big enough to accommodate lodgers, and his wish to exert control over the work patterns and morality of female workers. The Waltham boarding system used similar techniques to regulate the lives of women workers in both the United States and Japan. As Patricia Tsurumi has demonstrated, however, in Japan the companies' goals were often frustrated. There young women left mill work entirely in order to get away from company lodgings and physically remove themselves from the purview of their employers. In Paris young single women stayed on at work, but once they knew their way about town and felt safe, they took steps to evade supervision outside working hours. They did so by establishing themselves in independent households away from the scrutiny of either mill managers or male household heads, and, indeed, single women were more likely to do so than unmarried men.[13]

Girls who moved into town to work in the mills usually boarded. Some lived in one of the thirty rooms in the company-owned YWCA.[14] Many women in town took in boarders; some, especially among the east midlands migrants, ran boarding-houses accommodating ten or more mill workers. Conditions for boarders were cramped. Newspaper ads always specified that the terms were two 'girls' or 'men' to a room. Mildred Hopper, who came to work in the mills from nearby Princeton in 1939 and boarded in four different places before she married ten years later, remembered that 'we were three to a room. We all came from the country, knew each other. One would get married and another would move in from the country. We slept together and took our washing with us when we went back to the farm on weekends.' Boarding provided modestly priced accommodation and companionship for migrants newly arrived in town, and single men continued to find lodging satisfactory. Its advantages paled, however, for many women.[15]

In 1936, 10 per cent of Penmans single employees owned their own

Penmans workers Clara Robinson, Capitola Fick, and Beulah Robinson in the back garden of Mrs Fick's boarding-house, Walnut Street, c. 1905. Note the steep side of the Grand River Valley, rising immediately behind.

homes (fig. 1). The percentages are the same for female and male workers. Although the average age of employed single women and men was the same – twenty-seven – most women, having started to work younger, would have had more time to put money aside. Other single women established independent households in rented quarters. Bachelors rarely became tenants, preferring to continue on as boarders. But there were as many tenants as owners among women known in town as 'Miss' in 1936, when only 3 per cent of single, female mill workers were listed in lodgings. This pattern strengthened over time. In 1948 when only one in ten single men owned or rented his own home, one in three never-married women headed her own household.[16] A large number of single women, principally those without parents in town, bought their own homes and rented houses or apartments, living alone (an unknown circumstance for men) or sharing this accommodation with other single women. These women sheltered kin who came from the English east midlands or the countryside to begin work in the mill, participated actively in community life, and used their homes as venues for festive gatherings among co-workers.[17]

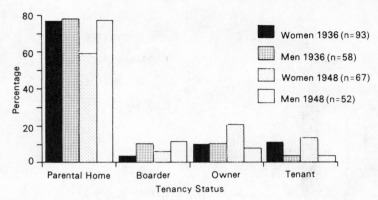

Figure 1

Tenancy status of single employees, all mills, 1936 and 1948

Single women, however, were not always more residentially autonomous than men. In 1936 three-quarters of unmarried mill workers in Paris lived in their parental homes, contributing to the family income. The aggregate statistic is the same for women and men, but, broken down by age and gender, divergence emerges.[18] Throughout the period, almost all teenaged mill workers lived at home; the majority in their early twenties were still in their parents' households. But single women were much more likely than men still to be at home when they were over thirty-six.[19] (See fig. 2.)

Why should this be the case? Financial need was acute because of low textile wages and the relatively high incidence of single-headed households in town. Many women lived alone with their children. Some were widowed, deserted, or never-married mothers who moved to Paris with their children because it was a place where they, with help from their teenagers, could assemble a family wage in the absence of a male breadwinner.[20] Other one-parent households resulted from the stresses of high male unemployment combined with the presence of stable female employment within the town. Women were reluctant to talk about the domestic tensions engendered when they and their children or they and their siblings were the earners who paid the rent and put food on the table. Absent males merely remained unaccounted for, or were described as having gone away looking for work, or as having returned to England.[21] Mothers alone then needed their wage-earning children at home, but this phenomenon does not account for the gender gap evident in those staying on in the parental household. Approxi-

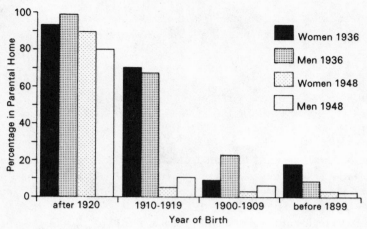

Figure 2
Proportion of employees living in parental home, by year of birth, 1936 and 1948

mately one in five of both single women and single men still at home in 1936 and in 1948 lived with single parents.[22]

The answer lies partly in the workings of the local marriage market. When mill workers said that Paris was 'a woman's paradise and a hard place for men,' they meant that it was far easier for women to find jobs. The search for a spouse was a different matter. Folk tales are legion about young men riding the radial track from Brantford or later cruising about in cars, attracted by the sport of displaying maleness in a woman's town. Perhaps the young men who filled the YWCA's Sunday afternoon prayer meetings or travelled to attend young people's groups in town churches had more serious intentions.[23]

Certainly, the local marriage market, as an inversion of the local labour market, did not favour women. Hilda Sharp Scott remembered, 'As it was more girls than men, if a man got a job in Penmans they thought it was something smart, the girls did – "oh," they would say, "we've got another man in town."' Among older mill workers, many more women than men remained single even in 1948 when cheaper and more accessible transportation made it easier for those men married to women employed in the mills to work out of town.[24]

Of course, as Gittins has observed in her study of a declining Devon woollen town from which men fled in search of better-paying jobs elsewhere, ready access, even to relatively ill-paid textile work, 'made women somewhat less dependent upon marriage for survival.' And if 'marriage partners became more scarce, marriage itself' became 'less secure.' The 'decline in marriage as a source of economic security made more women dependent on work in the formal labour market and upon informal networks between kin and neighbours.'[25] Migrant women, who had distanced themselves to varying degrees from family discipline by leaving home to seek work, found their steady and rising piece-work earnings sufficient to sustain independent households. Their workplace friendships were emotionally supportive and often the economic foundation for joint households comprised entirely of women. Many were joined in town by women kin with whom they were able to share housing and household work and upon whom they could rely for support in hard times.[26]

Although in many communities, of which the nearby steel town of Hamilton was one, parents mindful of contributions to the family income took pains with their grown sons' comforts, an unemployed boy leaving home took nothing from the family purse. In Paris, where girls' earnings began earlier and continued more steadily than their brothers' contributions did, parents were more likely to attempt to keep daughters at home. Parents in towns where boys' wages were larger attempted to inculcate a sense of family responsibility in sons,[27] but the task was easier with daughters. There was a much broader cultural reinforcement for female (than male) domestic obligations. In a community where women were well paid being a dutiful daughter implied both unpaid labour and cash contributions to kin. It was not unwomanly to take on the responsibilities and satisfactions of a 'dutiful daughter,' in the way that it might be unmanly to assume seriously the more clouded attribution of dutiful son.

Reinforcing the gendered distribution of familial responsibility in keeping earning daughters at home were the rigorous challenges of female respectability. A girl leaving home without leaving town seemed to shirk her primary personal obligations. She also, without sufficient cause, set herself outside the moral scrutiny of the family which unmarried females in particular were understood to require. More mill employees who were daughters than sons stayed at home unmarried, recognizing that they were materially better situated to contribute to the family budget but accepting as well that both their present sense of well-being as daughters and their future prospects as wives were best served in this way.[28]

The deep satisfactions found in being a caring daughter prudently preparing for married life and conforming to the ideological prescriptions of what a good woman should be predominate in the women's recollections of these years in the parental home. One woman bought her mother a dress with her first pay. Since they had quarrelled over whether she should take the job in her uncle's department at the mill, it seemed appropriate to ask, 'Was this a peace offering?' To the contrary, she replied, 'No, it was just because I loved her; she was a wonderful person, my mother.' Jean Hubbard, who worked for eight years at well-paying piece-work before she married, first 'saved enough money to put hydro in on the farm. It was quite an improvement. After that we got rid of the outhouse in the backyard.' Jean also bought her mother clothes and paid board. When she graduated from high school in 1939, an uncommon accomplishment among female mill workers, her parents had urged her to go on to university. She relished the thought of being a teacher, but deferred to her brother: 'I thought he had more ability than I had.' After the most pressing needs in her parents' household had been met, she began 'to put so much of every pay into something for looking ahead.' Describing the pattern among young women at the mill, she recalled, 'We bought cornflower, or some piece of china of your set and that sort of thing and linen. Probably a piece of each one every pay. Maybe not that much.'[29]

The average age at marriage among the women interviewed was twenty-six, twelve years after most had started work in the mill. As Jane Synge has noted in her study of Hamilton, however, there was more flexibility in the marriage age then than there is now. In Paris, the most frequent age at marriage was twenty-two. Anne Hedley remembered thinking, 'I was getting on then, we used to say that, at twenty-two. Not these days, but we used to think that then.' On the other hand, the late teens was counted too young, women who married at nineteen noting either that they had 'rushed into it' or that 'my first was on the way.' (There was a woman in town who performed abortions and in 1932 was charged and held on $10,000 bond in connection with the death from acute peritonitis of a twenty-one-year-old woman, but no interviewee mentioned her services.) Another group of female mill workers married markedly later than twenty-two, in their thirties and forties. Many of these had heavy home responsibilities, a widowed mother, or ailing parents. Some, having worked for many years, decided to postpone marriage further until they could afford and gain access to a home of their own, sometimes a difficult matter in the post-war housing shortage.[30] One-third of the wives working at Penmans in 1936 were married to men younger than themselves, an atypical pattern that was perhaps a response to the tightness of the local marriage market and perhaps, as Gittins has observed, also emblematic of the greater equality between marriage partners in textile towns.[31]

Meg Luxton has observed that the first generation of couples in the new mining town of Flin Flon got married far away 'from their natal families, and ... took pleasure in sharing the event with their friends. Couples in the second generation frequently noted that their parents organized their weddings,' that 'it was really my mother's do and his mother's.' In Paris, after Penmans work force grew in the first quarter of the century, the same pattern emerged. In the 1930s, marriages commonly took place on Wednesday afternoon, the bride in her travelling suit, the couple attended by two friends from the mill. The ceremonies were held at the parsonage, or the house where the bride had boarded. By the thirties, ceremonies had grown more elaborate, taking place on Saturdays rather than weekdays, the bride in a gown, accompanied by costumed bridesmaids, the ceremony in the church chancel or the home of kin and followed by a wedding supper. But almost never did marriage mark the end of the bride's employment in the mill.[32]

Penmans female employees worked after marriage and through their early childbearing years and left paid work only after their children grew old enough to replace them as contributors to the household income. In 1936 one-quarter of the Penmans female work force aged seventeen to twenty-six was married; 70 per cent of those aged twenty-seven to thirty-six was married. The drop comes among women over age thirty-six, only one-half of whom were wives. The pattern is similar in 1948. (See fig. 3.) Markedly more women gave 'home duties' rather than 'to be married' as their reason for leaving the mill.[33] In this sense, the pattern of work after marriage in Paris is like that found in the United States in the first third of this century by Mary Cookingham and Martha N. Fraundorf. As Fraundorf has noted, low male earnings 'made it necessary for many women with young children to stay in the labor force,' and as we have already seen in the case of Paris, 'the later substitution of the labor of the children for that of the wife was easier since there were fewer legal and economic barriers to the employment of children, and it was generally considered acceptable behavior.'[34]

Two further factors sustained this pattern in Paris. Wives' experience in paid work was long and for many satisfying. Going out to work was more familiar, and by community standards more fitting, than quitting

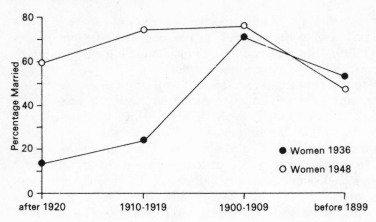

Figure 3
Proportion of female employees married, by year of birth, 1936 and 1948

to stay at home. Families, the firm, and the community, as we shall see, developed ways to accommodate wives working after childbearing. Between 1936 and 1948, as Penmans female work force grew older, the proportion who were married rose from 40 to 62 per cent.

Working while one's children were young was common in the mills, although having large families was not. Four out of ten married women at Penmans in 1936 had a child under the age five at home,[35] but one-half of the wives working in the mills in 1936 had no children aged five to twenty-one in their households. The average was one, considerably fewer than the mean for similar Ontario towns. Women who married in their thirties and forties rarely had children. In the older work force of 1948, 60 per cent of married women had no children aged five to twenty-one at home, and the average number of children among all married women employees was 0.8.[36] There were economic constraints on having larger families. 'Two was enough to keep,' Frances Randall said. 'In the Depression it was hard to keep them in clothes.' More children made it more difficult for a woman to stay on at the mill. Anne Hedley, a knitter and a Roman Catholic, who thought her family of four too large, noted, laughing in retrospect, 'Oh, I had a full house, I thought, I'm ashamed to go out, look at all the children I got. But I got over it, they had lovely curly hair and they loved to go out.'

The fit was close between the number of children women had and the number they thought ideal. Gittins also found this pattern in English textile towns, in contrast with mining communities, and attributed the difference to the greater equality and sense of joint responsibility among partners both of whom worked for wages. Most children were born to mothers in their late twenties, those who married at twenty-two delaying their first pregnancy, those who married later starting their families right away. Working through the first months of pregnancy was common, but most women quit at four and a half months, citing propriety: 'You didn't want to be down there when you looked like an elephant.'[37]

Principally as a result of childbearing, women's work histories at Penmans were more interrupted than men's. One-fifth of the women in 1936 and one-quarter of the women in 1948 returned to the mills after between two and six periods of absences away; fewer than 7 per cent of men had such intermittent work histories. The length of service records of both women and men, however, were considerable and not substantially different by gender: twenty-six years for women and twenty-seven for men in the yarn and knit-goods mills, eighteen for women and twenty-five for men in the hosiery mill in 1936. Women's absences for childbearing are often associated in discussions of gender division in the labour force with a short and scant attachment to wage work,[38] but this association is historically contingent. In Paris exceptionally long and regular work histories among childbearing women were made possible through adaptations by employers, family members, the community, and working mothers.

The knitting industry was vertically integrated through the garment-making stage, where most tasks required one worker to each machine and were labelled 'women's work.' By rating these jobs as piece-work, the firm gave women strong incentives to stay or return speedily to work so as to collect on their investment as young day workers and lower-paid piece-workers learning the machine. Managers and supervisors also encouraged women to return to the mill after childbearing, visiting them at home or sending word back with kin. They offered flexible hours, afternoon work while young children were sleeping, later starting hours than the 7 a.m. norm once youngsters were in school, or the option of working on a machine at home. As John Elliott, a supervisor in the hosiery mill, said, 'We had lots of work to do and were glad to get it done.'[39] Inflexible shop-floor regimes for men and the absence of breadwinner wages for any mill worker drove men out of town and kept women at the mill. Most women who returned less than a year after giving birth cited financial necessity. The husbands of many of these women were irregularly employed at jobs out of town, had difficulty staying in steady work in the 1920s and 1940s, and were even more dependent on their wife's earnings in the 1930s. Those who waited until their children were sightly older also noted that it 'took two of us working together to get by.'[40]

The lack of enough local jobs for men and any mill jobs paying breadwinner wages is at the core of why mothers worked in the mills. But it is not the whole of the matter. There was a different logic behind the familial division of labour in town, both within marriage and among kin, particularly female kin. Marriages among mill workers were more egalitarian than the norm. Many domestic tasks were allocated within the household in terms of wage work schedules rather than gender. When both husband and wife worked in the mills for similar remuneration, many aspects of the preparation for wage work became as individuated as collecting the wage.

Men were most likely to turn their hands to cooking. Female kin who did not live together did not, except on festive occasions, prepare meals for one another. Neither was food preparation commonly let to the market. The cooked-food shops of English textile towns were absent in Paris. The resolution to the 'meal problem' was internal to the household and more likely than any other domestic labour to be shared by men. The town was small enough that mill workers went home for their lunch hour so that women could get supper 'on the way' at noon. They cooked meat on the weekend to be eaten as leftovers during the week. When they rose in the late afternoon, men who had worked night shift put on the potatoes and steamed puddings prepared by their wives the night before and they took full responsibility for their own meals otherwise. One man with a unionized job in a nearby city, whose hours were shorter than those at Penmans, had dinner on the table by the time his wife returned from the mill. Seasonally employed workers, such as Mildred Hopper's carpenter husband, did both the housework and the meals in winter, just as the seasonally employed fishermen studied by Patricia Connelly and Martha Macdonald took on more household labour when the fishery was slack. Kathleen Jenner remembered proudly, 'Well, we were going to clean this one Saturday morning ... he was busy scrubbing the floor and a friend of his came by and he says, "What in the world are you doing, you're doing women's work" and he says "Indeed I am, Kate works longer hours than I so I can help her." '[41] Bill paying and grocery shopping were similarly divided in terms of which partner was free at the appropriate time of the day. A redefinition of the sexual division of labour within the household was thus a pragmatic – although limited and patterned – response to daily and seasonal schedules in the market economy.

Even among women whose husbands had been employed, sometimes for extended periods, none ever described a spouse assuming responsibility for child care or laundry, the home tasks defined as most onerous. Men played with children, took them on outings; waking night workers looked out for their offspring returning from school. No matter how minimally attached they were to the waged economy, fathers did not, however, change children, bathe them, or assume extended responsibility for their supervision, regarding these tasks as too unpleasant, intimate, or confining. Therefore, when exchanges among female kin were not possible, wage-earning wives turned to the market for help. Because the mill day began at 7 a.m., 'awfully early to be taking young ones out,' mothers of pre-schoolers looked for older women, no longer able or willing to do mill work, who would come into their homes during the day. Later they relied on neighbours to attend to their youngsters before and after school.

Laundry was, after child care, the real burden in the double day, almost a nightly chore because families had few changes of clothes; the mills were hot and full of floating fibres; and houses, until after the Second World War, rarely had indoor toilets. Even in the most egalitarian of households, men did not take on the heavy work of carrying water and pressing wet clothing through wringers perhaps because the end of the process, hanging the wash on lines to dry, had to be done in public view. Bert Russell, who like his wife was a mill worker, shared shopping, cooking, and bill paying, but when faced with laundry told her, 'You've got enough work; we'll send it out.' A Brantford laundry did a regular business among mill workers in the 1920s and 1930s, making pick-ups in Paris on Mondays and deliveries on Wednesdays. Women in town performed the same services, charging 25 to 45 cents per dozen articles, washed, ironed, and returned to the doorstep. There was a trade-off, of course, in contracting laundry out: full mill days and paid domestic help or shortened hours for wages in order to have time for household tasks. Jean Hubbard articulated the dilemma, 'sometimes by the time I paid them, they were earning more than I was.'[42]

The likelihood that men would share domestic work was thus related to local opportunities for male wage employment in mixed-gender workplaces. However the firm, although it wished for a stable pool of experienced female employees, had no interest in providing ample jobs for men in town (except during the English family recruitment phase, when male kin without textile skills were found work in the mills so that they could repay their passages). On the contrary, irregularly employed husbands were a strong inducement for women workers to continue at their posts after marriage and through childbearing. Men who found jobs outside Paris typically worked on men-only shop floors with co-workers for whom wage work and preparation for wage work were distinct and sexually segregated and who regarded themselves as breadwinners. Most women said that their husbands would not help at home 'unless he was asked,' an unsatisfactory foundation for a tightly timed struggle with the double day. Single women remembered days off, when work was slack in the early 1930s, as opportunities for country walks or excursions to Brantford; married women recalled them as 'good chances to get caught up on your housework.'[43]

The distinctive familial division of labour in the mill community extended beyond household boundaries. In fact, it was the openness with which women ran their own homes and regarded the domestic arrangements of their female kin that sustained women mill workers, providing an essential alternative source of help when there were tasks rejected by husbands as unmanly or when there was no man about the house. Women who shifted daily between paid and unpaid labour from their early teens as wage-earning daughters experienced these two kinds of work as complementary, interdependent, and shared. A different sense of what was time well spent developed among female kin in the mill community. Women were as ready to reallocate their domestic labour among households as they were to reapportion their own labour between home and the mill, in a system of exchange that acknowledged the value of both kinds of labour. In the spring of 1939 knitter Anne Hedley's son was a year and a half; her sister-in-law 'had two children and she wasn't going to work, and so she offered, "I'll mind Peter and that way you can go back to work."' For the next four years the boy went to this aunt's all week; 'she wouldn't let him come home nights, mind you.' Anne was back at work and earning but was relieved of the child-care aspects of a pressing double day. Her sister-in-law had part of Anne's pay packet, and they shared a sense of accomplishment in the efficiency of the arrangement.

Such agreements were frequent and often initiated by the non-wage-earning relative. They usually terminated when, by consensus, the pooled number of children became large enough to justify two full-time caregivers being out of the labour force. This number for Anne Hedley

Gilbert Milne, a Toronto freelance photographer, took this picture from the height above Walnut Street, 15 February 1949. Shown across the centre are the yarn, sweater, and underwear mills, backing onto the Grand River with the rest of the town beyond. The large buildings across the street from the mills are the Penmans printing plant and its general office. Much of the housing in the foreground was built by Penmans early in the century, some designed to serve as boarding-houses, others as modest family dwellings.

and her sister-in-law was five. Ida Pelton's mother suggested their sharing scheme, which also involved living together. 'They were very busy at Penmans, and we had this baby so my mother said, "I'm sure you could get a job at Penmans, what you do is what they need. Why don't you come with me and stay" and so she minded the baby while I worked and I gave her half of my pay.' This scheme relieved Ida's mother of the necessity to take outwork from the mill, which she found stressful, and allowed Ida to earn higher wages than she could have earned working on a machine at home. They revived the arrangement when Ida's second child was born. Stella Beechey and her husband lived with her mother for eight years after they were married in 1942. During this time their three children were born. Stella returned to work a year after each birth. Her mother took responsibility for child care and cooking; Stella did cleaning and washing at night and on weekends. Her mother used board from Stella's family and her other lodgers to cover her household expenses. When the Beecheys built their own house across the street, Stella's mother continued to be responsible for her grandchildren from 7 a.m. until after they had eaten supper. The Elliotts had a similar arrangement with her mother-in-law. Jean continued in the mill after her marriage, while her mother-in-law handled their home duties. As Jean said, 'It was just as well that I went to work, because she looked after the house and there was nothing actually for me to do here.' These women altered their households to make both staying in the labour force and remaining outside it more bearable, exchanging cash for child care and sharing domestic labour. Through time they adjusted both the nature and the parties to these exchanges and their domestic arrangements, moving between the market and the household economy and into and out of one another's homes.[44]

CONCLUSION

The domestic division of labour among the mill families of Paris was not as atypical as the gender configuration of the town's work force, nor was it consonant with the substantial, often equal, or preponderant contributions female mill employees made to their households through intensive wage labour. Women found that domestic gender divisions were mutable, but not mutable enough. It was easier for them to develop work and income-sharing arrangements with female relatives. These collaborations depended upon flexible patterns of co-residence that opened up the isolated patriarchal household and upon exchanges of cash and services among women which made moot the boundaries between the waged and the household economy. When female kin were unavailable to help with domestic labour, women mill workers frequently turned for help to the market, finding local definitions of what work might be done for pay more readily recast than the gender divisions that separated women from men in the household.

Most adaptation to lifelong female wage work occurred within the social practices of the kin groups that other town residents called mill families, and in the neighbourhoods by the railway junction and on the river flats where mill workers lived. In certain ways patterns in the whole municipality changed to accommodate the schedules of the mill and the habits of mill workers. Shopkeepers on Grand River Street expected to do most of their week's business between Saturday noon, when Penmans whistle blew to start of the weekend, and 10 p.m. that night. In these hours the town's single, long, commercial block became the precinct of mill workers and their families, promenading and exchanging news while laying in the week's provisions. There were businesses in town, notably the laundries, which existed only because mill workers had specific need for their services. The conventions about appropriate school-leaving age enforced by the town police chief were also an explicit adaptation to the needs of mill families and mill managers for adolescents, particularly girls, to be in the labour force rather than the classroom.

In Hanover working men consistently elected members of their group to municipal council to articulate working-men's concerns, often to forward a specific working-men's program. Hanover furniture workers were able to secure recognition of the distinctive class interests existing within town, and as men to act through the formal political structures of the municipality to forward those interests. Although the location of the lines dividing one class from another might be at issue, few would have denied that theirs was a community in which class interests were and ought to be represented.

In Paris mill families were accommodated rather than accepted. Some mill workers served on the Roman Catholic school board; others helped organize the municipality's recreational activities. But members of mill families were not present to articulate and forward the interests of their group before council. Formally the town behaved as if the domestic and neighbourhood customs of mill families were unspeakable. Paris was readily recognized by its demography as a 'women's town.' But culturally a wide distance yawned between what the townspeople, including mill workers, acknowledged as normative and what they observed as common practice within a large part their community. Immigrant, wage-earning mother was not the best social location from which to embark upon political action in a small Ontario town. By gender, provenance, and class, the female household heads of Paris were not well placed either to give their collective interests voice or to demand that acceptance replace denying and dismissive tolerance of their domestic values and family forms.

■ Chapter Five

Womanly militance, neighbourly wrath

On 18 January 1949 the members of local 153 of the United Textile Workers of America – AFL, certified the previous autumn as the bargaining agent for the Paris employees of Penmans Company, went out on strike against the firm. So searing was the experience that thirty-five years later townspeople remembered with unfailing accuracy who had struck and who had crossed the line; house by house, block by block, neighbours were known by which side they had been on during those three months.[1] Until the last of the knitting mills closed in town in the autumn of 1984, the women and men who worked for Penmans forswore the strike as a tactic and kept a wary distance from labour organization generally.

In the history of the mill families of Paris, the strike of 1949 stands uniquely in public view, an event structured by formal union and state institutions and subject to close and recording scrutiny. The dispute was amply reported in the local and national press of the day. Many union and federal labour department records of the dispute have been preserved. By the conventions of the historian's craft, these events should have been the parts of the mill workers' collective past most readily uncovered and reclaimed. Yet for me, they remain among the most elusive. Like Donald Smith, the experienced and skilled observer of the town who wrote an account of the dispute in 1981,[2] I remain unsettled and uncertain in my understanding of what happened in town that winter and spring.

In my interviews with townspeople the silences concerning the event were confounding, the commonalities in the accounts fierce and brittle in their conformity. Over the decades since the strike was lost the story of the dispute has been worn smooth, standardized in order, diction, and cadence; shorn of dissonance in pursuit of a guarded social peace. The contending stories from which this common representation was formed are not entirely submerged; incompatible parentheses break through at paragraph ends; the rhetoric of each narrative is two sided, both acknowledging and denying alternative renderings of the events.

From the start the actions and observations of the dispute were complicated by unfamiliarity; the unfamilarity of mill workers with public initiatives lodged through formal instruments; the unfamiliarity of union organizers, the national press, the provincial police and county magistrates with the particular local practices at stake in the dispute. Among mill families, the settled understandings about who worked and why were different from the implicit assumptions upon which the union movement had long relied. The many outsiders called in to manage and record the emergency worked from crisis reflex, recasting with their own familiar explanations all that they could not quickly reconcile with their own experience.

My portrait of the strike dwells most upon these dissonances among who mill families were and who they were said to have been, what they did and what they were said to have done, what actions they took and worried they ought or ought not to have taken. Perplexed by the complexity of the deflections, the silences, and the reconstructions in both the records and the recollections, I have not written so much about the events of the strike itself, as about the ways in which the ideologies of gender, class, and community limited, edited, and vanquished what happened in Paris during those months.

PROLOGUE

The United Textile Workers of America (UTWA) had begun organizing in Ontario in the spring of 1944. By 1946 it had established twelve locals in the province, seven in eastern Ontario and five within easy reach of Paris in the communities of Brantford and Woodstock. At the end of the war earnings in hosiery and knit goods were the lowest in the textile sector. The average manufacturing employee took home 50 per cent more than the average hosiery worker. The UTWA achieved its greatest gains, both in wages and in union security, in woven-goods plants where prices and profits were rising more rapidly than in knit goods. But organizers in the hosiery sector could take heart from their successes at the York Knitting Mills in Woodstock, thirty kilometres west of Paris, where by November 1946 Local 125 had achieved a considerable measure of union security through a maintenance-of-membership clause, as well as two weeks' paid vacation and a regular schedule of wage increases.[3]

In Paris the UTWA faced an uphill battle from the start. Jerry Regan, a veteran organizer among furniture workers, sizing up the community after his first weeks there in the spring of 1946, described it as 'one of the worst of the company towns.' There was a core of support for the union which coalesced quickly. By late April a quarter of the employees in the hosiery and underwear mills, and two-thirds of those in the sweater mill had signed cards. The lowest response was in the yarn mill. There an earlier attempt to organize a spinners union had been thwarted and a works council was in place. The local was chartered in June, but by July organizers were worried. The progress of the membership drive had been halted. The members of the works council had been reconstituted as a company union, and a vigorous campaign had begun to discredit the American Federation of Labour (AFL) as a 'foreign labour invasion' and the UTWA as communist led. 'The problem has become political rather than union,' Regan reported; 'the company have decided they can beat us.' In an attempt to consolidate its threatened position, the local applied for certification before the Ontario Labour Relations Board in August, but the application failed.[4]

Through the spring of 1947 the twelve members of the local executive, led by Charles Alexander, a boarder from the hosiery mill, tried to hold their ground, 'hoping for something to give us a break,' discouraged by how 'indifferent and self-satisfied' their co-workers seemed to be. Through 1947 the campaign was conducted under a dark pall.[5] The UTWA had been organizing and leading strikes among textile workers in Quebec, where Penmans and Dominion Textiles, a woven-goods firm with which Penmans had close corporate links, had several large plants. Kent Rowley and Madeleine Parent, members of the Canadian executive of the union, had been charged with seditious conspiracy in connection with a Quebec strike. The revelations of Igor Gouzenko heightened fears of communist infiltration in all areas of Canadian life. The widely reported trials of Rowley and Parent focused centrally on allegations that each was, or had been, a member of the Communist party. In Paris both the Canadian Textile Workers, the company union, and the Congress of Industrial Organizations (CIO) affiliated Textile Workers of America, which was competing with the UTWA to organize plants in southern Ontario, took up the anti-communist rhetoric of Duplessis' prosecutors. Several of the UTWA organizers were party members, most notable among them William E. Stewart, who led the strike in Paris in 1949 and later was leader of the Ontario Communist party. Anthony Valente, American president of the UTWA, long suspected the politics of his Canadian staff and in 1952 would fire twelve of them, including Rowley and Parent, on these grounds.

In Paris a concerted and sustained attempt to organize against an employer was unprecedented, in itself revolutionary. Many ordinary mill workers separated the workplace goals of the UTWA in town from whatever wider political agenda the union was said to espouse. Several prominent community leaders, among them Martin Hogan and Lawrence Brockbank from the school board and Donald Smith, a teacher and later principal at the high school, noted with alarm that was 'the communist label a good tactic' to discredit the legitimate demands of union activists at the mill.[6] It was indeed. When union membership was not customary in town and its local benefits were still prospective and unproven, when even the notions of demand and bargain were so different from the established patterns of request and wait, the teleology towards revolution, drawn out by rival unions and the firm, made more formidable an already considerable uncertainty.

In the spring of 1948 Local 153 applied successfully for certification. Signed cards were submitted from 452 of the 554 employees they considered members of the bargaining unit. When the vote was held on 2 April, in a unit defined to include 649, there were 328 votes for the UTWA, 240 for the company union, a margin of three votes above the level required for certification.[7] In the next three months representatives of the union and the firm met six times but made no major progress. A provincially appointed conciliator failed to effect a settlement in August. A three-man conciliation board was established in September and reported on 12 November.

The union had asked for a 20-cent hourly increase, 5 cents for cost of living and 15 cents to bring Penmans wages closer to average rates paid in the district. Citing the continuing activity of the company union group, it also asked for a maintenance-of-membership clause, requiring members to remain in good standing within the union for the duration of the contract. The majority conciliation report recommended a 5-cent increase and the very slim union security of the voluntary revocable check-off, agreeing with company claims that the leadership of the UTWA was 'irresponsible' and had shown itself entitled to no greater form of protection. The minority report, written by Drummond Wren of the Workers' Education Association, the union's nominee to the board, recommended a 15-cent hourly increase and, noting the continuing close associations between the company and the Employees' Association, a maintenance-of-membership clause and the provision that all new employees be required to become members of the union. The company granted the 5-cent increase in late November and thereafter declined to negotiate.[8] On 27 October, William Stewart, the field representative of the UTWA in Paris, in a letter to Drummond Wren had declared – using the diction of the tank commander he had lately been: 'We are making preparations to pull the pin in the event that this conciliation does not effect a settlement.'[9] Within the community opinion upon the best next step was less decided.

THE UNION-MINDED

Of the 693 workers on Penmans payrolls in 1948, 56 per cent were women; 42 per cent of the 433 members of Local 153, were female.[10] The union's own organizing structure may in part account for the lower representation of women among union members. The first female UTWA organizer in town, Helen McMaster Muller, only arrived after the strike vote had been held; Penmans workers were recruited through evening home visits and male field representatives of the union may have been less vigorous or at ease in their approaches to the many all-female households in the community.[11] Still, female militance in town was considerable. When the strike call finally came, 44 per cent of the those who responded by not crossing the line were women.

There were stark differences in the personal characteristics of female and male strikers. Women who supported the strike were on the average six years older than the men and four years older than the average among women employed by the firm. Single men were overrepresented among the strikers; among women the pattern was reversed. There were markedly more wives, and especially widows, among the strikers than in the work force as a whole.[12]

It is not surprising that older women, wives, and widows were most conspicuous among the female union activists. In Paris, as in New York and New England textile centres and the woven-goods districts of northern France, they had the most compelling and long-standing commitment to wage work. 'Over the years they'd been kinda ripped off,' a senior male worker recalled; 'this was a chance for them.' The oldest striker, reportedly, was sixty-two-year-old Florence Miller, a winder, who lived with her eighty-two-year-old husband in a rented house in town.[13] While in their young years female workers had been fearful of the boss, as they took responsibility for raising children and running households, fear turned to disdain. They grew less tolerant of the petty tyranny and favouritism practised by the foremen and lead hands, more confident of their own worth, more confirmed in their own sense of dignity and honour. 'I didn't want to feel helpless; I wanted my rights.' Lottie Keen, a skilled looper and a widow raising her son alone remembered, 'I thought it would give more security to people. That is what I understood unions were for the workers.' Betty Shaw's mother, one of the midlands immigrants who brought her kin to join her in Paris and by 1949 had worked thirty years in the mill, saw the strike as about fairness, a way to protect her daughter from workplace conventions she despised. The sense of generations passing arrayed itself as an investment and claim on the firm. 'I remembered how tired my mother was back about 1913 after she worked all day and then had to come home and get dinner.' 'They had always taken too much out of us.' 'I got up at that meeting,' Florence Lewis said quietly, her voice shaking slightly at the recollection, 'and I said I favoured the strike to make things better for my children. You wouldn't believe what it was like when I was a teenager in 1925. Everybody wants things better for their children.'[14] Long years of working side by side in the mill with neighbours and kin forged a sense of common predicament. Betty Shaw said of her mother and her elderly aunt, both fired after the strike, 'Everybody thought they had better stick together … I don't believe they ever would have retired as long as they were able to go.' For Mildred Hopper, a seamer in the sweater mill, the dispute was not about money: 'Myself, I figured I wasn't making a bad wage, but then I thought well if you don't stick together you are not going to get any place either. I think it was mostly to have somebody to go to and have some systems. I think it was just the principle of the thing of all being together to be able to do something.'[15] In earlier years this sense of needing 'to stick together' had sustained informal practices to 'help one another out' on the shop floor and extensive networks of exchange among households within the community of mill families. Hopper herself had worked away from Paris in unionized heavy industry during the war; by the late 1940s other female mill workers had brothers and husbands who were employed in union shops in nearby centres. To many, joining the union seemed a good way to extend and formalize long-standing habits of solidarity in town.[16]

NEIGHBOURLY WRATH

The feelings of belonging, of having cast one's lot with the town, of living within community traditions, by the scrupulous reckoning of obligations honoured and betrayed of living out community sanctions – all these responses gave townspeople cause to become engaged in the Penmans dispute, both for and against the strike. Those same habits of solidarity which made older women in town 'union-minded' formed a clear boundary between insiders and outsiders in the community, discrediting the advice of strangers, giving pause to neighbours about to break rank. They also gave force to criticisms of the masters of the mill and courage to plain folk who had chosen their ground.

The UTWA was not an institution indigenous to the town; its organizers had not come to live in Paris. While the rival unions railed against the AFL affiliate as an 'emissary from Moscow' and 'an American invasion,' within town it was the trespass across a boundary nearer to home that caused most disquiet. Even among those committed to the UTWA because 'an outside union could better bargain for our working condition' there was an undercurrent of unease, a worry that the organizers were 'sharp-talking fellas' who did not listen well enough, who did not value, and thus could not be trusted to make a separate peace concerning, important community traditions the work action put at risk.[17] When at the invitation of union organizers, men from unionized metal working plants in nearby Brantford arrived at Paris rallies, intending to raise morale and boost confidence, they heightened instead the apprehension of danger. Their cheers of support were heard as 'hollering' and 'hatred.'[18] 'In a small town like Paris everybody knows everybody else you see, especially if you have been working together.' Charles Harrison, weighing the implicatons of 'pulling the pin' in the midst of a circle of intimates, resigned from the union after the strike vote was taken. 'That small town bit of knowing what everybody did, and who everybody was, had repercussions. It became more intense when you had a difference of opinion. It was so intermixed with the life that you were living that it would never be the same again. It's because you were so close that once you split you would split wide open.'[19] Yet loyalty to the community of mill workers also steeled the resolve of women and men committed to the strike.

Tommy Curry, a long-time town resident but not a Penmans employee, claimed that unionists were motivated by 'a lively sense of responsibility towards the community welfare,' that they wanted Paris to be 'more than a barrack-room for industry.' When Bruce Wilson, a carder from nearby Princeton with only twelve months' experience in the mill, challenged Curry's right to speak about the strike, Grace Hockin replied, 'My family has been in and out of Penmans for the last 30 years. I myself started in the mill in 1938 for 18 cents an hour and in the past 10 years have put in seven years in the mill . Does Mr Wilson realize that he or maybe his co-workers are only seasonal workers, whereas the people in town have to rely on the Penman mill 365 days a year?'[20] As a non-striker told local historian Donald Smith, 'A lot of us owned our own homes. The company encouraged us to buy ... Many felt that since they couldn't leave Penmans the best thing they could do was join the union and try to get higher wages.' Remember, said Florence Lewis, a home-worker who ran a soup kitchen for the pickets from her back porch, 'we were all citizens of Paris.'[21]

The union organizers were not the only outsiders in town. By the late 1940s the older Penmans executives in Paris, men active in municipal politics and community organizations, frequently seen about the streets and the mill, were replaced by personnel transferred from plants in Quebec who were not 'town men.' The feeling was widespread, especially among veterans, that the management had grown calloused, divorced from community concerns, and preoccupied with profit, that the new men were not following the principles of fair play for which they had fought overseas.[22] For many in town the strike was a way to insist that the community should be more than 'a barrack-room for industry.'

But there were no local instruments with which to secure this claim. Both the cause and the apparent remedy to the town's problem lay outside community convention. Both the union and the firm were making decisions in Paris on the basis of industry-wide considerations. The more experience Penmans management had with the UTWA in Quebec, the more determined they were not to allow the union to gain a foothold in Paris. The more successful UTWA organizers were gaining union security and pay raises in other Ontario plants, the more convinced they were that Penmans, at least economically, could afford to yield to their Paris demands. In the final days, for both union and management, the issue came down to union security, a concept from industrial legality little understood in town. Without some effective measure of union security the company could continue to play on community loyalties to erode UTWA support. But a strike to gain union security entailed a greater risk for the workers than for the union, on an issue most meaningful to the outside organizers, on the basis of their experience in centres far away from Paris.[23] Charles Harrison, a skilled worker and veteran with strong views against Penmans management, became disaffected when after the conciliation report the union organizers 'just told us that this was the way it was going to be, as though we didn't know what we should be doing.' He and ten other senior workers resigned from the union. Martin Hogan, a thoughtful community leader with a sceptical view of Penmans tactics, judged the strike ill considered: 'an interested observer could see that they were making a terrible mistake by not accepting what they could get and then organizing from inside.' Like many Paris men speaking of that time, Charles Harrison favoured military metaphors:[24] 'the bullets were made by the people in Paris, but they wanted to hold the line before the bullet was fired, or they wanted to be the ones to fire the bullet themselves when the time came, but somebody beat them to the gun and pulled the trigger, and they didn't like that – some of them didn't like it.' Seven weeks after the strike vote was taken, the strike began.

WOMANLY MILITANCE

The boundary around the community was plain and public; to each piece of opinion or advice offered up concerning the dispute the suffix 'insider' or 'outsider' was readily affixed. Acts and thoughts were assigned citizenship, authority drawn from the place of residence of the person who displayed them. Citizenship might be contested, but this dispute, like the boundary, was arrayed in plain and public view.

The attribution of gender to acts and thoughts was less straightforward. The gender roles played for the duration of the strike were simultaneously assumed and ascribed, and the actor often found she had little control over how her part was perceived. Not only did gender ascriptions sort behaviour as manly or womanly, they obscured or removed certain ways of being from view. They directed not only what could or would be done, but what could be seen and said to have been done.

Respectability was the touchstone of womanly authority. As Ellen Ross has argued, women '*embodied* respectability or the lack of it, in their dress, public conduct, language, housekeeping, childrearing methods, spending habits, and, of course, sexual behaviour.' Respectability might once have been genteel, part of the regalia of a particular class, but it had become womanliness, woven into the whole cloth of the gender. Respectability was a virtue that resided in the self-image of women as mothers and homemakers but also formed their sense of their rights and responsibilities beyond the domestic sphere. It was a measure of conduct marked most in child rearing. Witness this response by a working-class woman in Paris to the 'sharp tongue' of a merchant's wife: 'I terrifically resent the way she snubbed me. Our family has always been respectable. That snob may have more money than us, but we're every bit as good. At least we have smarter and better-looking kids. They're better behaved too.' Respectability was also a sign of resistance, a claim by which female mill workers distinguished themselves from those managers and foremen who were 'no better than they ought to have been.'[25]

The striking female mill workers who were 'respectable married women' (and widows) came to their respectability by marriage rather than waged work. Decency was a virtue women felt they brought from home to the mill, a trait not incompatible but not indigenous to factory life. The honour and dignity they fought the strike to defend was challenged, not forged, on the shop floor. Women took satisfaction in their work skills but drew their worth from their domestic roles. Although the community convention was accepting and had long been accepting of working wives, in the crisis of the strike married respectability became rather like a modern Canadian pension; its portability was placed in question. Could a women bring to militance the presence she drew from her role as wife and mother? Would her authority, exercised by reference to domestic hierarchies rather than workplace relations, be acknowledged as relevant to the matters at issue in the strike? Once feelings became heated, women on both sides of the dispute used challenges to the virtue of wage-earning mothers (common enough in the mainstream culture and in communities organized around the male breadwinner wage) to discredit their opponents. A vigorous supporter of the strike, Florrie Horsfall, signing her letter to the editor '(Mrs) E. Horsfall,' berated Elsie Smith for working while her children were young. 'I came to Paris 28 years ago during the depression... My family grew to four in nine years ... I had to go out to work to make ends meet, and found it very hard to leave my children. To Mrs Smith I would say that as she is the mother of six children she should stay home and do justice to her family.' Elsie Smith, in turn, took on Grace Hockin, the strike supporter who claimed through her family thirty years' experience in and out of the mills. Hockin was doing Penmans work on a machine in her home before the strike, according to

Smith: 'able to make extra money, and still look after her home and babies without having to pay someone else to look after them while she went to the mill. After the little ones were tucked in for the night, and on Saturdays, she could make extra dollars, whereas we in the mill had regular hours ... I think Mrs. Hockin was very fortunate ... and should thank the company instead of running it down.'[26] Once there was an audience outside the mill community, once respectable women lent their standing as mothers to workplace militance, the local, implicit exception protecting the honour of wives who took jobs in the mill became contested. The genie was out of the bottle. All the ways in which domestic and workplace roles, gender, and class identifications might erode or reinforce one another came into play.

The reinterpretation of local events through the understandings of the mainstream culture masked the origins and muted the force of womanly militance. On the second day of the strike, the first Ontario Provincial Police officers arrived in town, at the invitation of municipal council after a month's pressure by the firm.[27] The next morning in what the Toronto press described as a 'wild melee' outside the hosiery mill,[28] OPP officers arrested Gertrude Williams, thirty-nine, and Margaret (May) Higgins, eighteen, and charged them with disorderly conduct. William Stewart, the UTWA field representative in Paris, summoned his best patriarchal indignation, portraying Williams and Higgins as vulnerable creatures by comparison with the real criminals at loose in the province. 'I hate their guts, every one of them. Why aren't they out looking for Mickey MacDonald? Why aren't they out looking for him instead of arresting the wife of Charlie Williams, and shoving little girls around on a picket line.' Mrs Williams, in her own account, was less willing to be dismissed from the fray by virtue of her gender. 'I was on the picket line not doing anything. There was some pushing and the next thing I knew I was arrested. But I took some arresting. It took three of them to put me in a car. They tried to scare me and say my place was at home. I told them my place is where I want to put it. My place is on the picket line, and that's where I'll be, every day until it's over.'[29] Mrs Williams was the odd one out in this exchange. From their perspective as men and outsiders, the male union organizer believed she would not, the provincial policemen believed that she should not, behave on the line in a way that would make her an effective picket. Mrs Williams alone among them seemed to credit her capacity for militance.

Horsfall, Hockin, Smith, and Williams all had worked for Penmans in the past and probably expected to be on the mills' payrolls at some time

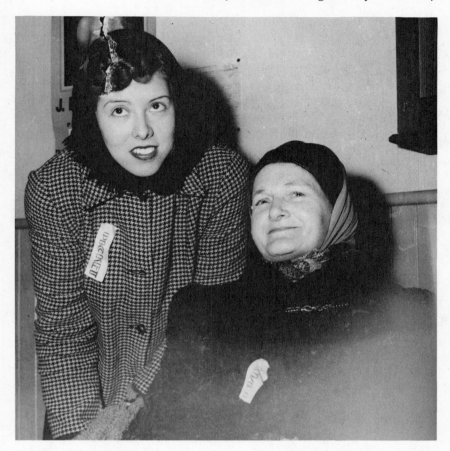

May Higgins and Gertrude Williams, still wearing 'picket' ribbons after their arrest, on the charge of disorderly conduct, on the picket line outside the hosiery mill, at dawn, 21 January 1949

again in the future, though none of them was a Penmans employee late in 1948. Women in the community commonly moved in and out of the labour force as the needs of their households changed and throughout their adult lives construed their own well-being as intimately connected with conditions in the mills. Those neighbours and kin who shared child-care responsibilties and fashioned collective living arrangements in order to make waged work possible were knowledgeable and concerned and considered themselves parties to the dispute even though they were not formally parties to the wage relationship. In Paris, as in the Lawrence strike of 1912, the female militance was forged and sustained in family and neighbourhood relationships. For women, it was within these relationships rather than through union organization that the need for change in the workplace was most compellingly articulated and the most formidable alliances both for and against the strike were lodged.[30] Friends and relations swelled the numbers of militants and widened their intelligence networks, their sources of sober counsel, their tactical resources. Among the most dauntless of the pickets was the wife of a man, once the boss in the shipping room, 'a real good guy to work for,' who had been fired one day by a universally detested manager and without apparent cause. When Eleanor Barrett, twenty-two, was 'plucked' from the picket line and charged with intimidation, her mother, who kept house for a family of five mill workers, immediately and publicly came forward to replace her. The day-care arrangements among neighbours and kin that had allowed mothers to hold down jobs in the mill now freed them to take their place on the line.[31]

Women controlled a considerable amount of housing stock in the town. More than a third of Penmans female employees in 1948 owned their own homes. Boarding-house keepers often ran their businesses out of more than one dwelling, and older women workers bought small rental properties as a security against the days when they could no longer go to the mill. The house owners were from the old mill families most strongly committed to the strike, and as a result workers arriving in town to take jobs during the dispute found few boarding places open to them. Mrs Clem Smith, declaring that none of her properties would shelter 'scabs,' evicted the tenants who had let rooms in one of her houses to four Nova Scotian strike breakers. The Nova Scotians had scuffled with her nieces and nephews on the line, and one of them had beaten up her nephew William in a Friday night disturbance on main street. Several women whose back gardens opened onto lanes near the mills kept their kitchens open through the night, dispensing hot coffee and encouragement. Florence Lewis suffered badly later for showing her loyalty to the strikers in this way, but Robert Fletcher, who from his car kept the night vigil on the Willow Street gate, remembered her as an 'awful good woman' who had been more effective than any of the unionists from nearby centres in supporting the strike.[32]

Family thus could be 'the institution *par excellence*' by which women combined 'to defend their collective interest,' and 'community based, female ties and networks' could 'be mobilized to produce forms of female control.' But the connection between gender and community solidarities and class-consciousness was contingent and volatile.[33] Florence Lewis's elderly neighbour, who worked at Penmans until she was well on in her eighties, felt Lewis had betrayed her and the accommodating employer who had given her work. They never spoke again. After a sidesman in the Baptist church refused to walk down the aisle with her to a pew, Lewis never thereafter attended a service.[34] The choice among family, community, and class interest which caused Charles Harrison and the ten other key union members to leave the UTWA in the wake of the strike vote was posed forcefully for the Pike and England families in the first week of the strike. On Thursday morning, Doreen Pike, a finisher in the sweater mill, and her husband, Arthur, a Department of Highways employee, were on the picket line. Doreen's mother would have been on the line as well, she declared later, but it was her turn to look after the children. Arthur Pike was arrested and charged by one of the thirty-seven Ontario Provincial Policemen now stationed in Paris at the request of Mayor William England. England was Doreen's father, Arthur's father-in-law. By Thursday evening there had been ten arrests. Those released were critical of the conditions under which they had been confined. Three hundred strike supporters marched through the streets to Mayor England's house, calling out that the police were 'outsiders' and carrying a petition protesting the presence of the provincials in town. There was shouting, singing, and a scuffle on the mayor's front lawn. The police intervened. The next day it was rumoured the mayor would resign; he did not, but Doreen Pike withdrew from the picket line, declaring: 'There was no excuse for them to make all that noise and disturbance.' Soon after this incident her father was hospitalized in a state of nervous collapse, out of the action for the duration of the dispute.[35] Ten days later Charles Alexander, the long-suffering president of Local 153, also left the picket line, claiming illness in his family, but also that he had 'wanted no violence and this had led him to stay off the lines.' The majority on council began to talk of the dispute as a '"family quarrel" in which the council should take no part.'[36] Some unionists and non-unionists alike came to use the imagery of family as a justification for retreat rather than engagement.

Like the fire that had destroyed the main street in 1900, like the spring floods that periodically tore through the mills and mill workers' housing on the river flats, the strike was a ferocious and fearsome physical presence in town. The struggle to think about social relations within the community in a different way, to understand, as Charles Alexander wrote to Val Bjarnason of the UTWA, 'the forces underlying the formation of a social system and the transmutation of individuals and families to that system,' to act on the basis of that understanding to claim rights, name abuses, to acknowledge the divide that lay between workers and bosses in town and finally choose sides had been arduous. While the members of the local had been pursuing certification, visiting co-workers and signing up members, there had been comforting similarities between the prospect of a fair hearing and a square deal in an organized workplace and honoured family, neighbourhood, and community values.

No one had ever behaved in public in town in the ways the script of the strike required. Parades had been cheerful national or seasonal celebrations in a commom cause, not angry assertions of claims or demonstrations of force. The mill gates had been places to exchange gossip and cigarettes, not curses and blows. On the first days, as the picket lines went up, a non-striker told local historian Donald Smith that many who went into the mill 'felt sick at heart' and went out at night to see that 'those fellows out in the cold got some coffee and sandwiches.' But by mid-week there were scores of provincial policemen, squads of big-city reporters, and several union organizers in town, giving 'the impression of a small invasion from some other part of the country.'[37] They were defining the dispute, and such simple neighbourly gestures were no longer reported. Many in the community remained heart-sick, but uneasily they played out their new roles. The pickets on the graveyard shift went for their coffee to Mrs Lewis, Mrs Corrigan, and the other ladies who kept their kitchen lights burning through the night.

The picket line was to provide a barrier between intending non-strikers and their workplaces in the mill. Its devices were silent shaming, verbal intimidation, and physical force. Of these, only shaming was womanly, but a picket that functioned using shaming alone would have won no public attention and served to discomfit but not inhibit workers passing through the line. Taking on the unaccustomed rhetoric of the bar-room and postures of the brawler both limited and enhanced women's effectiveness as picketers and affected both the way they were perceived and the way they felt about themselves. The resort to violence could compromise the acknowledged respectability upon which their claims to authority had been based or by the profoundness of its anomaly accentuate the urgency and the justice of their cause. The sensation of being out of bounds could be exhilarating and empowering, drawing women back again and again to savour its exotic pleasures; it could also cause them to retreat from the very possibility or, having glimpsed its fascinations, to draw back in self-revulsion.[38]

Mildred Hopper, who was early convinced that through the union Penmans could be made a better place to work, went home to her parents' farm in Princeton the morning the strike began 'and stayed there until the strike was over. I went out but I didn't want to be any part of it. I think that [being on the picket line] would be worst of all.' Lottie Keen, a widow who was one of only two women in the looping department to honour the picket, could not bring herself to join the line. 'Some of them [the women picketers] were very outspoken, like they'd follow you and call you scab and all this sort of stuff ... so I didn't feel bad about it, but it did make a lot of ... [voice tailing off].' May Phillips remembered most of the picketers being women:

> Most of them were women that worked there you see ... When that started I just stayed home. I lived in Brantford then, so I didn't see any sense in travelling up here and getting into a hassle. I don't like that kind of thing anyway.
>
> Q: What kind of thing do you mean?
>
> Getting into scraps all the time.

Her husband was a member of the autoworkers' union in Brantford, but he distrusted the politics of the UTWA and she deferred to his judgment. 'My husband says "you're not going up there while they are on strike" because he knew what that union was like.' Frances Randall's husband stayed out in respect for friends who had joined the union, but he gave clear orders to his wife, 'don't you dare go over there'; and she didn't.[39] Within the union movement, even among female activists, it was hard to acknowledge and defend womanly militance on its own merits. Jessie Bragg, five years a member of the UAW-CIO in Brantford, had helped the UTWA recruit members in Paris and spoken regularly at their meetings, but as the clashes on the picket line grew more violent and sympathy for the strikers appeared to wane, she felt compelled to reconfigure the dispute for the press: 'In looking over the picket lines, I have noticed at least 90 percent of the pickets are veterans from the last two wars and some veterans of both wars. We, as war workers ... were sure that those

The picket line along Willow Street in front of the yarn and sweater mills. Clara Farr is looking towards the camera, immediately to the right of the man carrying the sign reading, 'Textile workers want to live too!'

boys had the best during the war, so why don't we, as citizens of this town, whether it be the town fathers, Board of Trade, merchants or ministers of all denominations, get behind this affair and see that these boys have the best now?'[40]

Women's postures on the picket line were sharp-edged collages of their old and new roles, compelling for both their dissonance and their familiarity. In the first week of the strike, 'when the provincials got out of their cars and stationed themselves by the gates of the three mills, they smiled at the pickets and joked with some of the girls. The pickets found themselves responding in kind. The cops were pleasant.' 'Here come the other pickets,' a woman exclaimed, 'there's more in their picket line than in ours.'[41] In the second week when the weather turned bitterly cold, women 'far outnumbered' men on the line; 'they said the weather did not bother them.' Clara Farr remembered feeling queenly on the picket. 'Oh that was something! I never owned a fur coat in my life and somebody was good enough to bring me a fur coat so that I could go on the picket line.' 'My girl friends and I really had a lot of fun. It brought us a lot closer together. We became close friends.' 'We had dances; we had parties.' It was a non-striker who recalled for Donald Smith with barely submerged glee:

> One girl was very mouthy. She yelled all kinds of things at workers who were entering the mill. She even yelled them at a relative of hers. Finally the sergeant in charge of the police at that gate said to one of the relatives, 'The next time she yells at you, I'll turn my back and you slap her face.'
> Some of the women used hatpins, even jabbed the police in the rump. They carried them in their purses. They'd stick them into the cops when the cops were in line ... One cop had to go to the hospital for an infection in his rump. He was there for a few days. The stabbing was worse at night when the light was poor.[42]

Police, journalists, and pickets alike framed female militance in the imagery of feminine wiles.

Gender sensibilities could mute the force of the conflict. On the line, males who cursed females did no credit to their side; men who claimed injury from women's sharp tongues were objects of mirth; shouting matches between women neighbours were construed as cat-fights in the press.[43] Gendered identities were masks that changed in the shifting light and shadow of the dispute – mercurial, unpredictable in their effects upon public sympathy.

On 19 January Elizabeth May Cardy, a midlands immigrant who had run one of the large, flat-bed, full-fashioned knitting machines in the hosiery mill since 1929, was injured in an altercation, allegedly with Arthur Gignac and Lillian Gillow, as she tried to cross the line. Nine days later she suffered a stroke. At seven-thirty on the morning of 3 February charges of intimidation with violence were laid against Gillow and Gignac in connection with the incident of 19 January. The pickets and police were massed that morning at the Elm Street gate; Gillow was home with the flu; as Gignac, unaccountably it seemed to the other pickets, was dragged off the line into a squad car, what the press called a 'free-for-all' broke out. Hendrika Bethune, a twenty-two-year-old winder, was forced to the ground in the centre of a crowd; Robert Williams, whose mother had been arrested early in the dispute, thought Bethune was hurt and as he went to her aid was grabbed by a policeman. Helen Murphy, the secretary-treasurer of the local and at well over 200 pounds a formidable presence on the line, waded in to protect young

Williams and move the officer aside. There were nine arrests in the twenty minutes before the eight o'clock whistle blew. Murphy was charged with assaulting a policeman. Just after eight, the news came that Elizabeth Cardy had died. That day's front pages showed Bethune writhing in the ground surrounded by police. The next day a hundred pickets massed at the same gate. There were four arrests. Leta Morrison, aged thirty-seven, was run over by a car filled with non-strikers and taken to hospital. The newspapers showed Gladys Burtch, a twenty-three-year-old finisher, being carried from the scene in the arms of her father and Val Bjarnason from the UTWA after, the pickets claimed, she had been kicked in the stomach by a policeman.[44]

The arrests of 4 February brought the total in the first three weeks of the strike to twenty-seven. In the two months that followed, until the strike was settled on 9 April, the police laid seven more charges, five against UTWA organizers, only two against town residents. Though Coroner W.J. Deadman's report released 11 February determined that Cardy's death was not due to violence (she suffered from Bright's disease and previously twice had stopped work for extended periods),[45] and Morrison and Burtch recovered from their injuries, the will to make the picket a physical barrier around the mills was gone. The eighty to a hundred workers who still marched the picket lines substituted songs and snake dances for curses and blows. Coverage of the strike now concerned events in the courts rather than the street.

The trials began on 7 February. A court list, with charges against twenty-three persons, was unprecedented in Paris. By the time the accused 'and police and other witnesses have been admitted to the small Council Chamber,' the press predicted, 'there will be scarcely a seat available for anyone in the role of mere spectator.'[46] The standard charge laid, against male and female picketers alike, was creating a disturbance and intimidation with violence. Police testimony was commanding in the court. The rights of pickets were narrowly construed in the law. Three out of every four charges laid against strikers resulted in convictions.[47] But Magistrate R.J. Gillen of Brantford viewed both the witnesses and the behaviour required for a conviction through gendered expectations. In their questioning, both the crown attorneys and the defence counsel used presuppositions about what manly and womanly conduct would have been in order to elicit witness testimony about what had happened on the line. Neither strikers nor non-strikers had set aside their identities as women and men when they assumed their new roles on the picket line; yet women both recalled their familiar

This widely reproduced photograph shows Leta Morrison, 'just as she was thrown to the ground when struck by a car while on picket duty' on the morning of 4 February. The image, as carried by the wire services, was cropped a third of the way from the top, so that the other strikers, the police, and the occupants of the car were excluded, leaving Morrison alone in the frame raising her mittened hand against the shining grill and headlights of the vehicle.

The most frequently reproduced image of the strike nationally, this photograph shows Gladys Burtch, a twenty-three-year-old finisher at the hosiery
mill, being carried from the picket line on 4 February by her father and by Val
Bjarnason, in the fedora at right. Helen Murphy, the secretary of the local, is
behind at left; William Horsfall, behind at right. The photograph was presented cropped to show only the three central faces, with Burtch appearing
to have collapsed in the men's arms.

gendered reflexes to recoil and defend and listened as their unaccustomed postures of militance, so electrifying to claim and display, were made mild and conventional in legal summation. Looking out into the crowded council chamber, knowing their tale would be told and retold, they refashioned their recollections to become one of their sex.

The reaction rather than the act was key for Magistrate Gillen in ruling upon intimidation. The pattern in his judgments became clear in the first day of the trials. A male picket captain was accused of intimidating Gordon Parsons, a knitter-mechanic who had crossed the line. Parsons testifed that the picket had said, 'You're bloody brave while the cops are here, but I'll get you yet, you – – –,' but he insisted the threat had not made him fearful. Dismissing the charge, Gillen said 'that as Parsons was not afraid of the accused, there was no intimidation.' The requirement that the persons intimidated acknowledge before the court that they had been made afraid, when the avowal empowered their adversary and revealed their own vulnerability, ordered the court proceedings through patriarchal, and more proximate, political relations. Older women would agree they had feared younger women. Thus eighteen-year-old Margaret Higgins did intimidate fifty-year-old Rose Lewis. A woman threatened by a man would admit fear. Some older men would acknowledge fearing younger men. No man would own up to being frightened by any woman on the line, no matter how formidable her presence, with one exception. The crown attorney, by imputing that a union organizer, whether male or female, was a communist, could secure an admission of fear and a conviction against the accused from any witness before him.[48]

Men's actions to protect women or the elderly of either gender were viewed favourably by the court, but in the vicinity of violence, maleness could carry the implication of guilt. Lillian Gillow was a thirty-three-year-old widow, a finisher from the hosiery mill, living with her two children in her widowed father's house. She was charged with intimidation with violence after Mrs Cardy suffered her stroke. Gillow testified that she had been alone, holding Mrs Cardy's arm, attempting to talk to her, as two men, John Rogers and Martin Hogan, tried to help Cardy up the steps to a high loading platform outside the mill. Gillow said Arthur Gignac, the twenty-four-year-old knitter who was the other accused in the incident, was not nearby. Gignac testified he was several yards away, and defence witnesses concurred that he had not touched Mrs Cardy. Rogers and Hogan, however, claimed that on looking back they had seen Gignac grab Cardy's right hand. The court had heard that Cardy had been in ill health for two years, but in convicting both Gillow and Gignac, Magistrate Gillan reasoned: 'there could be no doubt that Mr Hogan and Mr Rogers were trying to help Mrs Cardy up to the platform and it would not have been necessary for them to help her, unless she were being held back. He believed that Arthur Gignac was holding her back and Mrs Gillow was pushing her.'[49] In view of the conflicting testimony about Gignac's location, the magistrate based his judgment on his appraisal of what force a woman might be able to exert, and even though Cardy was frail and the loading dock high, he determined that Lillian Gillow alone could not have dislodged her footing.

EPILOGUE

If men faced a more difficult time at the hands of the courts, women suffered greater non-judicial penalties as a result of their participation in the strike. The settlement agreement won only one concession from Penmans, that there would be no discrimination in rehiring, but this clause left the firm wide powers to determine the availability and suitability of candidates for jobs in the mill.[50] The longer experience with conditions in the mills and the more limited opportunities for them elsewhere in the labour force which made change at Penmans an urgent priority for women, made older women, wives, and widows exceptional in their militance and left these same women most vulnerable in the wake of the strike. The younger fellows who had been overrepresented among male supporters of the strike soon took jobs in electrical, metal, and wood-working plants in nearby centres. By comparison with other work available for men, as Roy Hawes, a thirty-four-year-old spinner, told a reporter in the crowd on main street the Sunday after the settlement, Penmans was 'not worth going back to.' Florence Miller was still chipper that afternoon, declaring herself rested for the return to work after the first 'holiday' in forty years at the mill.[51] But the rising post-war prohibitions against working wives, the reasserted sex-typing of jobs which was characteristic of the peace, closed this possibility for the most hard-pressed women members of Local 153. The last UTWA list of workers waiting, 'never sent for,' still hoping to regain their jobs at the mill, included thirty-one women and four men. Among them were Florence Miller, reportedly the oldest striker; Mathilda Crump, a fifty-nine-year-old widow, and her daughter Addie, a single woman aged forty, who lived together in a small house they owned in town; Mary Eames, a fifty-nine-year-old mender who had been at Penmans since 1904; Bridget Rook, sixty-five, whose forty-year-old son, a boarder, was also still unemployed; Eleanor Barrett, whose mother had stepped in to take her place on the line; Clara Farr, who had felt so resplendent in her borrowed fur coat; and Gladys Burtch, now recovered from her injuries and eager to be back in the finishing room.[52]

Summing up the reasons for the strike's failure, in the more friendly territory of Valleyfield, Quebec, where the mayor had opened the UTWA annual convention in the fall of 1949, Kent Rowley noted the 'lack of experience of Paris workers with union organization.' Women in town were more likely to think that they had 'picked the wrong union.'[53] In the longer term, however, their experience with womanly militance and neighbourly wrath intensified local distrust of class-based actions as a way to bring about social change. Disheartened by a renewed awareness of their limitations, the mill families of Paris turned back for meaning in their lives to the gender- and community-based solidarities in which their militance had been forged.

PART TWO

■ Chapter Six

As Christ the carpenter

The woodworkers of Hanover came into the watershed of the Saugeen River continuing a quest their fathers had undertaken for a world it was said their grandfathers had known. They were German speaking, principally from the southwest and the Rhineland, some of whom had sojourned for a generation among the Mennonites of Waterloo County, before travelling north towards the Bruce Peninsula. They came from anabaptist families which had lived on the cusp between agriculture and the crafts for several generations in Baden, Wurttemberg, the Rhine Palatinate, and Rhenish Prussia. Their forbears were not guild members sheltered behind the excluding ordinances of craft and town government, but small agricultural proprietors who fed themselves from their land and bartered their skills working in wood to meet other needs. The custom of partible inheritance in the region had over the generations made holdings too small to yield marketable agricultural surpluses. Families took up potato cultivation to sustain larger numbers of children upon their limited plots. Rural craftwork provided the means to remain on the land; the forest resources on non-arable slopes nearby provided particular opportunities for men who could turn their hands to woodworking.[1]

The contemporary political economist, Frederich List, characterized the forming pattern in the region as a *zwergwirtschaft*, a dwarf economy of tiny marginal holdings vulnerable to crisis. Craftsworkers had fared well enough behind the blockade during the Napoleonic Wars, but the steamboats and the new customs union which opened the Rhine valley to greater trade in the 1830s made cheaper, factory-made goods available in local markets. The pietistic small landholders who made ends barely meet by selling their handmade goods faced two choices, to set aside their agricultural and craft traditions and take up wage labour in the growing cities of the German Bund or to attempt by a longer move to effect a smaller change. Neither their anabaptist beliefs nor their village loyalties drew them towards the forming German state. Ironically the population growth that cottage industry had facilitated drove land prices too high to allow farmer/craftsmen to expand their holdings at home and high enough to finance familial emigration.[2]

Most German emigrants of the 1820s and 1830s chose destinations where land was abundant, in either Russia or the United States. Those who settled in British North America were relatively few but readily identifiable because they settled initially only where German-speaking Mennonite settlements already existed, particularly in Waterloo County. With their neighbours in the townships of Waterloo and Woolwich they shared the dialect of the upper Rhine, the language the eighteenth-century Mennonite emigrants to Pennsylvania brought north to the Grand River Valley after 1805. Dialect, however, was not the only feature of social life in Waterloo County in which the arriving farmer/craftsmen were to hear echoes of their German home districts.[3]

The German-speaking character of Woolwich and Waterloo was secured in 1805 and 1807 and exclusively maintained for a half-century thereafter through land title. Driven by land shortages to leave Pennsylvania, the Mennonites planned their new community to accommodate the needs of several inheriting generations. Their elders purchased over 100,000 acres in the two townships to be sold in parcels of 488 acres, five and ten times as large as the average Upper Canadian farm, even a quarter century later. This was not land to farm, however, but land by which to secure a future. Many brethern bought multiple parcels. By the 1820s all the German Land Company holdings were taken up, and, as the immigration from Baden, Wurttemberg, and the Palatinate began, Mennonites from Pennsylvania had turned from Upper Canada towards more propitious destinations.[4]

Some cheap plots of land were made available to the German newcomers, but in sizes below the threshold of agricultural self-sufficiency. The Mennonite farmers were pleased to hire their new neighbours as day labourers, for field work in summer and to help in the woods in winter, but their own family members were proficient in woodworking. The Mennonite community was, and preferred to be, largely self-sufficient in handicraft production. The emigrant artisan/

smallholders of southwest Germany had settled in a region where the limited availability of land made their workshop earnings crucial and where the market for their wares was, albeit for different reasons, as lean as it had been in the Old Country. As better horse-drawn farm machinery and the depletion of woodlots reduced the demand for wage labour on the land, the villages of the county remained small, 'held back,' Heinz Lehmann has argued, 'by the Mennonites, who opposed the creation of large towns on principle and would not release land for that purpose.' Many German artisans moved into the villages of Preston and West Montrose. But even the largest near locality, Berlin, still in 1852 had only 700 inhabitants, less than half as many as nearby Galt, and most Berlin craftsmen were tenants on Mennonite lands.[5]

By mid-century the bleak continuity of their German past and their present and future prospects was starkly apparent to the artisans and smallholders who had settled in Waterloo two decades before. Their craft livelihood was precarious; their relationship to the land mimicked the dwarf economy they had left. And population pressure was once again about to press them onward.

In Baden, Wurttemburg, and the Palatinate the potato harvest failed in 1842 and continued to fail for the rest of the decade. Local governments that had long opposed emigration began to sponsor the movement of whole communities overseas.[6] The population of Germany had risen by a third between 1820 and 1850, and the provocations to emigrate had become generalized. Among the almost 50,000 Germans who landed in Quebec between 1846 and 1860 and the 15,000 who stayed in British North America were East Elbian peasants from the Mecklenbergs, Prussia, and Pomerania freed from serfdom into land-lessness by the liberal Stein-Hardenberg reforms, and young men from Hanover, Alsace-Lorraine, Silesia, and Saxony fleeing conscription, the coal mines, and the uncertainties of the forming factory system. Most, like the emigrants to Waterloo in the 1830s, were seeking German-language communities where they could re-establish themselves in agriculture and practise their crafts.[7]

The heightening of the crisis for German-born artisans and small-holders in Waterloo and the new steady flow of arrivals from both the Rhineland and the east coincided with the building of a colonization road eighty miles north to open the counties of Bruce and Grey. In a movement, which an early local historian called 'Saugeen Fever,' thousands of Germans, resident for some time in Waterloo, joined recent immigrants in the southern townships of Carrick and Brant in

Bruce and Normanby and Sullivan in Grey. By 1870 these townships were settled; the majority of their inhabitants were German speaking. The town of Hanover, on the boundary between Grey and Bruce, arose from this migration. The community was culturally German and economically dependent, from the start, upon the interdependence of agriculture and woodworking.[8]

The town was named after his home province by one of the mid-century German immigrants, Christian Hassenjager, who in 1849 was Hanover's second settler. In its agricultural hinterland were many who came from the Mecklenbergs and the north. But its early industrial history was dominated by first- and second-generation immigrants from the upper Rhine who had practised their crafts and agriculture first in Waterloo. Pre-eminent among them was Daniel Knechtel, by the early twentieth century the leading furniture manufacturer in town and one of the most important woodworkers in the dominion.

The story of Daniel Knechtel's path to Hanover is like that of many of his employees in the years up to the First World War – not surprisingly. He chose them because they were like him, and his firm was able to expand because there were many like him about. Knechtel's father had come to Waterloo County in 1830 from a smallholding near Landstühl in the Rhine Palatinate, settled first with his family in Preston, attempted to support himself as a cooper in the village of Roseville and then secured land in Woolwich. With his wife, who had come from Kurhessen in 1841, he had thirteen children. Daniel, the second eldest, was born in 1843 and by 1853 was freed from school to learn carpentry and farming from his father and to work in the family interest. In 1861 he set out on his own, there being no future to inherit in Woolwich even for an eldest son. He worked with a group of carpenters building barns and houses in summer, spent a winter in a cabinet-maker's workshop in Berlin, and in 1864 with his brother Peter walked two days north to the farm in south Grey where his married elder sister had settled.[9]

Being without land or the resources to acquire it, Knechtel practised his craft in the countryside, hiring himself out to split rails and build barns, falling back on his farmer-brother-in-law's hospitality when his means became straitened, making furniture by hand in winter, carrying the farm produce with which he was paid into the village to barter. 1864 was late to start at farming in South Grey. Unlike his father, who had finished his life on the land, Knechtel never returned to agriculture. Those of his brothers who became farmers had to move on to the prairies to do so. In 1866 when he married Christina Stadelbauer, an immigrant from southern Bavaria, Knechtel moved into Hanover, built a workshop with living quarters in back, and cast his lot with the village. By 1911 he was employing 275 woodworkers in a four-storey factory on the main street of town.[10]

His partner from 1887 until 1912, Henry Peppler, born on a Waterloo County farm of Alsatian parents and there 'engaged in carpentry and other work,' joined Knechtel at age nineteen in 1875. His early finishing and upholstery foremen came from workshops in Waterloo; the first man to whom he delegated lumber buying had learned his woods in northern Germany. By the 1880s he was hiring not only Waterloo migrants and recent immigrants from the Mecklenbergs and the north, but the sons of first-generation settlers in nearby townships. Some of these men by their late teens thought of themselves as woodworkers, but all were without formal craft credentials.[11]

Frequently, right into the 1920s, Knechtel men were farmers' sons who began by farming, picked up some carpentry on the side, and turned to the furniture factory when their prospects in agriculture grew bleak. Many tried to stave off the day by going west on harvest excursions, hiring themselves out, renting land, or farming jointly with their fathers. They were younger sons of large pioneer families, but also inheriting sons and independent proprietors who lost faith in a future on the land and sold up.[12]

Agriculture and woodworking were bound in the region in a complex relation. By the 1880s hardwood stocks had become depleted near the larger urban centres of Ontario, and furniture makers were moving along the railways away from their markets towards their materials. The rich stands of sugar maple, elm, and basswood in south Bruce and Grey helped finance farm-making in the 1850s, 1860s, and 1870s. Until the turn of the century Hanover general merchants, ironmonger, tinsmith, as well as furniture makers, offered goods in trade for stove wood, furnace wood, and lumber. Farmers also bartered their wool and in 1897 subscribed to a co-operative wool and knit-goods mill in town as a market for their fleeces. The woollen mill failed and the furniture manufactories thrived because their relationship to agriculture in the surrounding district differed. After only one generation on the land, by the 1890s the farmers of the Saugeen Valley were having difficulty holding their own against prairie producers and the more intensive agricultural practices further south in the province. Village merchants were still complaining in 1897 of the effects of crop failures in the neighbourhood three years earlier. The region's lack of competitiveness in field crops and livestock, however, gave it an advantage in woods. The incentives to clear rough lands and stony soils for cultivation decreased; there were good reasons to tend woodlots carefully and good prices offered by village manufacturers when woodlands were offered for sale. In the winter of 1898-9 Knechtel bought two and three carloads of logs daily from nearby farmers. In late February 1900 John Schaefer hauled '2,800 feet of rock elm' into their yards in a single day. Into the 1920s Knechtel still advertised locally for maple, elm, and basswood sawlogs, knowing that farmers who had 'not been getting much money for their products the last few years and are becoming hard up' would sell from the bush 'to help out on expenses.'[13] After Hanover furniture manufacturers ceased to buy the majority of their lumber locally, they continued to turn to nearby agriculturalists, intermittently for their wood and regularly for the sons whom the land would not support. Here again was the meagre and familiar mutuality of wood and soil. In 1901, when raw material and labour each represented about a third of manufacturing costs in furniture, wages paid to woodworkers in Grey and Bruce were 60 per cent of those offered in Toronto. By 1911 furniture manufacture was the principal industry in both counties.[14]

That many of the late nineteenth- and early twentieth-century furniture workers of Hanover had been or would have been farmers does not mean that they were either indifferent or inferior craftsmen in wood. The superlative German cabinet-makers of Philadelphia came out of the same Rhine land/craft experience that formed the woodworkers of Waterloo and Grey/Bruce. Some of the finest furniture made in Upper Canada and Canada West was fashioned by craftsmen who worked in wood only when the weather kept them off the land.[15] The late nineteenth-century transformation from workshop to factory production of furniture was not nearly so stark a change at the bench and the moulder as the multi-storey exteriors and rumbling steam engines in the new plants might suggest.

In the late 1860s Daniel and Peter Knechtel ran a sawmill two miles out of town in addition to their Hanover woodworking shop. In the early 1870s they bought out a local furniture maker who had a steam engine and six woodworking machines and employed ten hands. A decade later Daniel Knechtel had fifty men working in a three-storey brick building making all manner of articles in wood, from sash, doors, and shingles to upholstered goods and cabinets. The firm sold hardware, groceries, and dry goods in addition to its own products, perhaps as incentives for farmers to bring in lumber to trade. Not until the early

1890s was Knechtel formed as a limited company to specialize in the manufacture and sale of furniture alone. By 1899 there were four steam-powered elevators and 150 machines in the plant, but neither the work Knechtel employees did nor the goods they made had much in common with modern mass production.[16]

Into the twentieth century furniture factories were craftshops serially replicated rather than workplaces fundamentally transformed by their increase in scale. The materials, the machinery, and the objects produced demanded craft sensitivities and skills from factory furniture workers. Factory labour divisions and the common practice of buying finished parts from other producers for assembly were carry-overs from the cabinet-maker's shop rather than introductions associated with factory production. Wood is a live material, responsive to changing heat and humidity, variable foot by foot in the opportunities it presents the sawyer, workable only by mechanical means, not susceptible to being hurried along or handled in larger lots by reduction to a liquid state through the application of heat.[17] Furniture was, and to some extent still is, a commodity in which buyers value familiarity and reject sameness. The evocations of known forms, whether the cabriole leg, the claw foot, or the carved back, were essential in popular furniture even if they resisted mechanical rendering. Yet, except in the cheapest lines, goods offered for sale needed to be continuously differentiated, defying the economics of specialty machine building.[18] It was in the sawmill that nineteenth-century woodworking technology excelled, in the cutting and ripping of boards, the planing of broad surfaces by powerful steam- and water-driven machines. These large saws, planers, and moulders performed their tasks without close analogies to the hand processes they superseded, ran with predictable results once set to the purpose, and could be operated by raw recruits. Thus was the preparation of the stock, already a modest part of furniture making costs, made cheaper.[19] Otherwise, late nineteenth- and early twentieth-century woodworking machines were power-driven hand tools which no matter how carefully set-up and jigged demanded care, judgment, and dexterity from their operators. Students of these machines often invoke designer David Pye's distinction between workmanship of risk and workmanship of certainty. Outside the sawmill, still in the turn-of-the-century furniture industry, 'the quality of the result' was 'continually at risk during the making.' As earlier woodworkers had sought precision through patterns and jigs, nineteenth-century furniture makers fashioned foot- and later steam-powered machines to reduce their margins of error in

making turnings, mortices, tenons, and trim. But such machines were more exact only when tended by operators of great skill. Until late in the nineteenth century fancy moulding, dovetailing, and carving machines did not yield gains over hand work sufficient to repay their capital costs.[20] In the precision and symmetry Ontario furniture makers valued as good work there was a strong continuity between the workshop and the factory. Consumer conceptions of good furniture were equally resilient, formed by tastes for fine hand work, persistently valuing features that resisted mechanization over design elements that could be deftly mass produced.[21]

In December 1900 the Knechtel plant on the main street of Hanover burned to the ground. While the owners of the building were hurrying back from Toronto by train, the men were rushing repeatedly into the the factory attempting to save their tools. In the days that followed it was uncertain whether Knechtel would rebuild in town. The furniture workers were fearful. They were craftsmen. Some had their tools. But their dilemma was akin to that of their fathers and grandfathers. The possession of the tools and knowledge of the craft alone were not enough to sustain a family.[22]

Knechtel did rebuild in Hanover, assisted by a $10,000 bonus and exemption from property taxes that the ratepayers of the village had approved by a margin of 254 to 11.[23] The years before the First World War were salad days for the firm. It built additions to the plants purchased in the late 1890s in nearby Walkerton and Southampton, expanded its Hanover building twice, and in 1911 built a new factory for the manufacture of office furniture. Each year from 1904 to 1911 the shareholders received 7 per cent or more in dividends, save 1909 when funds were reserved to buy a warehouse in Winnipeg and finance the expected purchase of new timber lands.[24]

The company grew with the country. Between 1901 and 1911 the population of Canada increased by 34 per cent; the population of Hanover grew by 68 per cent; nationally the value of furniture production rose by 77 per cent. From its three plants Knechtel sold

---

Two examples of Knechtel furniture. The ash bedroom suite, with curly ash veneer on raised panels and serpentine drawers, is from the 1900 catalogue. The dining room suite, called William and Mary pattern, was made from solid walnut posts and frames, with tops, fronts, and gables of veneer. This example is from the 1922 catalogue.

The Knechtel main plant, 1901, as it was rebuilt a year after it was destroyed by fire. In the foreground is the Durham Road, Hanover's commercial street. The town hall and municipal library were immediately across from the plant. This rendering shows local farmers hauling logs from their woodlots for sale to the firm, and sawn boards, piled to air dry behind the plant.

under $300,000 worth of goods in 1901 and over $700,000 in 1910. There were more Canadians and more prosperous Canadians who chose large houses and massive furniture as ways to display their wealth.[25] In 1901 Knechtel had a travelling sales staff of five in central Canada and after 1903 a permanent representative in the west.[26]

It throve in a tariff-sheltered market. Duties protecting Canadian furniture rose from 15 and 20 per cent under the pre-Confederation Galt-Cayley regime to 30 per cent in 1896 when maritimer W.S. Fielding and his cabinet colleagues began to scrutinize the rates. Canadian manufacturers stoutly and successfully defended their level of protection, which was 5 per cent higher than United States duties against Canadian goods, claiming that even at that level American makers were dumping wares across the border, and that Canadian manufacturers could not survive on a reduced market share.[27] Their industry lobby, one of the earliest organized under the Canadian Manufacturers' Association umbrella, was also able, through the first decade of the century, to keep duties levied on the mahogany and quarter-oak veneers they themselves imported at a low 7.5 per cent.[28]

And Knechtel, with other modestly scaled small-town firms in Ontario (where 80 per cent of Canadian furniture was made in these years), succeeded at the expense of bigger plants in larger urban centres. As W.B. Rogers, a Toronto retailer, argued to Fielding: 'It does not hold good in furniture that the city can manufacture to better advantage than the small towns.' Specialty producers were more successful in the trade than large multi-line firms. In an industry in which there were few economies of scale, manufacturers located in small communities where skilled workers had strong local cultural ties were strategically well situated.[29]

In 1911 70 per cent of the inhabitants of Hanover were ethnically German. The German character of the town continued to be an important reason to settle in the community and to stay there, both for German-speaking migrants from other parts of North America and for newly arriving immigrants. Into the third generation German remained the language of the home. In the years before the First World War, when German ancestry was more honourable than problematical in Canada, advertisements for shop clerks and domestic servants in the town newspaper frequently specified that applicants be German speaking.[30] The town library held a German-language collection, and the town council, apparently inconclusively, debated in 1908 whether to hire a German-speaking teacher for the public school staff. In the two Lutheran churches of Hanover worship was in German morning and evening, although after 1897 the Evangelical Lutherans held an additional afternoon service 'to which all English friends are invited.' Not until 1921 did the larger Lutheran congregation, St Matthew's, consider instituting English church classes for their youngsters.[31] The local Baptist church retained close links with the German Baptist Churches of North America, held its services in German, and taught English-speaking youngsters German vocabulary in its Sunday school. Daniel Knechtel, and his son after him, prominent among Hanover Baptists, spoke German within their own homes.[32]

From 1870 there was a German-language paper in nearby Walkerton which carried a column of Hanover news and reports of political events in Germany. The *Glocke*, however, ceased publication in 1904 even though German remained the common language of home and church in the district. Perhaps its vigorous, well-read editor had overestimated local interest in German news.[33] Like many long-established ethnic communities overseas, the Germans of south Grey and Bruce had gone their own way. The German cultural connections of the majority were with the anabaptist faith and the language and land/craft traditions of Rhine villages in the 1820s and 1830s, not with the unified modern German state. The smaller stream of later German immigrants adapted to the older patterns of the majority. Unlike the early twentieth-century midlands emigrants of Paris, the recent arrivals to Hanover did not form a distinctive group within town or maintain their European ties through transatlantic visits. Many of them shared with their pietistic early nineteenth-century predecessors an aversion drawn in village culture and anabaptist principles to growing central government. Several men who had joined the community in the 1860s and the early twentieth century were known to have left Germany to evade military service. Two nationalisms were not contending in Hanover, Ontario. There were well-attended patriotic concerts during the South African War, which John Mitchell, editor of the *Hanover Post*, emphasized to refute reports the community was pro-Boer. Those adaptations there were to the preponderantly non-British-Canadian character of the town seemed harmless enough. Hanover held its municipal celebrations on 1 July, Dominion Day, rather than 24 May, Queen Victoria's birthday and the favoured choice in neighbouring Chesley, Harriston, and Walkerton. The reticence that Scots farmers in other parts of the county claimed to detect in Hanover was not born of disloyalty. It was an understandable enough hesitation in a community, without military and nationalist traditions, identified first with hearth, craft, and church.[34]

Soon after war was declared in 1914 the Canadian government issued a proclamation assuring immigrants of German nationality that 'they would not be interfered with so long as they pursued their ordinary avocations.'[35] This the German-born men of Hanover were content enough to do. Among British Canadians in the first months of the war, manliness became equated with the patriotic willingness to serve. So long as the contingents were readily filled with volunteers it was not politically necessary to articulate a wider social identity between virility and enlistment.

Hanover was in the federal constituency of South Grey, a riding in which by 1914 the villagers and townsfolk were more likely Germans and the farmers British. The elections of 1908 and 1911 had been hotly and closely contested. The Liberal was H.H. Miller, a Hanover conveyancer long associated in business and politics with the Knechtels. The Conservative, R.J. Ball, had been born on a farm in the riding and taught school in the countryside. He had worked for a time for Knechtel and Knechtel's banker, James H. Adams, before severing his ties and establishing a chair factory in town. Miller won in 1908; Ball was the sitting, though largely silent, member from 1911 through the war years. Miller was more closely identified with the town and the ethnic German community and this connection seems to have figured in his 1911 defeat.[36]

It was Miller who came to the defence of his German neighbours when their loyalty was first called into question in 1914. Citing sources from Owen Sound, in the more British northern part of the county, the Toronto *Globe* on 1 November reported that ministers in South Grey had been raising funds for German soldiers' widows and orphans. In a reply to the *Globe*'s editor, Miller traced the incident to one German-American cleric in Neustadt, who had taken up the suggestion in a denominational newspaper from the neutral United States and since recanted his error in judgment. The defeated Liberal MP from South Grey then took the opportunity to summarize Hanover's patriotic works, noting that while the town had six German churches, a German-born mayor, and a council dominated by German Canadians, it had sent off each member of its second contingent with a ten-dollar gold piece and done best raising money for its Patriotic Fund among its German-Canadian citizens. Castell Hopkins, in the *Canadian Annual Review* of that year, edited the letter to misconstrue its message. Miller referred to 'a very few townsmen who talk disloyally, and who should be arrested,' but his intent had been to emphasize that 'though full of sympathy for the German people who are the victims of the Kaiser and his war-lords,' the German Canadians of Hanover 'sincerely desire the Kaiser's defeat and the maintenance of Britain's power.'[37]

During the next three years the community escaped outside print comment upon its loyalty. Within town, business and municipal leaders attempted to chart an uneasy middle way, to raise money through the Patriotic Fund and the Imperial Order Daughters of the Empire (IODE), but without evoking a demonology of all things German, to support the war without demanding that the community deny its origins and its fears. Daniel Knechtel headed the Patriotic Fund. Charles Witthun, the man he trusted to buy lumber for his factories, remained privately pro-German.

The dilemmas were most personally intense for young men; called simultaneously to serve for, and to serve against, to self-assertion and self-hatred, some set against their fathers in a community where traditions of filial loyalty were strong. Clyde Dankert, a Hanover teenager during the First World War, who was later a professor of economics at Dartmouth College in Hanover, New Hampshire, remembered arguing against both his father and his uncle Charlie Witthun in favour of the war. Dankert had two older brothers who had crossed over to 'the States' rather than be drafted into the Canadian army and two older sisters who had lost their beaux on the Front. Dankert's brothers later resolved their conflicts about manliness and honour in service by joining American army lumbering units on the Pacific coast.[38]

In the *Post* editor George Mitchell noted, as his father had done during the South African War, each new recruit and the festive send-off of each new contingent at the train station. But while most British-Canadian journals gave appreciative prominence to women's shaming white feather campaigns against young civilian men and applauded recruiters' beefy rhetoric diminishing those who would not enlist, Mitchell's frequent accounts of petitions for exemption under the Military Service Act of 1917 were unadorned. His reports of boys' suicides by hanging and shooting rather than serve were regretful. His accounts of local draftees doing 'battle within themselves against tears' as they waited alone with their families on the railway platform offered sympathy and comfort.[39]

If refusal to serve pressed young men towards self-destruction, agreeing to fight, possibly to prove themselves commanding warriors, only reconfigured the gender dilemma. Mitchell carried this letter on his front page in early June 1918 from Private Herman Diebel to his sister Ornetta:

> Dear little sister,
>
> ... What do you think? They won't let me go to France on account of my name being too German. I suppose they take me for a German spy. Well, I would just as soon go to France as some of my chums from Hanover have to go. There are about a dozen that were not drafted for France. I am now a dining room girl serving out meals and washing dishes. Won't I be an expert when I get back. Bill Boeking is with me ...
>
> From your brother
> Herman

Because of their German surnames, Hanover boys saw themselves denied men's work, left behind to be girls doing women's tasks. They could claim loyalty by their willingness to serve. Many did get to the front, Herman Diebel among them. Still they sensed that away from the uncertain shelter of their home town in the heightened racialism of the times, manly prowess in the bearing of arms was a troubling trait for their fellow Canadians to acknowledge in the sons and grandsons of the German born.[40]

As the war lengthened, popular sentiment challenged and overwhelmed the federal government's assurances that aliens and naturalized Canadians might pursue their 'ordinary avocations' undisturbed. In September 1918 the spirit of total war came to Hanover, in the person of Stanley Russell, a South African veteran from nearby Walkerton. Identifying themselves as Dominion Police, Russell and his colleagues had arrested three local men, Otto Bluhm and Herman Miltz, both Knechtel employees, and Henry Osthoff, a town merchant, charged them under the Alien Enemy Act, and whisked them off to Walkerton, where a British-Canadian justice of the peace obliged each to pay $250. The fines were retained in the municipality where the court action took place, and Walkerton residents were reported pleased to 'pave their streets with money of pro-Germans from Hanover.' In exuberant coverage in the Toronto and Owen Sound papers, Bluhm was described as a German naval reservist, Miltz as a reservist in the Landstrum, and Osthoff as a former Prussian artillery man. Russell was congratulated for his 'smooth detective work' in 'rounding up delinquents.' The action was one of a common enough kind in the last months of the war, outside the law, but well within current popular conceptions of justice.[41]

The pro-German allegations extended beyond the three accused. It was rumoured that the military police had a list of one hundred men who ought to be charged under the act, who should have registered as aliens and had not. From press reports it appeared that the town council and police had been involved in this deception, because they had not established registration procedures in their municipality.

James Adams, the town's bank manager, A.R. Currey, a Hanover barrister, and George Mitchell, editor of the *Post*, came to their community's defence. They noted that the German-born inhabitants of Hanover were long settled in town and thus fell not under the order in council of 20 September 1916 governing 'the floating alien population' by which they had been detained, but PC 2721, the Alien Enemy Registration Ordinance, passed into law in the early months of the war. PC 2721 left to the minister of justice the initiative to designate which cities and towns should establish registration offices and required

The Hanover Band. Through the early twentieth century, the town paid a
bandmaster, and these local musicians competed provincially with considerable success. Otto Bluhm had been a musician before he emigrated to Canada, but several other Knechtel employees and active unionists also were
members of the band.

registration only of aliens of enemy nationality residing in or within
twenty miles of these locations. No office had been gazetted for
Hanover, nor for any place within twenty miles distant. To avert further
controversy, however, within a week of the Bluhm, Miltz, and Osthoff
arrests, council had despatched their constable, Tom Beamish, to
Ottawa to be sworn as a Dominion Policeman and to be supplied with
registration forms. Adams, Currey, and Mitchell made sure newspaper
readers in Toronto and Owen Sound were aware that one of the men
fined had a son fighting overseas. Five days before the war ended the
three convictions were quashed and the fine monies retrieved from the
Walkerton treasury. The day the armistice was signed 100 festooned
cars from Hanover packed the square in front of Walkerton town hall.
The speeches were cordial but the symbolism was clear. A mounted
Walkerton horseman stationed himself on the steps before the town hall
entrance. The Hanoverians then returned home to burn the Kaiser, Von
Tirpitz, and Hindenburg in effigy. Miltz and Bluhm, both members and
sometime leaders of the Hanover Band, probably played for the
occasion. Bluhm, always active in the church life of the community, later
became prominent in the town's labour organizations.[42]

In the inter-war years more Hanover churches began to conduct their services in English, and German came to be regarded as a language that parents rather than children spoke. But immigrants continued to arrive from Germany during the Weimar period. In the hard times of the 1930s, the community made it a priority to retain night courses for newcomers from Europe who wished to learn English. Its German character remained a valued feature of town life.[43] The recollection of the town's leaders' wartime accomplishments crafting a Canadian loyalism that did not shame German origins or rob troubled young men of their manliness influenced skilled workers considering pursuing higher wages in larger centres.

The furniture industry of Hanover arose in and from its agricultural hinterland. Along their way to south Bruce and Grey, in the Rhineland and Waterloo County, the settlers of the Saugeen Valley had lived on the land and by their crafts. In their German home districts and in Waterloo, their smallholdings limited their agricultural returns. In Bruce and Grey they secured land, but within a generation they found their market position weakening against western competition.

They were craftsmen in wood, skilled if not accredited, who by building, timber making, and cabinetry extended their households' resources and lodged their claims as breadwinners. The woodworking shops of the village came together into factories and began, with tariff shelter, to serve a growing national market, but the materials, the machines, the process of making was fundamentally the same. Craft sensibilities and dexterities remained essential. As agricultural fortunes waned, the surrounding countryside provided more wood and more woodworkers for the furniture factories in town.

Chapter Seven

Manliness, craftsmanship, and scientific management

Daniel Knechtel was the most prominent man in Hanover from the mid-1880s when his firm became the largest employer in town, until 1936 when he died at the age of ninety-two. For a half-century the example he set for masculine behaviour was as difficult to overlook as the four-storey Knechtel factory which dominated the main street of town. He governed his whole life by a single stern code, setting his will, his theology, and his personal authority against the changing times. His obituary described an austere man who remained to the end 'mentally alert and physically active,' living 'the strenuous life of the pioneer,' refusing to spare himself, a man 'without hobbies... ever engrossed in his business, his home and his philanthropy,' an 'example of Christian manhood.' He dressed plainly, ate simply, lived without ostentation among his workmen in a house near the plant, refusing leisure as weakness.[1] 'He was brought up in the pioneer atmosphere of building up a new country, and his nature compelled him to be "up and doing," even in the quarter-century when he might easily have followed the quite general practice of men who "rest on their oars" and are satisfied to clip coupons and lead a life of ease.' Daniel Knechtel believed that work had intrinsic merit. He worked for work's sake, and he worked to serve God. He saw his work as drawing him towards the men he employed rather than distinguishing him from them.

He was not a patriarch, who by distancing himself infantilized his male employees, but in his own mind a craftsman among craftsmen who through common gender shared a set of Christian responsibilities. When the businessmen of Hanover held a grand banquet to celebrate the reopening of his factory after the fire of 1900, they presented Daniel Knechtel with a gold-topped cane to symbolize his standing as the best among them and as a captain of industry. Knechtel[2] resisted the ascription. He called the cane 'too good' for him as a craftsman, and better suited to Mr Miller, the local conveyancer who gave him financial advice: 'If I have any ability I owe it all to a kind Providence, and my talents were given to me so that I might work in the aid and for the betterment of mankind. I appreciate the kindness of the people of Hanover, who, it seems wish to do me honour, but which will make me proud, which I do not wish to be. I don't consider myself any better than those situated in the humblest circumstances in life.' Dan Knechtel ran his factory as he had run the workshop from which it grew. He thought of himself as a workman, if the chief workman, drawing his authority over his employees from his longer knowledge of the craft they shared. While his managers and salesmen were salaried, Daniel Knechtel in the early twentieth century preferred to be waged, paid '50 cents for every hour actually spent in the company's service.'

He believed in setting an example of a whole Christian craftsman's life, in the pace of his work, his thrift and his public service, emphasizing that as they too were workmen, the men employed in his factory could have all he had. As a pietist, Knechtel's sense of manly work extended to good works. He financed the town's hospital, its library, its park, and its YMCA. He was the first reeve of the village of Hanover and mayor of the town for three terms.[3] He was proud that his men lived in homes as fine as his own and that employees left his machine room and cabinet shop prepared to take charge of factories in other parts of Canada and the United States and run them successfully.[4] His was a social analysis theologically grounded. As in the next world salvation was accessible to all, if attained only by the few, so for the rewards of this life all men shared a common possibility.

Daniel Knechtel measured his worth in his powers of self-control, to work past physical weariness, to stick firmly to a prudently laid plan, to lay away savings against tests of his faith – by his later years to resist the temptations to leisure, physical comfort, and personal vanity which his wealth had laid in his way. This was not, as he claimed it, a power to establish or maintain social distinctions but an individual discipline of faith which drew him and the men he employed together in a common purpose.

Yet through all these actions, which he undertook and understood to serve otherworldly ends, Daniel Knechtel forged a dense net of personal obligations, rarely spoken, rarely forgotten. When Knechtel took Frank Stoldt to Toronto for an operation to restore use of his paralysed side, the local paper noted that young Stoldt 'will have reason to revere the name of his benefactor.' As the new Knechtel factory rose on the main street, an irreverent columnist from a neighbouring town mocked: 'Every time they take a squint over at the Knechtel big block it seems to tickle them and make them think that Hanover will give us all plenty of bread and butter in the future. How they depend on the old furniture king, I mean a large number of poor old chaps who can hardly do anything else than shop work.'[5] Knechtel did not see his role as that of king to subject. He thought of himself as bound with his men in common cause, exercising the shared male responsibilities of craftsman, house owner, church leader and civic office holder, governed by a common code of manly conduct in social roles that were at once male obligations and arbiters of masculine identity.

BUSINESS CONDITIONS AND BREADWINNER UNIONISM

Gradually, through the early twentieth century Daniel Knechtel passed the management of the family firm to his son, Jacob, known as J.S. By the 1920s the furniture industry in Canada was no longer the congery of workshops providing for local markets it had been in the 1870s, nor the vigorous group of prosperous firms serving an expanding national market it had been in the decade before 1912. The changing predicament of the industry posed problems that the first generation of Canadian factory owners turned craftsmen had not faced; the transformation in the wider economy towards mass production industries presented solutions that the new generation of owners and managers in the furniture industry – no longer craftsmen but designers, engineers, and 'finance men' – found alluringly authoritative, modern, and scientific. The new stresses in the industry and its changed market circumstances placed pressure upon established social relations, both class and gender relations, within individual firms. The gauze of common gender identity, which had obscured the differences between masters and men behind a veil of craft fraternity, began to tear. The new ideology about how and why working men worked did not arise from conditions at the point of production in the furniture industry or from observation of sawyers, joiners, and finishers working with wood, but its force was no less considerable for this incongruity.

The company J.S. Knechtel had taken in trust from his father was in straitened circumstances by 1915. Though in retrospect it is clear that

Three generations of Knechtel Furniture Company presidents: Daniel, his son J.S., and J.S.'s son, Karl

his troubles were industry wide and not, finally, within the power of any one man to remedy, J.S. felt personally responsible for the decline in the firm's fortunes. During the war years most Canadian furniture-makers had kept barely afloat. Knechtel managed to pay modest dividends to its common-stockholders only by forgoing depreciation allowances. Industry profits averaged 2.6 per cent on capital in 1917 and 3 per cent in 1918.[6] The exception was 1919 when Knechtel sales rose by 50 per cent over 1918 to $1.3 million, as men returning from overseas established new homes, and families who had postponed buying during the war moved into larger premises.[7] The decade of the 1920s was not generally a prosperous one, and furniture was a discretionary good. Input costs for lumber, glass, and finishing materials rose under demand pressure from automobile manufacturers. In the ten years before 1924 increases in furniture prices exceeded those in general commodity prices by 30 per cent.[8] Most importantly, familiar bureaus and bedsteads were not holding their own against the parade of new consumer durables of the age, particularly automobiles and electrically powered domestic appliances. Even in 1919 Canadians spent $2 per capita on furniture, and $4 per head on automobiles.[9]

The essential problem in the industry was excess capacity. As population growth slowed and new commodities lured buyers elsewhere, there were too many furniture makers, both owners and workers, producing more furniture than Canadians would buy. The problem was not a temporary dip in the business cycle. Relatively there would never again to be so many new households needing to be furnished all at once as there had been during the immigration boom and the opening of the west. In the consumer culture grand furniture would now be one among ever more ways to display taste and social position. In retrospect it is clear that the sector had to shrink to conform to the smaller continuing demand for its products. This insight was neither available nor particularly useful to individual manufacturers in the early 1920s. It was not apparent that the decline in demand was long term nor, had it been, which firms would be best placed to survive in the new conditions. What owners could do was take evasive action and wait to see how it all turned out.

The structure of the sector had not changed. The post-war industry still consisted of many small competing firms run as elaborated artisanal shops. Because small firms were more efficient than large firms in the production of furniture (there were few economies of scale in the industry), the common structural resolution within capitalism to the rigours of competitive pricing, consolidation towards a smaller manageable number of sellers (oligopoly) or a single seller (monopoly), did not attract woodworkers. Instead the Furniture Manufacturers' Association (FMA), of which J.S. Knechtel was a prominent member, turned to price fixing. Hanover chair maker and member of parliament Robert Ball defended this practice as no more 'criminal for merchants and manufacturers' than for working men who 'conspire together not to sell their labour lower than a certain price.' Most furniture manufacturers, facing the complex problem of how to price a diverse array of goods produced in small lots, set prices as Knechtel said they did: 'to meet the competition with some regard to costs.'[10] Even in the buoyant pre-war period, this greater attentiveness to competition than costs created instability, and the FMA considered a compact among producers to prevent its members from undercutting one another.[11] In 1918 the accounting firm of Clarkson, Gordon, Dilworth, employed to investigate the failing health of the industry, recommended a standard costing system for all members of the association incorporating a minimum net profit of 15 per cent. James E. Ferguson, an experienced executive with the Canada Furniture Company of Woodstock, was hired to implement such a system. Under his guidance, FMA collusion in restraint of trade functioned satisfactorily through 1924. Manufacturers checked their cost figures with the cost-accounting department and agreed to 'stand firm with prices that' would 'yield a living profit.'[12] Thereafter, as the pressures from excess capacity intensified, the individualism of owners reasserted itself, and the operations of the cost-accounting department were suspended.[13]

The days were past when an inattentively managed company might 'not only exist but even have a modified share of the general prosperity thrust upon them.' Costs rose, demand fell, and furniture manufacturers careened close to bankruptcy. The challenge, industry leaders said, was 'to cut prices to the very bone' by seeking out more modern methods, to treat the problems of excess capacity in the industry by striving for 'cheaper instead of greater production.'[14] Industrial engineers who earlier had concentrated their analysis upon metal-working mass production industries, began to turn their attention towards the problems raised by the short production runs, variable material quality, and high cutting speeds in woodworking.[15]

In the nineteenth century the resolutions to problems of industry health had been found in the political economy, principally in the tariff, an instrument that owners and workers could champion in common cause. The men who made furniture in Canada were still arguing with one voice before the tariff commissioners in 1920, defending their right to work, condemning as shoddy the cheaper foreign goods that were encroaching upon their territory.[16] Each of these claims – to wage work, to arbitrate quality, to defend territory – had credibility and gained political force because it was a valued attribute of male gender identity, a masculine prerogative that transcended class difference. Employers with female work forces could not make the same arguments in concert with or on behalf of their women employees to similar effect.

In the twentieth century attention turned to 'the domestic economy of the factory'[17] and to labour productivity as both cause and remedy when profits paled. In the growing mass production industries, organized in monopolistic firms, run by managers and engineers, the quest for efficiency brought to the fore the divisions between men. Control meant control by one group of men over another, in pursuit of productivity, so that manliness divided by class into two reciprocal tasks, to exercise control and to resist being controlled. Labour productivity, it was said, was the modern manufacturers' challenge; whether it was a challenge which arose on their shop floors, furniture manufacturers accepted it as an appropriate priority among men of their class.

Whether furniture manufacturers' problems with labour productivity were as real as their dilemmas in setting prices and dividing market share is doubtful. It was the historically low level of wages in the furniture industry relative to other sectors that they worried over in print during the post-war years, as inflation eroded their employees' real earnings, and upholsterers, joiners and mechanics left to ply their skills in the auto plants of Detroit. 'Now the furniture industry has not [such] a glut of highly-skilled mechanics,' a foreman wrote to the *Canadian Woodworker* in March 1921, 'that it can play fast and loose with those it has already got. Therefore at present I think it would be a poor policy to reduce wages.' By convention furniture makers regarded one-third of sales as labour's share of their revenues; as a group they were more likely to celebrate than criticize the work habits of their men; they reported no slacking in the intensity of work in their plants.[18]

But the quest for greater labour productivity was a sign of the changing social relations of the time. J.S. Knechtel was a founding member of the labour committee the FMA organized to gather industrial relations intelligence. Through the post-war years in this capacity he received regular reports from the National Council of Furniture Association meetings in the United States on experiments in labour relations and from the Corporations Auxiliary Company of Ohio on American unionists' responses to these plans.[19] This advice, predicated upon experience in the new mass production industries, assumed that the interests of employers and employees were different, and regularly in conflict, and that working men left to their own devices had neither the capacity nor the inclination to work efficiently. It justified the growing social divisions between masters and men, the growing disparities in their habits of life and entitlements. J.S. Knechtel did not know that his men were cheating him. He did know that lacking both his father's craft skills and personal presence he could not be one of the men. The new ideology of management, by locating his problems in the labour productivity of his firm, told him why he ought not to be.

The first productivity-enhancing device Knechtel tried was profit sharing, a strategy predicated upon a quite different story about men at work than heretofore had been told in the firm. Gone were the craft pride, personal loyalty, and mutual respect that had been at the core of Dan Knechtel's relations with the men he employed. Advocates of profit sharing claimed that it was 'incentive for gain' that motivated men to do good work, that a commitment to stay with the firm was established by the prospect of 'participating in year-end profits,' that co-operation was thus forged between owners and their employees, such that workmen would report 'carelessness on the part of their fellows' and press the pace on the job in a spirit of 'friendly competition.'[20] J.S. Knechtel turned to profit sharing, hoping to increase output sufficiently to counteract rising costs. The plan was implemented in the wake of a strike among unionized furniture workers in Stratford, Ontario, early in 1919, impelled by escalating living costs in the presence of strong industry sales.[21] He presented the scheme to the men, not in the diction of the new story about workplace relations, with its emphasis upon individual productivity and disciplining calculus of rewards, but in words Dan Knechtel might have used.

February 28, 1919

Dear Sir:

For a number of years the idea of Profit-sharing has given us much food for thought but it is only recently that it has taken practical form ... We were making very good progress on this idea when we were suddenly faced with the depression of 1913, followed the next year by the Great War. This war involved our very existence ... We had to concentrate our mind and energy towards one end – that of surviving.

We are now emerging from these years of difficulty and horror and can again turn our minds towards the better things. The war has been a good teacher – if nothing else. It has given us a new and broader outlook on life and greater consideration for our fellowmen. We have learned that co-operation is the Life of Trade; that competition whether it be in the markets of Trade or of Labor, carries with it many evils. It is hoped that all of us have come through this terrible ordeal chastened in spirit, more fair-minded and more willing to hand out the square deal.

Now you will see by the enclosed, this plan of Profit-sharing has been worked out on the bonus idea – really dividends on Labor earned for a given period. The minimum has been set at 5 per cent but may be more, and will be more in any year when the Company's earnings warrant the payment. It is a voluntary proposition on our part and entails nothing in the nature of a bargain, but it is up to you to make good if you wish to derive the benefits ...

In unity there is strength. Let us work together.

Yours truly,
The Knechtel Furniture Company, Limited
per J.S. Knechtel[22]

Here were the homely metaphors, 'food for thought,' the 'Life of Trade,' the 'square deal'; the sermon rhetoric of chastened spirit and minds concentrated towards better things; the craftsman's penchant for practical form. Only the medium was dissonant; the elder Knechtel had never communicated with his men by so indirect a means as letter.

The accompanying flyer detailing the terms of the plan made the departure in labour relations philosophy more clear. The bonus was to be made once yearly on 15 December, not as a per capita payment but as a fixed proportion of each man's yearly earnings. Only those who had been in continuous employment with the firm through the year would receive their share; a worker discharged 'for any cause whatsoever or who shall quit work on his own accord' would 'entirely forfeit' the bonus.[23]

Following the conciliation board report prepared as part of the Stratford strike settlement, in April 1919 Ontario manufacturers agreed to two industry-wide pay increases, the first through a reduction of working hours from sixty to fifty-five per week at constant pay on 1 May, the second a 10 per cent raise beginning 1 June. To avoid seeming to acknowledge that any factors other than productivity might be considered in determining pay, J.S. instructed his superintendents to assign these raises 'at their discretion,' to some men above and to some below the average, calling the change 'simply an increase in pay,' never mentioning a 10 per cent raise.[24]

These increases notwithstanding, by autumn furniture factory workers in Hanover and other northern furniture towns became convinced that they, like the men of Stratford, needed a union. Former Hanover men, now Knechtel employees in Southampton, thirty-five kilometres away, and members of the two craft unions in the trade, the United Brotherhood of Carpenters and Joiners and the Brotherhood of Painters and Finishers, addressed the first meeting in town, where a third of the local men eligible for membership signed on. Three weeks later, when salaried union officals arrived to speak, half of the 600 Hanover furniture workers had joined.

The unions organizing in Hanover were conservative and wage oriented. They used the craft as their organizing unit but had set aside craft sensibilities concerning quality and control in favour of a philosophy of work that, like that lately articulated by furniture manufacturers, emphasized earnings and output. In this they took direction from their American parents. In the United States the United Brotherhood of Carpenters and Joiners' leadership was committed to continuing its patriotic wartime pact with employers, arguing that drives to maximize productivity benefited both managers and men. The Carpenters and Joiners were also at great pains to distinguish themselves from the syndicalist unions gaining public prominence, and anti-Bolshevic opprobrium, at the time.[26]

In Hanover J.F. Marsh from Niagara Falls, the Carpenters' organizer, spoke first of the 'financial benefits' of joining the union, but he encouraged the men to 'be satisfied with a little at a time' so that their home town would grow. 'The unions didn't want to cripple the industry,' he said. 'They wanted business to grow but they also wanted part of the profits.'

This union appeal placed a strong emphasis upon the men's responsibilities as breadwinners, shifting the balance among the roles by which furniture workers could define their worth as men towards providing and away from producing:

> We men marry, in our opinion, the best girl in the world. We take her home and she finds her work cut out for her. If, like some union men, we are able to supply her with $35 or $45 a week in wages she has a fairly easy time, but imagine the worrying and pinching she has to do if she only gets $20, $18 or

as is often the case only $15 a week. She wants her children to be on a par with other children but how can she do this when she has $18 a week to expend ... No wonder she worries and becomes nervous and we men merely add to the flames when we grumble if meals are not ready.[27]

The message Marsh carried was that cash would smooth the way to domestic satisfaction, to all those good things a couple shared when the wife was not nervous and the husband was doing what husbands should do. Charles Green, a former Hanoverian then working in Southampton, in turn argued for higher wages so that furniture workers could keep their children in school past the age of fourteen; others said that 'the men owed it to their wives and children to organize' and demand shorter hours because 'their homes demanded their presence.' The union man they described worried about the quality of his home life, found his autonomy there rather than on the shop floor; he was a 'sane' man, willing to 'give the best there is in him' to help the manufacturers, knowing that the bosses 'acted like gentlemen' when 'the men are behind the firm.'[28]

In early November the unions, led by William Weigel, a town councillor and representative of the Finishers, and Ed Winkler, municipal fire chief and president of the union local, initiated negotiations with the manufacturers. The owners agreed that they too desired 'manly, wholesome, co-operative and mutually beneficial relations' with the men, but when presented with a pay demand, which they acknowledged was justified 'through the high cost of living,' at the same session at which they were informed that bonusing (the union reference for the companies' profit-sharing schemes) was 'contrary to the spirit and rules of the union,' granted the raise and cancelled the bonus.[29]

The objection in union practice was not to profit sharing per se, but union organizers warned the men that the bonus was really deferred earnings rather than a good-faith offering from management. They argued that a year was too long a period for an employee to risk his savings with an employer who could confiscate the sum by arbitrary firing. They urged the bonus be paid monthly.[30] Knechtel insisted that the bonus 'was meant as a reward for continuity of service' and refused to change the term.[31] His upholstery foreman, Bernhardt Urstadt, then circulated a petition in the factory, which 134 men signed, requesting profit-sharing be reinstated, and Knechtel demurred to their request. Through this deft coercion he kept the plan in force and cast doubt on the consistency and representativeness of the union. In a community

Knechtel employees outside the machine room windows, along the front of the rebuilt main plant, c. 1901

where men still measured their work histories in decades the risks of arbitrary dismissal, in 1919, may have seemed small. In any case, without the protection of union grievance procedures refusing a request by a foreman would have been tricky. The men later felt the profit-sharing scheme had been little more than a bribe, a bribe they had been ill advised to accept.[32]

In reaction, through the next two years the unions' activities became more community focused; James Marsh, Arthur Martel, and other representatives from the labour hierarchy came to town less often. As short time in the plants grew more common, while living costs continued to rise, the local union turned away from wage negotiations towards remedies that were within their control. In concert with the area branch of the United Farmers of Ontario, they bought out two local merchants and established a co-operative department store which sold groceries, dry goods and hardware at reduced rates. To save on fuel costs the local unions secured cutting rights on a nearby woodlot, and on the winter Fridays and Saturdays in 1920 and 1921 when the factories were closed, they worked there 'taking a cord of wood instead of wages to help out.' Fire Chief Winkler, who ran a tenoner in the Knechtel machine room, wrote spritely doggerel worthy of Sarah Binks to celebrate the solidarity and satisfaction derived from this project.

> With an ax on our backs, and a saw in hand,
> We go marching along, like a little brass band,
> Into the woods we hide our lunch,
> And start to work like a united bunch,
> The axes they swing, and the trees they fall
> While the saws they sing at every call ...[33]

Whatever the non-material benefits of this autonomous initiative in union policy, as plant inventories grew yearly through the early 1920s, pursuing wage unionism according to the organizers' model seemed increasingly bootless.

The organizers from the United Brotherhood of Carpenters and Joiners and from the Painters had presented a view of why men worked that emphasized their role as breadwinners and focused upon the quality of life they should defend as providers more than the quality of life they experienced as producers on the shop floor. They organized the furniture workers of Hanover by craft but did not seek to mobilize them centrally around the values of craft work. The profit-sharing plan J.S. Knechtel launched and defended in 1919 was predicated upon a philosophy about why men worked and what forged common purpose among men across class lines starkly different from his father's belief about men at work and men together. But he 'sold' the scheme, the word is his, pencilled in in his hand on a proposal for industrial democracy from the American National Council of Furniture Manufacturers, in the rhetoric of the craft fraternity. In that first prosperous year after the war he made no changes in the production process within the plant that would have called attention to the differences between himself and his father.

THE SON, THE STOPWATCH, AND HIS FATHER'S MEN

In fact they were very different men who crafted their gender identities from jarringly incompatible elements. J.S. was the son of a powerful father, born to wealth, one of a new generation of Canadian industrialists[34] who had never known the workshop, who conducted their businesses with the advice of engineers rather than craftsmen and shared the lifestyles of other captains of industry rather than those of the men they employed. J.S. would have accepted the gold-topped cane Dan Knechtel had regarded as too good for him – but living out the implications of being manly in ways his father would not accept caused him grave difficulties to the end of his days.

J.S. Knechtel had much more formal education than his father. He attended school in Hanover and at the Baptist mission at Grand Ligne, Quebec, where he went to learn French in order to do business with Quebec dealers. He also went to business college 'to fit himself for the accounting end of the work.'[35] In turn he sought more schooling, and more exclusive schooling, for his own sons and daughters. He sent Max to St Andrew's College north of Toronto; Fritz graduated from McMaster, Xenia from Johns Hopkins in nursing; Renata became a high school teacher after completing her BA.[36]

He lived grandly in town, collecting a salary of $7,200 per year. The house he donated to the municipality as a hospital was valued at $50,000 in 1921 and included bedrooms enough to accommodate twenty to thirty patients. In later years he maintained a summer home on the Lake Huron shore at Southampton and a winter home at Delray Beach in Florida in addition to his Hanover residence. The site of the Knechtel sawmill at Stokes Bay was turned into the Tamarac Island Fishing and Shooting Club where he and other industrialists from Bruce and Grey counties took sport in like company.[37]

Yet he guarded his privacy intensely. His reclusiveness was described at his death as 'a boyish shyness that made it an ordeal to appear in public' and drove him to retire 'to the comparative obscurity of his office and his home.' 'The field of public service,' the obituary writer noted tellingly, 'he left to his father.' It was the design work of furniture making, in its technical rather than aesthetic dimensions, that gave him most pleasure. Separated from the bustle of the plant, in a sunlit second-storey room above the main office, he perfected mechanisms to be attached to the wooden frames being cut below, sliders for drawers and table leaves, hinges and supports for the reclining chairs popular at the time.[38]

J.S. Knechtel was a more distant, technical sort of man than his father, looking for less personal, more rule-based solutions to the problems confronting the firm. In his aversion to the highly personalized exercise of authority that had characterized his father, J.S. found professional validation and reinforcement from the industrial engineers, efficiency experts, and 'scientific managers' of his day. It had been the express purpose of Frederick Winslow Taylor, the leading early polemicist for scientific management, 'to set up a factory which could run effectively without an outstanding executive on top,' where technically grounded rules would substitute for exceptional ability and judgment in the employer, where an intermediary cadre of managers and a machine-like organization separated the owner from personal contact with the men he employed, from disorder, intense emotion, and pain. The characterization of business leadership as an engineering problem to be resolved through the command of technical expertise rather than personal presence suited J.S., who like Taylor himself was more comfortable in 'the quiet of the laboratory and the study' than amid 'the diverse and clashing activities of the shop.'[39]

From the turn of the century, J.S. had derogated the craft knowledge and craft autonomy his father had honoured. He claimed to be most proud of the younger employees of the plant, to find them most valuable. 'They are not so set in their ways and can adapt themselves better to our manner of doing business, and having a future before them are most ambitious.'[40] J.S. Knechtel wanted craft knowledge sceptically scrutinized and scientifically systematized, what worthy remnants survived the test secured in the 'hands and handbooks' of managers and engineers.[41]

The notion that masculine identity could be found outside manual work, in the explicit rejection of craft knowledge, in the delegation of workplace competence to others – this took some selling. Recall the warm praise for Daniel Knechtel in 1936 because he was not a man to rest on his oars, content to clip coupons and live a life of ease. Owners and superintendents of Dan Knechtel's day had demonstrated their manliness and earned their authority over the men they employed by practising craft skill. The temptation to prove virility by turning a hand to uncontestedly manly production tasks remained strong among managers in the 1920s, newly sequestered in offices and told to be thinking rather than doing. 'Is your superintendent a thinker, or just a worker?' the trade journals asked, positing the classic Taylorite distinction between conception and execution and insisting that supervisors separate themselves by clothing, demeanour, and setting from men who merely worked. 'Give me the superintendent who sits in his office and figures. With a mind more or less free from details he can concentrate on a job and figure out a much more profitable way of doing it.' Distrust the plant where 'you can't tell the super from one of the machine hands,' where 'he dresses like them, acts like them and looks like them in every respect.' Realize that the superintendent proud to help 'to load stuff on a wagon at the shipping room door' has made himself 'the highest priced porter around the place' when 'his time might have been better employed trying to figure out how to cut a corner somewhere and save money.'[42] This advice assumed class distinctions craftsmen-owners had implicitly denied. But class identification was not what was at issue. Being middle class was indisputably preferable to being working class. Superintendents, managers, and owners played at labouring work not because they longed to be working class, but because they worried that by their white collars, clean hands, and quiet offices, by their separation from physical work, they might have gone over to the feminine side and lost their claims to be men.[43]

If managers were uncertain about the manliness of thinking about doing, rather than doing, owners were at one further remove from established claims to masculine identity in a small agricultural and manufacturing community. Under the new business regime, the owner's task was to choose other men – because they had competence superior to his own – to run the firm from which he would profit. In a perfect inversion of the old order of things, the new captain of industry was to be judged successful not by his capacity to work but by his capacity to secure leisure time for himself by hiring others. That a man who 'little by little let go of the reins' would be attractive to women, that a man who left the office for an afternoon of sport could still count upon the dedication of the managers he left behind – these propositions required selling too.

The new ethics of masculine identity among the industrial elite required that virility be separated from physicality. The claim was that money could trump muscle in the ranking of manly prowess. It was a hard claim to make stick. The admiration of physical power among men was too deep. As managers played at labouring work, industrialists turned to sport, seeking in the physical prowess of the game a display to compensate for the manual dexterities absent from their work. The need to insist upon a new coin of masculinity was compelling among monied men of the 1920s. The refinements cultivated by the new bourgeoisie to mark social distance in an uncertain world evoked the dandy and the fool. The forming culture among the industrial elite was all the more threatening to the foundations of masculine identity because it confined bourgeois men to business roles which, in their privacy and mediated indirection, looked like women's parts.

LIFE'S LITTLE JESTS—No. 41144   *Forgive us, Mr. Goldberg*

ISAAC AUGUSTUS JOSEPHUS McCANN
TO HIS OFFICE FORCE POSED AS
EFFICIENCY MAN;
HE PAWED OVER ESTIMATES MORNING
AND NIGHT
IN AN EFFORT TO BUY ALL HIS
LUMBER JUST RIGHT.

NOW HOBART McFIFE HIRED MEN
WHO HAD BRAINS
AND LITTLE BY LITTLE LET GO OF
THE REINS.
SOME PEOPLE HAD CALLED HIM AN
INDOLENT FISH,
TO WHICH HE REPLIED,"I HAVE CHOSEN MY DISH."

BUT WHEN TIME FOR VACATIONS HAD
FINALLY ROLLED 'ROUND,
EFFICIENCY IKE TO HIS OFFICE WAS
BOUND;
SO COMPLEX WAS HIS SYSTEM OF BUYING,
YOU SEE,
THAT HE HADN'T A MOMENT TO
GO ON A SPREE.

WHILE McFIFE SAID," NOW FELLOWS
I CANNOT DENY
THAT YOU KNOW HOW TO RUN THINGS
AS WELL AS DO I;
SO I'M OFF FOR A MONTH WHERE
IT'S NOT SO PROSAIC—
AND FOR LUMBER—YOU KNOW, BOYS,—OUR
FRIENDS, WOOD-MOSAIC."

WOOD-MOSAIC CO., *Incorporated*, LOUISVILLE, KY.

Wood-Mosaic

Veneers~Hardwood Lumber~Flooring~Dimension Corestock

'Life's Little Jests,' from *CWFM*, July 1926, 39

Through the early 1920s J.S. Knechtel's personal sense of failure and inadequacy became more intense. He wanted more distance from the everyday running of the firm and more time for the design and patent work that gave him satisfaction. For these reasons he found the 'scientific production incentive plans' being recommended in the trade journals attractive. They were ordered, rule based; they delegated responsibility from the owner to experts; not only did they allow the owner distance; they demanded he keep aloof from his men. Industrial engineering made his doubts about whether he could fill his father's shoes into scientifically grounded reservations about his father's methods.

Unlike the profit-sharing experiment of 1919, the remedy to which he turned in 1922, a timed incentive wage system, involved fundamental changes in work relations on the shop floor. More than a philosophical reinterpretation of why men worked, it was a direct intervention in the pace and pattern of the labour process. Like the plan of 1919, however, it was designed to increase labour productivity, a difficulty often diagnosed in mass production industries, but still in 1922 probably the least of Canadian furniture manufacturers' worries. Making labour productivity a priority had several advantages. Improved worker efficiency was a goal each manufacturer could pursue on his own; the essential problem in the woodworking sector, excess capacity, would be resolved outside the firm by the grim hand of the market through plant closures; all each owner could do was pursue palliative action in hopes that his was not the name to drop off the FMA membership list. Concentrating upon worker efficiency kept the burden and the blame far from the front office. The manufacturer who located his firm's problems in labour productivity need not change himself but merely direct others to change. The strategy, however, profoundly challenged the craft practices that had governed labour relations and gender relations in woodworking plants. If J.S. was looking for peace through the stop-watch he was looking in the wrong place.

Knechtel chose Forest Products Engineering of Chicago, a leader in the Woodworking Division of the American Association of Mechanical Engineers, to bring modern management and increased labour productivity to his firm. The contract he signed in April 1922 was to install 'process methods, quality and performance standards, and labor wage incentives' in Knechtel plants. Forest Products engineers began working in Hanover in May 1922 and continued to travel regularly between Chicago and Hanover until May 1923.[44]

Their system, called an 'earned hours plan,' was one of the second-generation scientific management schemes, trumpeted as an improvement over Frederick Taylor's union-baiting, timed-production systems. For each task in the plant the engineers decided the amount of production for which an hour's wages should be paid; workers who could produce the rated amount in less than an hour had the remaining time to earn extra pay. The second-generation schemes acknowledged that wages were properly 'a matter of bargain between employer and employee' (Taylor had regarded wage fixing as a technical problem) and set rates of production only; the plan also accommodated seniority differentials in pay between old-timers and newcomers in ways that straight piece-work systems had not. None the less the rates were fixed by an outsider with a stop-watch, who measured the quantity and not the quality of the work performed, in the stated intention of replacing the craft routines on the shop floor with a scientific 'foundation for production control' which would reduce labour costs.[45] As it turned out, the plan did not alienate the craft union. It did alienate the craftsmen employed in the plant.

The plans to bring in industrial engineering experts coincided with a period of great personal distress for J.S. Yearly under his leadership the capital his father had built up in the company was being eroded. Long-time employees of the firm were working short time, or not working at all. As he was arranging to pass authority over production in his factories to American experts, he suffered a nervous breakdown. For many months thereafter he was unable to make business decisions. In December he contracted pneumonia. By February 1923, when his workers struck against the 'earned hours' plan, he was described as severely ill. Years later when required to account for the state of the company to a firm of investment bankers, he described the spring of 1922 as the beginning of three years during which his incapacity caused the management of the firm to be 'passive.' While his father continued to be active in other business concerns in town, J.S. was obliged to take to his bed. He spent many of the next months away from Hanover trying to find some peace of mind by the lake and the ocean.[46] The firm that his father had passed into his care was left in the tending of American technicians. When the engineers' demands provoked Knechtel employees to strike for the first time, it was Dan Knechtel and his friend Max Armstrong who had to manage the crisis.

Reaction against the time-study men and their system was swift. A month after the Forest Products engineers arrived in the Knechtel main plant, ninety-six men signed a petition 'vigorously' protesting the use of the stop-watch and the absence under the new regime of 'fixed prices or wages' the men 'could rely on.' In June a committee, led by Paul Dressler, a forty-year-old carver, and John Fleet, a forty-four-year-old cabinet-maker, pressed these issues with management. They were unable to achieve changes. Times were slack and many men laid off in 1921 were not yet back to work. Fleet and Dressler agreed for the men that the system should be given a trial.[47]

During the next seven months animosity between the engineers and Knechtel employees grew. The benefits of the earned-hours plan were spread unevenly among the men. Those aged forty to forty-nine gained most from the intensification of work under the timed production system. Herb Hallman, a forty-two-year-old employee in the machine room who signed the petition against the timed rates, increased his earnings by 25 per cent in 1923 through the bonus. But 70 per cent of men fifty and over, unable to keep up with the heightened pace, never beat the production threshold that would have accorded them extra pay. Similarly, most younger men, not yet so thoroughly in command of their tasks, earned nothing in bonuses. Stamina and skill were not enough to beat the system when its rewards structures were ill grounded. Under the rates established in the finishing and rubbing rooms, the majority of the men earned extra pay; in the cabinet room most did not, and few machinists matched the finishers' considerable gains from the scheme.[48] Some men were fired for refusing to be timed and for speaking out against the unfairness of the system. Feelings grew particularly intense against E.A. Dietz, the Forest Products engineer who had been in the plant steadily from May 1922. Dietz was accused of threatening the men with firing if they did not meet the production quotas he set for each hour's work and of mocking older employees who could not keep up with the rates.[49]

Fearful for their jobs and without support from the hierarchy of their union, which by 1923 had embraced productivity improvement as the foundation for wage increases,[50] the employees at the Knechtel main plant vented their growing frustration with covert actions. The Forest Products engineers were worried enough by the volume of threatening mail to telegraph their headquarters in Chicago. Chicago alerted Washington; Washington approached Ottawa from whence a telegram reached town 'stating that these experts were American citizens and must be fully protected.'[51]

J.S. Knechtel too received warnings. One protest letter against the system, in fine script, in pencil and unsigned, reminded J.S. of his own frailties and his obligations as a Christian man.

Mr J S Knechtel –

As the good Lord is sparing you yet another while, may you consider well your faithful employees. What have they done for you in the years gone by? Your surroundings and wealth speak for themselves. They have been true to you (the majority and old standbys at least) and appreciate what you have done for them.

This system you are now trying to establish is causing *breakdowns, worry and sickness*. Why should you do it? Wouldn't it be pleasanter to create happiness among your men than causing trouble? Think it over.

'Fear God. Honor all men' –I appeal to you as a Christian man to take it to the Lord in prayer & he will guide you in the ways of right.

From one in sorrow.

'The Lord will hold you responsible for what happens.'[52]

The retribution threatened here was divine. J.S. was accused of betraying a trust, taking from the men in ways his father had not – 'Your surroundings and wealth speak for themselves' – and returning to them not the honour they were due as men, but 'breakdowns, worry and sickness.' His departures from his father's ways had first made J.S. ill, they seemed to say; now the plague caused by his broken faith was spreading through him to the men who had been his father's loyal employees.

In February 1923 the Forest Products engineers began to introduce their system into the Knechtel desk and kitchen cabinet plants and the factory of Peppler Bros, the next-largest furniture manufacturer in town. Nine months of reports from the men at the Knechtel main plant convinced other Hanover furniture workers that they should try to stop the stop-watch men before they got started. On Monday, 12 February the men at Peppler's struck; by Friday, 16 February all Knechtel employees, including the men at the main plant, had joined them to protest the 'efficiency bonus system.' Although the strikers were members of the union, from the outset union officials made it clear that they had 'no hand' in organizing the strike.[53]

On the afternoon of Monday, 20 February 250 of the 300 men on strike paraded through the streets of Hanover following a large banner inscribed:

They have faces of brass
  And hearts of stone
    There will be no peace
      Till the stop watch is gone.[54]

Meanwhile eighteen representatives of the employees were meeting a committee of eight local employers at the Town Hall. Daniel Knechtel and the firm's secretary-treasurer, Max Armstrong, represented the main plant. J.S. did not attend.

That afternoon the furniture workers of Hanover spoke for craft sensibilities rather than science as the guide to good furniture making, good labour-management relations, and manly conduct.[55] With passion and eloquence they championed a set of principles that neither their bosses nor their unions were any longer willing to defend and exposed contradictions neither management nor the AFL unions were willing to acknowledge.

They began by insisting upon standards in workmanship, arguing that 'the quality of the furniture produced under this system must eventually be detrimental to ... the manufacturers' themselves. 'These efficiency men know nothing about furniture-making. They're smart, all right, but they are theory men, not practical,' insisted Cameron Peppler, the Knechtel saw filer and the most highly skilled man in the machine room. Under the timed system wet lumber, bad cuts, poor fits, and finishes with no foundation became routine; the rubbers at the end of the production line had to turn back goods that wouldn't stand final polishing. Robert Cripps, a twenty-eight-year-old finisher, who was bettering his earnings by 20 per cent through production bonuses, reminded the employers that when the samples were made for the furniture exhibition the men had been put on straight time – because 'we couldn't make it good enough under the system.'

As a code of personal relations, the furniture workers found the system unworthy, 'the principles of those men who are installing it beneath contempt.' No man, they argued, wanted to slight on his work, and then shove it on to other men. The system was impractical because it broke down trust, bound the men in servitude rather than brotherhood, and sent them home swearing at a time of day when they ought to have been whistling in satisfaction with the work they had done.

The men described their experience of the incentive system as a physical assault. The engineers 'put the stop watch on them,' forcing them to work at a pace that made them ill, that they could not maintain day after day, let alone year after year. 'He believed in doing a good days work,' the *Post* reported Bob Cripps as saying, but under the system 'he felt he couldn't stand the pace, one morning it took him two hours to get out of bed in the morning. His back was like a board and felt as if somebody had a knife in him.' The system took so little account of bodily health, James Thompson said, 'that a man lost if he spat or took a drink of water.'

They disputed both the morality and the business sense of a system that caused most suffering among the older men, who knew the trade best and had 'laboured good and faithful to their masters since their boyhood.' And they demanded that a share of control over the pace of production be restored to them. 'Why didn't they ask us or consider us? Why didn't they discuss it with us when we asked them to?' The working man had 'a right to say under what conditions he should work' and should be consulted about how the work was to be done, not only as a matter of manly fair play, but also because he knew best how to make good products.

Daniel Knechtel remained absolutely silent throughout the long afternoon meeting. Max Armstrong, an accountant, not a woodworker, but like Daniel Knechtel a former mayor of the town, tried to placate the men. 'You fancy the system reflects upon your ability. I don't think so,' he said, even as he defended the new ways. 'The idea is to try and train the men to work more efficiently – not necessarily harder.' Yet he, too, was plainly perplexed. The engineers worried most that the men would dawdle while being timed. It was apparent that at Knechtel they had done just the opposite. 'Fleet, why in blazes did you work so hard?' Armstrong asked the cabinet-maker who was the most compelling spokesman for the men. John Fleet had increased his earnings by 25 per cent in each of the three pay periods preceding the strike but he knew he couldn't maintain the pace year in and year out.[56] 'I sweated trying to do good work,' Fleet replied, and the gap in understanding between the engineer and the craftsman yawned wide.

The engineers believed the men had no standards save their standard of living. The men, having agreed to give the system a fair trial, had taken on the engineers' goals in addition to their own. Fleet felt responsible, having persuaded them in the previous spring to try to work on the efficiency men's terms. The system failed at Knechtel because the craftsmen would not suspend their own sense about what made good work, a sense the system men disbelieved, denied, and in practice set about to destroy.

The strike was ended that afternoon with a resolution that kept the efficiency system in place, but gave the dismissed men back their jobs, established monthly conferences to discuss grievances, and guaranteed that for a year no man would have to take a reduction in hourly pay through failure to 'come up to standard time.'

The system itself lasted another couple of years and then faded away. The goal of scientific management was to move the questioning and deliberation from work on the shop floor to a front office planning department; to give the furniture workers themselves such simplified tasks that they would need work only physically, in actions that could be observed and calibrated. The men argued that the pondering and discrimination had to happen by the machines and at the benches if they were to be effective. In time the owners and the engineers came to agree with them on this technical point. As 'no two pieces of wood of the same species can be regarded as absolutely identical' and 'a piece of wood which is just so long and so wide one day, may be perceptibly longer and wider the next,'[57] there remained good reasons for the man with the material in his hand to make the decision about how best to cut or match or polish. From break-out to packing, the quality of each man's work depended upon the care taken at each previous stage. Badly dried wood would not machine well; hurried imprecise cuts caused grief for the cabinet-makers; imperfect joins marred the finishing. By the middle of the decade owners writing to the trade journals claimed that in their experience 'piecework had a tendency to make a man crooked,' to make 'a good mechanic a careless workman,' to induce men to 'cut corners' rather than take 'time for the finer touches.'[58] Manufacturers had come to realize that techniques derived from mass production industries did not apply in furniture.

But the legacy of the strike of 1923 and the men's nine months' experience with the new diminishing and distrustful view of who they were and what might be expected of them lived on. In targeting labour productivity as the problem facing furniture men in the 1920s, owners, J.S. Knechtel among them, were guided by expert and, as their employees emphasized, 'alien' advice rather than observation of their own shopfloors. Although incentive wage schemes were discredited among furniture manufacturers and did not re-emerge at Knechtel until the 1950s, the explanations forged by experience with mass production industries, such as automobile and electrical appliance manufacturing, concerning how men were known and came to know themselves, how they came to be and could be understood as gendered social beings, did not rely for their validity in the community upon their practical usefulness in town workplaces. The industrial engineers and the AFL union organizers came and went, as the city journalists and the military police had before them, the settled sensibilities of the community never quite the same for their passing.

CONCLUSION

In the 1920s the grounding of masculine identity in the physicality of manual work was being challenged. In the mass production industries, where the economy was growing rapidly and the sleek authority of modernity shone most bright, tasks were subdivided and hierarchies elaborated.

Experience in these industries in wartime and after led craft unionists to reconsider how a working man might define his worth. They abandoned the minutiae of modern factory jobs as a ground upon which to claim authority and autonomy and embraced drives for increased productivity as the foundation for raises in pay. They reinterpreted the relationship of work to manliness, emphasizing men's roles as providers rather than producers, the authority of the breadwinner rather than the autonomy of the craftsman, the quality of home life over the quality of life at work.

Many male workers were unwilling to follow them along this route. For them the connection between manliness and craft practice – the arbitration of quality, the control of pace, the mutuality of confraternity – was too close. They fought their battles apart from their unions, until more politically minded industrial labour organizations came along.

In the 1920s managers and owners too were offered their manliness in cash. In return for better salaries and better profits they were to forswear manual activities, take on the sissifying refinements in dress and demeanour that would distinguish them from men who merely worked, and to act indirectly and at a distance in the manner of wives rather than warriors. Partitioning virility from physicality, putting it in a pay packet, a stock portfolio, in kid spats over polished leather shoes – none of these quite sufficed.

On both sides of the class divide there was watchful apprehension. Amid all this change, where were the elements from which manliness was made?

■ Chapter Eight

For men and girls: the politics and experience of gendered wage work

MEN WORK WOOD

In an essential and visceral way, in their connection to the wage, the men who made furniture in Hanover in 1900 were different from the carpenters and cabinet-makers who had tramped the Garafraxa Road into the new counties of Grey and Bruce. Both in making and in earning they had lost that equivocal but discernible autonomy artisans had claimed. Few had lived or could even recall the craftsman's day, 'going out through the snow to a board pile, selecting stuff, carrying it in and after scraping off the snow in winter, or sweeping off the dust in summer, laying of the stuff with a chalk-line ... dressing it up with a jack plane ... mortising by hand, cutting tenons and shoulders with a backsaw.'[1] Yet to assert that 'the working life of the furnituremaker changed from that of skilled craftsman to day labourer'[2] would construe too narrowly what gave the work meaning. In the factory the processes of craft production retained their distinguishable satisfactions. Furniture remained a good appreciated for its beauty as well as its usefulness, still valued most for the careful hand work which made it rare and distinctive. A Canadian poet writing in 1925 captured a continuity that withstood changes in scale and technology.

> Each man to his trade. Thank God for mine.
> To fashion out of the hearts of trees
> Some lasting beauty, from oak or pine ...
> To make the cradle, to shape the chair ...

> Each men to his trade – each is good ...
> But we who work with pungent wood
> Are serving mortals and serving art ...
> A greater boon I would never ask
> Than curling shavings around my feet,
> And the sawdust smell that is always sweet.

The sensual pleasures that came from working in wood, the honour of making something that would endure and be treasured because it had been crafted – the best and right word – with care, infused the tasks in the distinctive departments of the furniture factory with a significance drawn from grounds entirely separate from the wage. A man who had worked in the machine room at Knechtel with his father and his uncles and gone on into public life to work in cabinets of another kind spoke as a craftsman's son of factory-made goods, 'I think of the designs they made, those older traditional designs, and the quality. There is something deliciously heavy in wood. You have to have a certain love for the stuff and for what they put into it.'[3]

John Richards, thinking about the transformation from workshop to factory production, thought 'the wood workmen's occupation ... greatly changed' but not 'like Othello's, gone.'[4] The wood workmen's work continued to confer manliness. There was a comforting certainty that making these strong and aromatic materials into beautiful, useful, and timeless goods was fitting work for a man, work that both secured and constituted his manly identity. Perhaps this is why Othello came to Richards's mind. The contrast he wished to draw was not defensive but observing. Neither wage payment – nor steam power and the belts and gears of modern machinery – had severed the vital essence that made masculine the men who fashioned objects from wood, no matter how partial their participation in the process of the making had become.

Woodworking was a vocation that fathers passed to sons, that men learned by watching other men. In its resplendent variety it seems to confound easy attribution by gender. From some it demanded strength, from some the toleration and taste for danger. Amputations were 'the woodworker's trademark.' From others it called for the most scrupulous discernment, the ability to capture and render the most subtle variation, to work to fine scale with the most delicate of tools. The unity and honour in this diversity made, and was made in, gender. In the noise and danger, the proudly hierarchical work relations of the machine room, in the quiet deliberating equality of the cabinet shop, the heat and

Men and boys from the Knechtel machine room, posed in front of the belting that carried power to their machines, with a stack of saw blades at right, c. 1904. The men in the back row, left to right, are Alex Peppler, Norman Peppler, George Schwindt, and Fred Bluhm. Paul Dressler, the carver, who with John Fleet led the resistance to the scientific management schemes of 1921–3, is number 12 at right. Alex Peppler, the Knechtel saw filer, was the father of Cameron, an active unionist who succeeded him in this job, among the highest paid in the factory. Norman Peppler and his father, Henry, left the firm in 1911 to found their own furniture company in town.

rush and vaporous pall of the finishing department – the experience of work was starkly different but the claim to and by the work was the same.[5] Paul Willis has made this point well: 'whatever the specific problems of the difficult task, they are always essentially masculine problems, requiring masculine capacities to deal with them.' The factory system, the partition of craft skills, and the subordination and vulnerability of the wage had taken away from the significance of the work within class relations. But burnished and cherished as continuity and compensation was the value of this complex of tasks as a way to mark

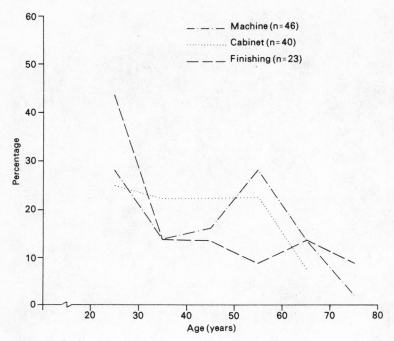

Figure 4
Age distribution of employees by department, Knechtel main plant, 1938

worth between men, as men, and to mark them in their gender as apart from that saliently absent other.[6]

The most hierarchical workplace within a furniture factory was the machine room, where parts were shaped from dimensioned stock, and its antecedent annex, the break-out department, where rough boards were cut and glued into standard sizes. This was where most entry level jobs in the plant were located and where the differentiations between men retained the closest analogies with the relations between fathers and sons in agriculture and masters and apprentices in the crafts. Most men felt indebted to older male kin – fathers, uncles or elder brothers – for intervening to secure them their first place in the plant: 'if he knew the foreman, he would maybe say, "Give him a chance." That's possibly the only way you would get a chance.'[7]

Most began as the junior helper, the 'tailer' taking away stock being fed through the machine by a senior worker on the 'front end.' Evidence of the ladding system which governed work in the machine room

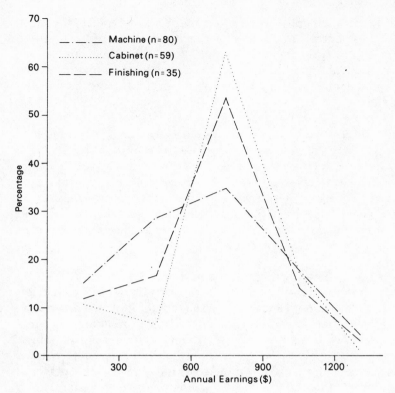

Figure 5
Distribution of annual employee earnings by department, Knechtel main
plant, 1938

emerges clearly in the twin peaks in the age distribution of the
department (fig. 4). There were exactly as many men in their fifties as
men in their twenties at work in the room in 1938, with a scattering of
other workers spread in between. Here, too, was the full hierarchy of
earnings in the plant most readily apparent. The best paid and the least
well paid of Knechtel employees were about equally represented in the
department (fig. 5).

Progressing through the hierarchy in the machine room was a
schooling in patriarchal relations, which young men learned and later
reproduced. As boys got their jobs through the interventions of male
kin, so later they gained the experience and knowledge they would need
to succeed to a machine of their own through their personal relation-

ships with older men in the room. Even after Knechtel tried in the 1920s to install a scientific management regime in the plant, machine operators in practice retained the right to choose their successors. Young men amiably bore a measure of deprecation in token for this dispensation. Henry Gateman, describing events of the late 1930s, remembered:

> Sam Colby. He run the mattison lathes. He was getting older and they wanted somebody to take it over. There was different ones suggested and he said no, they're nice fellows to me, but I'm not teaching them anything. They said, who would you suggest? He said, get Henry down, that's me ... I was grateful to him because, I asked him one day, why are you showing me all this. And he said, well, I always got along with you and I like you. And he said, one thing about you is you're a little like an elephant – when I teach you something, you never forget.

In later years Gateman confidently replicated this pattern. 'If I had a somebody working with me and I didn't care for him, I wouldn't tell him a lot of things they should know. Where if I did, I'd explain it down to as much as I knew about it.' A young man could not learn enough to run a machine merely by being present in the room and observing; older men were frugal with their knowledge, their only job security, willing to train only a successor who would acknowledge the teaching as a personal favour and not betray the trust by displaying precocious mastery of the work. In this patriarchal thicket of patronage and deference, by definition the best-placed men were sons with fathers working in the room. Karl Ruhl was candid about the process. Although he benefited by his kin connections, he saw the highly personalized barriers to knowledge about the machines as 'one of the big faults' at Knechtel. He recalled as a tailer asking the router operator for whom he worked how to read the design drawing for their machine and being told, 'Go ask your Dad.' After months of doing what he called 'joe boy' work in the veneer room, Ruhl got his first good job in the plant, doing waterfall bending, an intricate process that his father had been the first in the plant to master. Among relatives the passing on of knowledge was a legacy and in practicality a loan. Male kin kept some joint entitlement to whatever earnings the bequeathed information might command.[8]

There was no shift work at Knechtel. Each operator retained exclusive responsibility and control of his machine.[9] Each piece of equipment was demanding in its own way. The highest paid man in the machine room, and in the plant, was the saw filer. His job was to braze, or fashion, and

Machining a table leg before the open revolving blade of the shaper at the Knechtel main plant.

then properly tension band-saws, a task that required many years of study and experience to master. In 1938 when the average Knechtel employee took home $639 for the year, the saw filer, Cameron Peppler, earned $1,367. Cameron, age forty-two, had learned this work from his father Alex, who in 1938 was sixty-seven, and continuing as the only other filer, part time.[10] Next best paid were the men who ran the shaper, the moulder (colloquially the 'sticker'), and the router, all of whom earned over $1,000 in 1938. These workers had to grind their own knives from small, quarter-inch-thick plates of steel, mounting and balancing the knives in revolving cutter heads to suit the demands of each new design.[11] In each of these cases the capacity of the machine was both limited and extended by the ingenuity and experience of the operator. Much sanding continued to be done manually in the inter-war years, but if a firm had an expert belt-sander, one 'of those alert inventive men, the kind who is always devising new forms, new hand blocks and new devices for holding and in some cases moving the work,' the continuously running band of abrasive on a mould sanding machine could be jigged to do a large proportion of this work. Here too the best worker was a man of long experience who could remember just that wrinkle that had worked once years before.[12]

The work-horse of the machine room was the double-end tenoner, a substantial piece of equipment which could tackle a piece of stock from four sides at once. The tenoner was fitted with multiple cutting heads, powered by separate motors which could be set to run at different speeds. The operator needed considerable facility in interpreting the designer's drawings as well as the ability to grind knives, position heads and set speeds to achieve the specified effect. The two Knechtels tenoners each earned 50 per cent more than the average wage in 1938.[13] Although furniture workers' skills had become more specialized, like craft proficiencies they continued to be regarded as personal attributes, which gave a man worth and allowed him to command authority over other, especially younger, men.

In the machine room men most valued the variety in their work and the sense of control and autonomy they experienced as they appraised the stock and retooled the equipment for each new task.[14] They gained stature among their peers, and extra pay, because their work was dangerous. Cutting speeds were much higher in woodworking than metalworking plants; variations in the density of the stock and shifts in the direction of the grain might cause a board unaccountably to buck back against the operator's body, or the cutting head to explode in a

A router operator embellishing glued-up panels in the Knechtel machine room, 1955

dangerous shower of flying knives. Because the cutters were being repositioned frequently, it was difficult to design effective multi-purpose guards. On the mattison lathe and the shaper, where 'the woodworker's trademark' frequently was made, there were no automatic feeds; each piece of stock had to be manhandled into contact with the spinning knives. There could be no 'day-dreaming' on the machine room floor and, even in jobs that demanded considerable forward planning from the operator, no 'thinking about something other than what you're doing at the time – even though it is pertaining to your work.'[15] The danger, both emanant and imminent in the work, lurking hidden in the grain and texture of the fine and fragrant wood, men tolerated, even embraced, for the extra pay such tasks were assigned – but as much, and perhaps more, for the manly character the work demanded and conferred – the toughness, the steely nerve, the hardiness which could be called courage.[16]

Technological change did not alter radically the experience of working in the machine room during the inter-war period. In unadjusted dollars,

A row of spindle carvers doing fine detail work by a row of windows in the
Knechtel main plant, c. 1904. The carvers moved pieces of stock past the
open blade to create forms such as those shown on the bedroom suite made in
1900 and illustrated in chapter 6, p 130.

earnings in the department were about the same in 1938 as in 1928,
although the dispersion of the income distribution had narrowed.[17]
Briefly in the mid-1920s Knechtel experimented with the use of teenaged
workers in front of rip saws and jointers. But the picture of Jane
Kunsenhauser, the only female employee in the Knechtel machine
room, often used in Canada Machinery Company ads was deceptive.
The new equipment installed in the main plant in the 1920s and 1930s
substituted electric motors for steam power, and ball for babbitt
bearings. Higher-speed, steel cutting heads were built into heavier
frames. Together these changes meant that each of the eight to ten
set-ups an operator installed in a day could be put in place more quickly
and accurately and was more likely to hold its tolerance, without
adjustment, for the length of the run.[19] Rather than taking experienced
operators from work they had mastered, younger men usually were
assigned these machines, on the grounds that they had less to unlearn
and would be more willing to press the new equipment to its higher

Two young people running a planer, smoothing the surface of sawn dimensioned stock, in the Knechtel machine room, early 1923. By her sex Jane Kunsenhauser was exceptional as a tailer. The boy at right seems young to have been an operator. Kunsenhauser worked in the machine room for some time during the 1920s. Featuring her in this advertisement, and with so youthful a companion, was probably part of the machine manufacturer's campaign to sell equipment as labour saving.

production limits.[19] This, and the depression concern to provide work for men with young families, probably accounts for the decline in the average age of workers in the machine room from forty-eight years to forty-three between 1928 and 1938. Men still read drawings, cut knives and blocks, calibrated set-ups, and scrutinized stock, but the most ornery machines in the room had, in some measure, been tamed. Older skilled workers were not displaced, but the proportion of machine-room operators in the upper tail of the income distribution, those earning over $1,200 yearly, declined from 10 per cent in 1928 to 4 per cent ten years later. There was a certain levelling but not a lowering of earnings in the room, and the key instruments to confer patronage and demand deference among the men remained intact.

Boys grew in manliness as they rose, by favour and deference, through the ranks in the room. But all, from the tailer to the saw filer, were secured alike in their self-respect as men by doing work that was men's alone to do. 'I got out of school and I got working, even though I didn't keep my money, I got working with other fellas. And I always liked working with other fellas.' For a time during the Second World War, women worked in numbers in the machine room, but the discomfort with their presence was acute on all sides. Accounts of their injuries were made exceptionally graphic and were explicit about gender differences: 'This was in a machine that was about five feet long. A chain that goes right in the knives. She got her hand in there and she run it half way through the machine. I was on the other side of the room and I seen it happen and I run quick and caught it before it got up to the knives and took her hand out. It was just about that thick, just squashed flat. And she fainted, and I grabbed her and carried her to the office.' The coda to this story, 'They took her to the hospital. She was back again though. Just crushed,' was not meant to matter as much to the listener, as the depiction of the event itself. Men were described as having been carried out of the room unconscious, but never as having fainted. The girl's response was made womanly by the man's diction, and she thereby was defined, whether she came back again or not, as an inappropriate co-worker in the room. Women themselves described the work as unfitting, not because of the danger, but because of the readiness to take charge which being in front of a machine required.

> I worked about five years. Mostly take away. The men had the upper hand there and so they should as far as that goes. We were just their helpers. None of us were trained. We just went in to sweep floors, whatever we could do that we could be hired.
>
> Q: Most men I've talked to weren't trained when they arrived there either.
>
> They were men, so they stepped in and took over.

The dynamic in gender relations here – 'The work was for men. For the responsibility, the danger, for everything else' – is very much like that Cynthia Cockburn describes among printers. It mattered terribly that there be a settled understanding of who men and women were, that there be confirmation that this was work women could not do, and that men were superior because they could.[20]

Upstairs in the cabinet-making shop work relations were very different from those in the machine room. The age distribution was remarkably even, by comparison with other departments in the factory. In 1938 men in their twenties, thirties, forties, and fifties were about equally represented in the cabinet-making shop (fig. 4). One by one, younger men were taken into the department, as one by one, older men left. The average age in the room remained steady through the inter-war period, at about forty-one years.[21] Newcomers worked beside old hands, working with them, rather than for them, in stark distinction from the 'tailers' down below. Many had been first employed in the machine room, that was where the most 'first jobs' in the factory were to be had, but they entered the cabinet shop on a footing of relative equality. Despite the broad range of ages working in the room, the earnings of cabinet-makers did not vary greatly from man to man. The majority of the sixty men in the cabinet shop in 1938 earned somewhere around $700; only one earned over $1,200; only six took home less than $300 for the year (fig. 5).[22]

There was a progression through the range of tasks in the shop, but a man moved from working among men doing one job, on to working among men doing another. There was no ladding in the room. Newcomers began putting together small pieces, usually drawers, and after a time moved on to the case clamps, where they assembled the supporting members, the gables, for cabinets and chests. Those longest in the room worked 'on the bench', selecting and trimming parts for each assembled case. The bench hands worked doors and drawers so that they moved smoothly but with a pleasing sensation of solidity in the case, choosing pieces that came together visually and physically into a harmonious whole.

Whereas within the machine room, hierarchy was a sphere of action in which each man played his part – young men worked to form deferential relationships as helpers which would smooth their succession to their own machine, older men appraised and selected among pretenders to their station – in the cabinet-making shop work histories were recalled in the passive voice: 'They moved me along to making drawers. So I was there eleven years making drawers. Then they decided that I should go on bench and hang doors and drawers and fit them. Dining room, bedroom, cellarettes, wine cabinets. Anything on hinges. That's how I got there.' The 'they' was a single 'he,' the foreman, but in the cabinet shop he seemed outside, almost marginal to, the significant workplace relationships. He is almost never identified by name. Cabinet-makers recalled exactly who had worked beside them, at

Knechtel cabinet-makers constructing cases and fitting doors and drawers, at right, their individual work-benches facing the large windows looking onto Hanover's main street

the desk clamps, the case clamps, and the bench, but they did not see being put to that task as the product of a personal relationship; they made plural and anonymous the single man who had selected them for the work. The process of succeeding towards and to the bench was described in organic rather than political terms, as a matter of mortality: 'They put a newcomer in when one fellow would drop over and die. They mostly died off. They'd put a man right beside you. I had them on either side of me. You'd teach them and do your own work too, you know.' Teaching was not a matter of discretion or patronage, but a matter of course.[23]

The emphasis upon horizontal rather than vertical work relations in the cabinet shop emerges clearly in discussions of work pace. Pace and quality were seen as closely related, and necessarily and appropriately within the purview of the cabinet-makers themselves rather than the foreman. 'You'd set a nice little pace to that work and you carried it on day after day ... You had an idea of how long it would take you to do this and how long it would take you to do that. You just went along. You could see what the other man was doing ... the two guys on each side of me, that's Bill Colby and Sam Wise, they worked on each side of me and they were very steady guys [that made them] very good cabinet-makers.'[24] The setting made it easy for cabinet-makers to observe and confer with one another. The men on the bench line worked at stations set six feet apart along the windows facing the main street on the third floor of the factory. With no machinery, there was 'not near the noise in the cabinet shop. Just maybe when they're hammering something together and that's only a few minutes,' and no belting or equipment to disrupt lines of sight. Younger men who tried to rush the pace learned by observation rather than instruction that steadiness, the cabinet-maker's highest compliment, and deliberateness and economy of effort yielded the best results.

Q: Is bench a hard job?

I wouldn't say that. It's steady. It's really interesting. That's what I like about it. You always learn something ... I know some of the fellows would come up to me and say, I don't know how you do it. You're taking your time and we're going like heck and you're keeping up with us. Well, I said, you have to deal with your common sense. I said, the more you hammer, then the more you have to fix it. That's where they got behind. They were trying to speed up.

When the firm tried an incentive production scheme after the Second World War, the whole bench line opted out for two years. Their settled 'steady' pace was rated as 70 per cent of a day's work. 'We says, no, 70 per cent was a day's work. You could make more if you want to. We just worked – 70 per cent was a day's work so that's what we did. Then you could make your job right, you know, too. If the wood was warped, or something like that, you've got to straighten that out. That's what we did.' Even piece-work for cabinet-makers was an oddity in the industry. Early on the industrial engineers came to realize that, whatever might apply in the rest of the plant, 'one' [was] 'just as far ahead with a crew of reliable cabinet makers working at so much per hour.'[25]

In the 1920s the cabinet-makers had been, on average, the least well-paid workers in the factory; by the late 1930s their earnings ranked highest. The 'hand skill'[26] that cabinet-makers admired and emulated in one another retained its authority with the employer as well. The bench hand's initials on the back of each cabinet he completed were not only a device by which the quality of his work could be checked, but an affirmation of the standards he espoused. Work relations in the cabinet shop, where a man worked among men rather than for a particular man, where learning was by self-directed observation rather than submission to authority, created a group of men confident in their identities as men and as workers, who would play a leading role in industrial unionism in town in the 1930s and after.

It is possible to say least, and in fact nothing at all, from the point of view of the men themselves, about work in the finishing room. No one who had experience as a finisher in the inter-war years survives in Hanover. In retrospect it is plain that the work was the most dangerous in the plant; at the time the finishing department probably was most conspicuous for the rapid rate at which technological change was transforming the finisher's work. The new manner of working was more hazardous than the old, but neither the health implications of the change nor the appropriate remedies were immediately apparent.

Until the First World War most finishes at Knechtel were applied by hand. An experienced man dipping a brush into a pot of oleoresinous varnish, the standard coating at the time, could finish four chairs per hour. After the war, an entirely new technology, borrowed from the automobile industry, was put into place. Finishers now worked with spray guns rather than brushes, applying nitrocellulose lacquers. Because four times as much lacquer was emitted into the air as came to rest on the furniture, each finisher worked inside a booth which confined the dispersion of the spray. The new process was prodigal of materials but, in the strictly technical sense of the word, labour saving. One man with a helper could now process twenty-four chairs per hour.[27] Engineers, aware that naptha gas, seeping down towards the boiler, might cause an explosion and that fumes from fillers and stains escaping from the finishing department would make workers in other parts of the plant nauseated, emphasized the need for proper ventilation. At the time nitrocellulous lacquers were acknowledged as more 'capricious' but not as more pernicious than varnishes.[28] Even in 1923 finishing was a young man's job, and it became ever more so as the years went on (fig. 4).

Two thirds of the men in the plant worked in the machine, cabinet, and finishing rooms; the rest were employed in the last stages of the production process, rubbing down finishes, upholstering chair seats,

A finisher, unprotected by a face mask, working at a spray booth, the Knechtel main plant, c. 1950

affixing mirrors and trimmings, and preparing the goods for shipping. The only long-term female employees here were Augusta Krug and Elizabeth Wisler, both widows, who ran sewing machines in the upholstery department. Wisler and Jane Kunsenhauser were the only two women working in the factory in 1923; ten years later the number was the same. By tradition, furniture making was men's work, 'for the danger, for the responsibility, for everything else.' In the inter-war years in Hanover the claim was undisputed. In learning the work boys learned to be men; the performance of the task both tested and secured their manly identities. Both for the local political economy and for the dynamics of family life in the community – and indeed for the men themselves – what was essential about the gendering of this work masculine was not its apparent and considerable diversity, but the agreement that by right if not by reason it was men's alone to do.

GIRLS CAN WORK

Women's work in town remained largely outside the market. For a time in the 1890s there was a small woollen and knitting mill in Hanover which employed young women for wages, but the firm was never a thriving enterprise, and by 1901 it had ceased operations.[29] The wives of town manufacturers and merchants hired girls to do light housework; the proprietors of the two town hotels employed dining-room girls and linen maids; but servant keeping was not general in Hanover and most daughters who remained in town worked at home alongside their mothers until they married.[30]

The score or more female artisans in Hanover were dressmakers and milliners. Unlike the wood workman's crafts, those of the women bespoke trades that had not been consolidated into large-scale enterprises. Some female craft workers became proprietors, but their businesses remained small, sustained by the skills of one woman and usually conducted in premises loaned or leased from a man. Milliners were waged employees, engaged spring and fall by the three general merchants in town. Only one local milliner, Miss Barltrop, ran her own fancy-goods shop and engaged her own apprentices.[31] Dressmakers were more commonly proprietors conducting their businesses from rooms above the stores on the main street. They, like the milliners, emphasized the skill and knowledge they had gained by working in larger fashion centres, usually Toronto or Detroit, yet at the turn of the century their new position as independent proprietors retained elements of the itinerant seamstresses' role. Under the heading 'Fashionable Dressmaking' Miss L.M. Bricker advertised herself in 1897 as 'late of Detroit, now permanently located in Hanover' and willing to 'take in or go out sewing by day. Style and satisfaction guaranteed. Rooms above Lorenz store.' Other women did millinery or dressmaking work part time, from their own homes, or those of male kin.[32] This craft work, especially millinery, was important in town life, part of rituals to affirm respectability, to distinguish rank, to claim connectedness with the wider world, but in a community of 2,000 souls, half of them men, it did not provide employment for many, or financial independence for any more than one or two.

There were glimmerings of the new, white-collar female occupations in town; the furniture factories employed women as stenographers and clerks; the Portland Cement Company engaged a female lab technician in 1899; the manager and chief operator of the telephone exchange was a woman who employed an all-female staff. Most of these salaried workers, however, were not local girls but women who came from away.[33]

There were, of course, many young women in town, not, as in Paris, half as many more women than men, but in the years before the First World War just about as many girls as boys, leaving school and looking toward adulthood.[34] When boys went into the machine rooms at the furniture factories, what did girls do? Plainly there was lots of work at home. Both families and dwellings were large in Hanover, and girls' help in garment making and seasonal food processing made a real difference in the household economy. Farm traditions were not far away in Hanover. There were large gardens and poultry to be tended; some households also kept a cow. A girl who married in her late teens would not have too long to bide her time at home before she had a household of her own to run. Still, the example of the co-operative woollen mill of the 1890s remained. There had once been a payroll in town, collected by daughters and added to the community's store of cash. There might be a social interest at issue concerning how teenaged girls spent their time.

In 1910 a local tailor, Andrew Hamel, construing the absence of waged work for young women as an opportunity, organized a group of town businessmen to build a factory which would 'employ girls especially.' A firm of shirtmakers used the premises for several years as a branch plant. When the branch closed, many young women from Hanover followed their jobs to the main factory in Kitchener. Through the war years the *Post* carried lists of scores of Hanover girls, often in groups of sisters, returning to their home town for the annual two-week summer plant closing. Recruiting advertisements from out-of-town firms directed particularly at young women who had never before worked for wages appeared with greater frequency in the town paper. Some tried to anticipate the preferences of daughters (and their parents) on neighbourhood farms with offers of 'steady work for the winter, at good pay and in a clean, warm mill.' Others addressed uncertainties about the transition, both to waged work and life away from home, with promises that beginners would be 'paid salaries from commencement,' and given 'valuable training in agreeable work for the inexperienced' in 'clean, airy, sunlit workrooms,' with transportation provided and 'boarding houses secured.'[35] Hamel's plan had tapped a local interest but inadvertently initiated a troubling pattern. Teenaged girls were experimenting in increasing numbers with waged work. Their employment was acceptably different from that of their brothers' and appropriate to their gender in two ways: (1) they worked among women with textiles rather among men with wood, and (2) they worked as girls rather than women – expecting to learn womanliness later in marriage rather than through their work behind a machine. In another way, however, the waged work of young women was unacceptably different from that of their brothers. Against all good sense about how girls and boys should be guided, the new pattern meant that while young men stayed in town under the watchful eyes of male kin, young women left the protecting gaze of the community, to do work their mothers had never done, in places their mothers might never have been.

Thus by 1920 the interests of adult men in town, as ratepayers and as fathers, converged around the question of a 'factory for girls.' The town now owned the plant Hamel's group had built. In April, by a vote of 367 for to 28 against, the community agreed to give a Toronto firm $30,000 and tax-exempt status to reopen the building as the Hanover Cotton and Woolen Mills, the sum to be raised by issuing twenty-year municipal debentures. The town kept a 6 per cent mortgage for $45,000 on the building, but not the equipment, and agreed to forgive $1,500 of the principal yearly if the firm maintained a payroll of 200 or more. In two years the Toronto proprietors of the factory, R.G. Long and Company, were gone. By 1926 the plant had opened and closed again. The new holders of the mortgage, Allen Silk Mills of Toronto, sold out to a firm of Wisconsin knitters in 1929, who went bankrupt in 1938. By this time the town mortgage had been repaid. Subsequent manufacturers of hosiery and denim clothing were not seen as creatures of the community will in the same way.[36] But through the rocky inter-war years each failure and resurrection of the 'factory for girls' reopened the discussion of whether and why the daughters of town ought to work for wages.

Hanover was an unpretentious community, never aspiring to be the county seat, pleased to be known as a 'mechanics town,' proud of the modestness of its civic buildings, holding fast to a civic creed of spare efficiency. Bringing daughters into the labour force appealed, especially to the Board of Trade, on these grounds, as a way to expand the number of wage earners in town, without expanding the number of residents with claims upon town services. Succeeding occupiers of the 'factory for girls' assured council that they would not 'bring in an army of outside people' but employ largely local help. In the early 1920s, when times were lean in town, the prospect of a larger and stronger economy provisioning a stable population within the current town limits had great appeal. After several years of short time in the woodworking plants, having 'men and boys get work in the furniture factories, while girls work' in the mill, seemed a prudent way to ensure that households would not be left for long stretches without any cash income at all. The crisis of the early 1930s underlined this principal: 'every manufacturing centre should have both heavy and light industries, the men of each family being employed in the heavier work, and the girls of the same family in the lighter work,' so that the community had some protection from the vagaries of national markets.[37] Female employment, thus, was an economic failsafe for the community as a whole and the individual households within it.

But always the females to be employed were closely specified. They were to be local girls, not strangers. They were to be daughters, not mothers or wives. Parents were not averse to strangers in town; they were averse to having their unmarried daughters hive off to strange places just at a time in their lives when they might get themselves in trouble. The demand put to succeeding mortgagees of the 'factory for girls' that they give preference to young women from Hanover, even though they might be inexperienced in the work, was part of the strategy to try to keep daughters in their home town and under scrutiny during the years when they might be sexually active outside marriage, or, to use the phrase of the time, courting. The availability of waged work for young women in town not only reassured parents that their daughters remained under the watchful gaze of neighbours and kin; it also by deft and effective indirectness, by seeming inadvertance, increased the likelihood that local young people of both sexes would marry persons whom their parents knew.[38] Inauspicious as the location proved to be for the first five firms that took up the space, the 'factory for girls' served the purposes of the community relatively well.

Some early managers of the factory stepped outside the local consensus and tried to recruit married women for work in the mill. They did not succeed. Unlike the situation in Paris, where women married and stayed on at their jobs, in Hanover all the workplace festivities surrounding marriage were celebrations of parting. The factory was a place for daughters to work, but only until they became wives. The plant was planned to bring more money into the community, by bringing young women into the labour force. But in terms of gender relations in town, it was a conservative measure, a way to protect existing courtship patterns and regulate sexual conduct. It secured the established path towards marriage for the daughters of the town. But the 'factory for girls' by design was no place for wives.[39]

CONCLUSION

The creation of jobs was a matter of public interest and municipal policy initiative. Both the interest and the initiatives, however, varied as between men and women. The town fathers took steps to safeguard the jobs of working men in the municipality when it became clear, as it did after the fire that destroyed the Knechtel main plant, that town capitalists must be paid to give community needs precedence over their individual class interest. The bounty paid to Knechtel to rebuild in Hanover rather than another town seemed the only way to hold on to the men who both directly and indirectly provided the financial foundation for town life. There was a strong local consensus that town monies should be spent to keep a 'factory for girls' employing young women in town, but women's wages were seen not as a foundation, but as a failsafe, for municipal fortunes.

As men's and women's pay packets played different roles in economic relations in town, at the level of both the household and the community, so, in gender relations, waged work took on different meanings for men and women. Through waged work, boys learned manliness; they mastered disciplines and discriminations, ways of appraising their work and one another, which they would practice through their adult lives; varied though these ways of being manly were, they shared one trait: they were lessons males alone might learn. Girls did not learn womanliness through their paid employment. Their experience of waged work in the town-sponsored 'factory for girls' was important in their growing into womanhood because it became them to remain under the protection of male kin while they waited for their life's work, in marriage and outside the market, to begin.

■ Chapter Nine

Single fellows and family men

This chapter is written almost entirely on the basis of evidence gathered from men, reflecting upon their perceptions of their own pasts, and from newspaper accounts of men's pursuit and defences of their livelihoods outside waged work. The elaborations and the silences here are created by men's understandings about what was important to say about their behaviour and motivations and what it was inappropriate to speak about with a woman they had known for only a short time. In some senses this is but a complement to the voices of the women of Paris, revealing and falling silent, as they considered their lives inside and outside marriage. But in many ways it is not. The women of Paris had long known that there was something distinctive about the way in which households in their community were organized and were sometimes comfortable sharing their conclusions about both *why* and how they had worked out their separate way with their kin, their bosses, and their co-workers. For the men of Hanover, households headed by male breadwinners were, even in the hardest of economic times, 'natural,' traditional, and commonsensical, not problematic subjects for reflection but relations governed by the most visceral reflexes of everyday life. Their conscious or willing recall about their family lives is less densely textured than that of the women of Paris. The axioms about domestic gender roles fit closely enough with their own experience to rest comfortably as the whole of the explanation for why their households were the way they were. Men spoke clearly about their obligations and entitlements, both as single fellows and family men, and their understandings about the divergences and convergences between their claims in these two stages of their lives. Though the revelations are often by inadvertence, they leave no doubt about the resoluteness of their authority as family men. They readily distinguish their fit claims before and after marriage; there are glimpses of how male authority was worked out within marriage; but reading through the silences has been, and will be, frustrating here.

Men's credibility in the community was not grounded in their maleness per se, not in their market allegiances alone, but rested as well in their demonstrated responsibility as family men. The distinctions between single fellows and family men are plain in masculine entitlement to public office. From the early 1920s there were always members of the municipal council elected to represent the working man's interest. These councillors also were family men. It is usual to explain men's participation in municipal life in terms of their class interest and to link women's concern with community issues to their domestic concerns. There is a considerable literature on social mothering and maternal feminism. But the importance of married status in the choice of community leaders makes it reasonable to ask in what ways men's electoral office holding was informed by convictions about what a good husband and father should be. It is surely not coincidence that few single men of any class were elected to municipal office, and that communities routinely levied poll taxes on their single men on the grounds that as unmarried males they were paid more than their due for their waged work.

There is much about the union interest in Hanover municipal politics that looks like social fathering. The leaders of the labour unions in Hanover were typically not single fellows but family men. In the early 1920s, Ed Winkler, a Knechtel tenoner, moving force behind the woodlot project, and later town fire chief, together with his fellow labour councillor, William Weigel, a finisher and union leader at Knechtel, took up consumers' and well as producers' causes, pressing for a town-controlled weigh scale, so that householders could feel confident they were getting the amount of coal and hay for which they paid. In the 1930s William Fischer, the fiesty upholsterer who had made common cause with the Workers' Unity League organizers in town, known to his peers as 'a good worker and a family man,' led a labour delegation before council arguing for a municipal swimming pool. He noted that 'many parents were anxious during summer' because children went down to swim in the unsafe and contaminated waters of the Saugeen River. The union men volunteered to donate their labour to the project if the more cash-rich Kinsmen would provide money for materials.[1] More frequently money matters set the union men and the representatives of the commercial interest in town at cross-purposes on the basis of their domestic concerns. Clayton Planz, a labour councillor in the 1940s and 1950s, saw his role as a working man's representative 'to keep the tax rate down; then it would be easier for us to own a home and even your rent would be that much cheaper.'[2]

Rates of house ownership were high among Knechtel employees. More than half of all woodworkers employed at the Knechtel factory in the inter-war years owned the dwellings in which they lived; the rates were higher among married men. The pursuit of clear title to domestic space was most urgent of all in the depths of the depression. In 1933, 72 per cent of the married men on the Knechtel payrolls owned their own houses.[3] And these men succeeded to ownership relatively early in their lives; throughout the inter-war period one in four men in his twenties and one in two men in his thirties owned his own residence. Ownership provided households with a measure of security, not only because it exorcised the spectre of landlords bearing eviction notices in hard times. As British researchers interviewing unemployed men in the 1930s observed, in defending their homes men insisted upon their pride, dignity, and respectability.[4] In Hanover, the values defended through ownership were not only ideological but material. Hanover homes were the touchstones of a way of life that included considerable domestic production, valued both in goods and for the sinews of mutual care and responsibility it secured. 'Fine homes, like new factories,' Adam Seiling of Knechtel claimed, were 'evidences of a town's progression.'[5]

Hanover men spoke with great pride both about their handiness and about their homes. Few began as young family men in fine residences, but they took over ruins of one sort or another and over time made them admirably habitable. This process went a good deal beyond do-it-yourself decoration; these men were really describing non-market ways to add to the usable housing stock of the town. Asked whether he rented or bought accommodation when he married in 1946 at age twenty, Clayton Planz replied that he had done neither. 'I rebuilt. It was a barn on my father's property. At the time you couldn't rent. There just weren't too many places to rent. We took it down and made a small three-room house out of it. All on one floor.' When his family outgrew the space circumscribed by the barn's stone foundation, he acquired land under the Veterans' Land Act, and built another house. Lot sizes were large in Hanover, and it was commonplace for parents to help out a son or daughter by allowing them to build on the side lawn or backyard street frontage. Three woodworkers, Clarence Bluhm, Gus Heldt, and Walter Boettger, each were allowed to buy a lot for $10 in tax sales during the housing shortage of the late 1930s after they agreed to build themselves houses, of a specified standard, within the year. Thomas Reis began in 1928 with a shed which over time he turned into a two-storey, three-bedroom house. All this building relied more upon men's craft skills, and labour volunteered or bartered informally among neighbours and kin, than it did upon cash or the services of contractors.[6]

In good times, when the furniture factories were hiring single men from out of town, wives could use this houseroom to bring in cash. One in five unmarried woodworkers boarded in town in the lean years of the early 1920s and the 1930s, and one in four did in 1928, when local plants were running up to and above normal capacity. In more difficult times, families doubled up. In 1933 a quarter of Knechtel married employees shared their dwelling with another family; this proportion had risen to a third by 1938; by contrast, in 1928, 96 per cent had lived in houses that functioned as single family residences. These adaptations occurred rapidly, in ways that recall Hareven's characterizations of the 'malleable' household.[7] In the five years between 1928 and 1933 the average number of households per dwelling in Hanover increased from 1 to 1.3; the number of persons per dwelling rose from 4.9 to 5.2. Some of these extras in the houseful did not board, but paid rent for what the English would call a 'bed-sit.' Clarence Helwig was one of these: 'I had two rooms. A bedroom on one side of the room and a kitchen on the other. The bathroom and the living room we shared ... In the morning I'd get out of bed and be right at the table.' Others of the extras were whole families of kin – children, siblings, or cousins of the owner – who moved in to share the space, work, and expenses. In this way the houseroom stretched everyone's resources, although the remedy clearly at times demanded deep reservoirs of patience as well.[8]

A large portion of the town's food supply was produced and exchanged in the informal economy, and never saw the grocers' shops on the Durham Road. Many woodworkers had barns at the back of their properties where they kept a cow, a few chickens, and some pigs. Most families, tenants and owners alike, kept large gardens to meet their own needs for root crops year round and other fresh vegetables in summer. Serph Gingrich, a Knechtel rubbing department employee and an active unionist in the Workers' Unity League years, kept his family of ten off relief during the depression by gardening: 'There's a lot of land up here. I'd plant lots of potatos and sell them by the basket. Oh different things, vegetables, corn. The children were small. We had really hard times, but we pulled through.' Relief funds were never adequate during the early 1930s, but there was no protest when, in order to save more of the budget for winter expenses, the municipal committee in charge cut support all round each August for several months. The non-market production of fruits and vegetables was so well established in town that the assumption that 'most everyone has a garden' and that people were able for a time 'to supply their own food' was uncontested.[9]

There was nothing casual about gardening in Hanover; for the men of the town growing things was a serious pursuit, an affirmation, a validation, more nourishing than the stocked larders come autumn alone measured. Sam Howell, the knitting mechanic who had lived in both Paris and Hanover, described the whole town through the imagery of its backyards: 'Up in Hanover, what struck me when I went up there was their gardens. Everybody had a garden and you could look down almost a whole block and everybody would plant their things, like they'd plant them in rows here [Paris]. The next people would watch that and they would do exactly the same thing; you could look down there and see them all lined up. This is what German people are like; they are very disciplined.' Clyde Dankert, the Hanover boy, later Darmouth College professor of economics and biographer of Adam Smith, recalls with pleasure not only the order, but the aesthetics and the confident, knowledgeable discriminations that gave cultivation its satisfactions:

> A large part of the area behind our house was devoted to a garden. On one side we had a number of small plots, about eight or ten feet square, with well-kept paths between them, and each devoted to certain vegetables. The first one, for instance, was devoted to onions, and had an attractive border of lettuce. This part of our garden not only yielded very useful vegetables for the family but looked very attractive. The potato patch was beside these plots, and apart from its lower portion was not good land. The upper part was largely clay. At the end of the potato patch we had raspberry bushes which continued to yield good 'crops' for quite some time.

The young Clyde was also willing to acknowledge a certain romanticism in the Hanover approach to gardening, and wrote a poem, in the manner of Wordsworth, about Charles Oppertshauser, a Knechtel chair driver who lived next door, silent and still in meditation among his flowers. Dankert's lifelong friend, the painter Carl Schaefer, evokes the

'Summer Evening in Town, Hanover,' Version v, 20 July 1942, by Carl Schaefer, Edmonton Art Gallery. The Knechtel main plant forms the backdrop of this view down the back gardens of Victoria Street, where Schaefer as a boy played with his neighbour Clyde Dankert. Schaefer's maternal grandfather was Samuel Fellman, Daniel Knechtel's finishing-room foreman and prominent shareholder in the Knechtel firm. Backyards were busy worksites where cattle and chickens, as well as vegetables, were raised. Many also included small craft workshops.

oneness of these pleasures, the seamlessness of the furniture workers' world, in his 'Summer Evening in Town, Hanover,' Version v, 20 July 1942, as viewed from his grandmother Fellman's yard, south past his pal Clyde's to the outline of the Knechtel factory on the Durham Road.[10]

Buying meat retail was also unusual in town. So many households acquired their meat through the informal economy that local butchers in protest withdrew their services from the community for a month in the summer of 1920. The butchers wanted a municipal tax levied on the meat pedlars, mostly farmers from the surrounding district, who were undercutting main street prices as they sold door to door. When the labour councillors, Winkler, Weigel, Devlin, and Laidlaw, swung the council against the tax, the butchers closed up. But even in high summer, when their refrigeration facilities gave them their greatest advantage over the street vendors, the butchers found their withdrawal of services had little effect, save that even more townspeople were patronizing the pedlars. Come mid-August they reopened. In 1938 William Fischer found himself, once again taking up where Weigel and Winkler had left off, arguing against taxes on meat pedlars 'because of his interest in the working man.'[11]

The yards of Hanover houses also included a plethora of sheds and back kitchens converted into craft workshops where men made cabinets, sharpened saws, repaired engines and cut hair. As a young man, Carl Schaefer worked for a neighbour on a small lathe, turning out beer-keg spigots. Dankert helped a backyard saw filer. Other Knechtel employees tramped about the surrounding countryside practising their craft skills or working as extra hands on the land or in woodlots.[12]

The activities by which Hanover men supported their families, thus, went a good deal beyond their factory waged work alone. They valued their waged work for more than the cash it paid; they also looked for their livelihood to a broad range of household and neighbourhood activities in addition to their factory employment. Their participation in the informal economy, in the non-market provision of foodstuffs, housing, and services, contributed to their material resources and to their spiritual and political resilience in troubled times, creating a sense of worthiness, competence, and confidence as it widened the tactical options at their command. The presence of a vital informal economy did not blunt the force of waged workers' struggles against employers in industrial disputes. Indeed, as we shall see, exactly the opposite was the case in Hanover, through both the inter-war and the post-war years.

But what influence would the presence of a vigorous informal economy have upon the domestic relationships of the family man? The question is not much considered. Gershuny reports in an afterword that he expects sexual segregation in unpaid work to change little with shifts in the relative sizes of the formal and informal economies. The evidence from field-work for Pahl's claim that women's stronger position in the formal economy leads to a shift in the sexual division of labour in the household remains scant. On the basis of her cross-sectional study of England and Wales, 1900–39, Gittins reports the highest rate of egalitarian marriages and joint-role conjugal relationships in communities where wives worked for wages full-time. But her evidence also suggests, although she does not draw out this implication, that in many localities it was the high value both spouses placed upon work done outside the money economy that provided the foundation for the

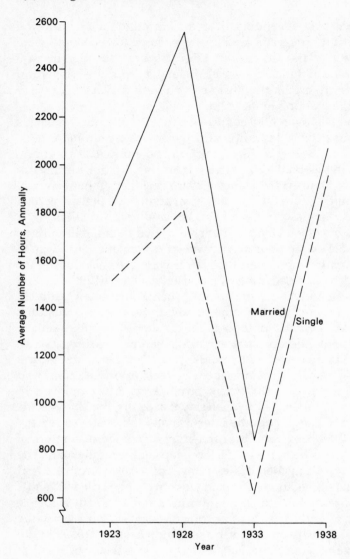

Figure 6
Average number of hours worked yearly by marital status, Knechtel
employees, 1923–38

joint-role relationship in marriage. These beliefs about the value of non-market work reduced the priority of labour-force participation, both absolutely and as a ground for authority, in household decision-making. Trevor Lummis, finding that family men in early twentieth-century, East Anglian fishing communities bore little resemblance in recollection to the stereotype of the brutal working-class father, suggests that not only material conditions in the national and domestic economy, but also community social conventions about same and mixed gender sociability, shaped men's views of their rights and their due as family men.[13]

Certainly their burdens as family men varied with the numbers and ages of their children. Men with many children, or more particularly, many school-aged children at home, were not paid more per hour in recognition of the greater needs in their households. In this sense, as Hilary Land has argued, the breadwinner ideology discriminated between male and female wage earners, but not among males between bachelors and family men.[14] Fathers did not cope with this incongruity on their own. They managed to be good providers because they received both social and familial support. But in the cultural conception of the responsible family man the distinction between the good provider and the bad provider was highly individuated; the credit or blame was attached to the breadwinner alone.

Working extra hours was one way family men could try to resolve the gap between standardized hourly wage rates and their undeniably non-standard-sized families. Over the course of the year at Knechtel in the inter-war period married men always worked more hours than single men. So long as there was work available, family men increased the time they spent earning wages at the plant for each child they had living at home. In domestic terms, this was an unsatisfactory resolution to the family wage problem – one parent was most often away working in the market economy in those households where the burden of domestic labour was greatest. Wives most in need of help were least able to call on their husband's time. Fathers with the most children had the least time to spend with them.

And, of course, whether fathers with larger families could work extra hours at their regular factory jobs depended upon the availability of overtime and the conventions by which the extra hours were allocated. Thus in 1928 the relationship between the number of hours a man worked in the Knechtel factory and the number of children he had at home was direct and linear. Men with five children at home worked 50

TABLE 2
Total hours worked yearly, Knechtel wage-earners

	1923	1928	1933	1938
Marital status				
Married	1842	2539	848	2079
n	(107)	(96)	(92)	(119)
Single	1510	1802	628	1975
n	(35)	(24)	(16)	(36)
Number of children				
0	1794	2078	643	2088
n	(12)	(16)	(10)	(26)
1	1665	2492	786	1775
n	(25)	(21)	(21)	(23)
2	1772	2424	883	2242
n	(16)	(20)	(20)	(30)
3	1773	2686	1099	2115
n	(28)	(15)	(15)	(16)
4	1948	2973	971	2023
n	(10)	(7)	(9)	(11)
5	2178	3105	605	2242
n	(12)	(11)	(9)	(6)

n = number of observations

per cent more hours than men with none. There was more work to be had than many men wanted. Those with larger families accepted and those with smaller families refused overtime. But in 1933, when the pressure of family needs was most acute, no one at the plant was working even a regular week, and men with many children could not be sure they would get extra hours of waged work. That year the nine Knechtel workers with five children at home worked fewer hours than those who had none. Throughout the plant married men were offered more hours to work than single men, but when all the family men were feeling the pinch, and the man with the large family was hoping for hours others with fewer children felt they needed as well, who got the work depended more upon accommodations negotiated among small groups of co-workers. Sometimes co-workers were willing to recognize the needs of men with large families and cede them a larger share of the

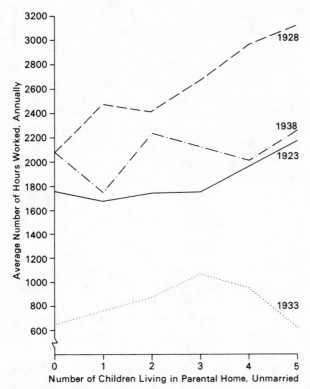

Figure 7
Average number of hours worked yearly, by number of children, Knechtel
employees, 1923–38

scarce work being offered at the plant. Sometimes they refused to
acknowledge a group obligation of this sort, and left the overburdened
breadwinners among them to their own devices. Thomas Schaus
describes this process in the rubbing room:

It slowed down again in the thirties, 1929-thirties. I know I was only
working two half days a week. There was four of us, the foreman and two
other men. The other man had a large family. I only had two children and he
had seven or eight. So the boss and him, they worked four days a week and
the other man, he just had adopted a son, and him and I, we were supposed
to work four half days. So I made out with him, well you work two days,
and I'll work two days. Then, if you wanted to go away or do something else
you won't be split up all the time.

His co-worker Seraph Gingrich, father of eight, remembered how he benefited from this arrangement: 'I got pretty near as much as everyone did, maybe a bit more, because they knew I had a large family. Some of them got laid off for four or five months. They didn't lay me off.' But neither all foremen nor all co-workers were willing in the clench to honour the entitlements of those with larger families. 'Some of them had too big families – more than they could take care of,' a man from the machine room remembered, 'it was their own fault.'[15]

Many of the men who worked at Knechtel during the 1930s came from families of eight or more, but this demographic pattern was changing. Henry Gateman, whose own family of four children was smaller than that in which he had grown up, when asked whether he had ever wished for either more or fewer children, replied: 'Never more. I've often thought that if I'd have had less, I maybe could have helped my children more ... If you only had one child you really could – But it's nice because there is somebody here [to visit] every day.' Through the inter-war period the number of children in the households of Knechtel workers in their twenties declined steadily, from 1.7 in 1923 to 0.95 in 1938. Couples, weighing the limited resources at their command through either the formal or the informal economy, were beginning their families later and were likely to achieve a smaller completed family size.[16]

Through work in addition to their waged work, through additional hours of waged work, and by delaying beginning a family, married woodworkers attempted, with the acquiescence of their co-workers and the assistance of their wives, to overcome the rigidity and inadequacy of the male breadwinner wage as the material foundation for family life. But all the while they held adamantly to the notion that only men should be breadwinners, and that a wife's place was in the home. For most this position was axiomatic: 'My mother stayed home and raised us as best she could. I think life would be a lot better. There would be no unemployment for the men if women were to do the same as they did years ago.' 'A woman should be a homemaker.' 'To look after the home, look after the house, that's a woman's responsibility.' 'It is the man's job to look after the woman and not let the women go out to work ... If the man is able to work, the man should be able to provide enough money to support his wife at home.'[17]

There is no doubt that husbands measured their personal worth as men by their ability to meet their households' needs for cash. They were particularly likely to compare themselves in this regard with their fathers, and their wives' place in the household with their mothers. This was a long-standing part of masculine gender identity. In the agricultural and craft-based economy that had preceded industrialization in the district, men took the goods the household produced to market and controlled the flow of cash into the domestic economy.[18] In Hanover, men who happily took on household tasks so that their wives could engage in the neighbourhood and community production of goods and services refused to allow their wives to work for wages. Apparently the question was frequently raised. While men always seemed certain the household could get by without the extra cash, from the 1920s, when more factory-produced clothing and foodstuffs were available in local stores, women saw cash as giving them more leeway as managers to decide what to produce domestically and what to bring into the household from the market. Men won these disputes by insisting on the worth and priority of household work, particularly of mothering, and by arguing the moral superiority of having less and making more at home. In the household he headed, Henry Gateman enforced the rule of 'no two.' 'My wife often mentioned about going out and getting a job. My wife isn't – she's pretty good, but I told her, no two. If you want to get a job, alright I'll stay home ... I said, if she worked, I wasn't going to work. I said there's got to be somebody home with the family.' Through the 1930s and after, as we shall see, Hanover woodworkers were engaged in radical unionism. Their participation in the informal economy was, on one level, a way to broaden their resources, by decreasing their dependence upon waged work to increase their resilience in industrial struggles. But in Hanover, just as Elizabeth Jameson has found in the mining community of Cripple Creek, the more successful men were in both achieving wage gains and sustaining alternative sources of livelihood, the less likely was it that their wives would work for wages, the more likely both men's roles and women's roles would persist little changed amid the tumult.[19]

Men typically replied to the question, 'What work did you do around the house?' with a list of the activities that kept them from home.

> You mean housework. No. I always did extra work. Some call it moonlighting. I don't know. I tended bar at nights and weekends for twenty years. I caretake at the Lutheran church and the Baptist church. So I always did extra work.
>
> Me? I didn't do too much, no. I played in the band, so I wasn't home very much.

Within the household, the sexual division of labour was marked by the walls of the dwelling: 'I did all the outside work. Sometimes I'd help with the inside work, spring housecleaning and things like that. She done that pretty well herself. I was working down at the greenhouse on the weekends, and holidays for about thirty years.' Although early in their marriage, Mrs Lang, the wife of a cabinet-maker and trusted union leader, had wanted to remain in her job at the knitting mill, having lost the argument, she anxiously assumed all the 'real work' of housekeeping and child care.

> As far as work in the house, no. He had a lot of work outside and his mother lived at that time and lots of time he was helping her yet. He was quite busy, so I didn't expect him to help. I was home alone with the children. I loved working so I didn't mind him not helping me then, but he helped with the dishes when I needed it and he helped put the kids to bed and he babysat. As far as real work, no. I felt guilty when he had to do anything like that, you know, because I felt that was my job until I couldn't do it.

Mrs Lang was scrupulous in the distinction; what she did in the home was 'real work'; the labour her husband did within the walls of the house, his 'helping' and 'babysitting,' was not work in the same sense. A good wife could not in conscience ask her husband to do real work in the home when he had so much real work of other kinds to do, never mind that this burden, made by his refusal to allow her to share in wage earning, was self-inflicted, self-aggrandizing, hers to accommodate, and not of her choosing. The rule of 'no two,' with its implication that a wage-earning husband cared more for the welfare of his children than did a wife who wanted to enter the paid labour force, by shaming powerfully enforced wives' sense of their domestic obligations.[20]

Upon what was based the authority of the husband to exclude his wife from the paid labour force? Why did the tactics of absence and shaming work so effectively to minimize his domestic labour responsibilities? Beginning with the assumption that 'economic competence' was 'the chief ground' upon which the authority of breadwinners was lodged, social investigators observing household hierarchies in a wide variety of communities in the 1930s pursued the question, 'What happens to the authority of the male head of the family when he fails as a provider?' Most found that their initial assumption was unfounded, that the authority of the husbands they observed was not defined by their competence as a provider, was not necessarily diminished by their

reduced ability to meet family needs, was not instrumental but
ideological in its justification. Men had authority in households because
they were husbands and fathers; their authority was intrinsic to the
social definition of their familial position. That definition included
breadwinning, but it included much else as well. Paternal authority was
an existential state, more being than doing, hedged by but not defined
by performance.[21] In retrospect it is even more clear that 'the depression
attacked and sometimes shattered fathers' "effectiveness" as providers;
but the role itself survived until the return of better times.'[22] Reflecting
upon this paradox, that 'depressions involve massive disruptions of
capitalist production ... but not of households, or at least not on the
same scale. Indeed a vast amount of energy goes into keeping
households going in the worst of circumstances, and the volume of
domestic production probably rises in depressions,' it is difficult to hold
on with much conviction to the notion that the vitality of the patriarchal
household derives primarily from its sustaining connection to capitalist
production.[23]

There is no doubt that the depression put immense stress upon both
men and women in Hanover as it did in many other communities. In the
social triage of the early 1930s, the claims of single men in the factory and
in the family were most tenuous. Unmarried men were the first laid off
at Knechtel. The proportion of single fellows on the payroll fell
markedly between 1928 and 1933. Although household sizes rose, as
daughters returned home, sons accepted that it was unmanly to 'put
feet under mother's table' once they had no wages to bring home. 'I
couldn't expect my mother to feed me so I went to the farm. I walked five
or six miles until – just to work for my board.' Whereas at Knechtel in
1923 and 1928 half of the young men aged twenty to twenty-nine still
lived with their parents, in 1933 the proportion had fallen to under
one-fifth. Gordon Peck left town to work near Toronto when he was laid
off – 'There was no work at all here,' and returned only when he decided
to marry. Many of his peers delayed their marriages. Although there
were fewer single men in Knechtel work force as a whole in 1933, among
men in their twenties there were fewer married men than there had ever
been before.[24]

Relief officials were clear about the contingency of male entitlements.
They had no intention of using public or charitable funds to replicate the
inefficiencies of the breadwinner wage, by paying all adult males as if
they had families to support. In February 1932 Mayor Max Armstrong
sternly lectured a group of single men who appeared before council

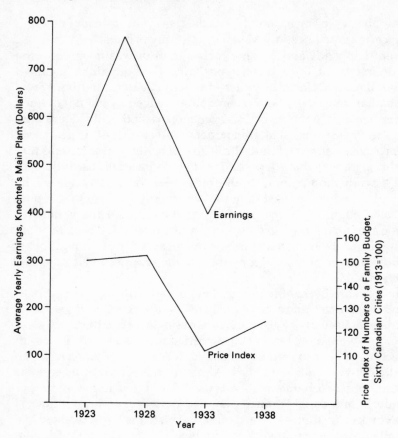

Figure 8
Yearly earnings and cost of living, 1923–38

asking for work: 'You need not sit down and expect the town to feed and clothe you. That's pretty plain talk but I believe that's the case. The town is at the end of its tether so far as money is concerned ... [We] will have to combine to provide food, clothing and fuel – not to single men, or even married men, but to the latter's families. Don't get it into your head that the town must provide food – we haven't.'[25] Single men were urged to pack up and go. As labour councillor Wright insisted, 'Young fellows should be the first to take farm positions. One could hardly blame a man for not wanting to leave his wife and family in town while he worked on a farm.'[26]

In good times men had marked their own steadiness and dependability, these traits of personal, manly character, by the regularity of their waged employment. Insisting upon high standards of craftsmanship in waged work had been one way a man affirmed his personal integrity. Loosed from the schedules and standards of the factory, woodworkers felt they had lost touch with themselves. Paul Lazarfield and Samuel Stouffer suggested in 1937 that an unemployed man who knew that many of his 'fellow workers in the same occupation at the same income level' shared his predicament would feel this disorientation less keenly, but in Hanover the stigma and pain of being on relief remained intense even when public dependence became a common predicament in town. Disputes between relief workers and their foremen were frequent; men insisted that they were 'always willing to go out and work, but they could not be expected to work hard and fast' at heavy manual tasks, especially when 'they were not getting enough food to do so.' Authorities called relief workers 'touchy' and claimed they were not showing 'decent, manly co-operation' on the job. Even when every plant in town was shut up tight, the implication remained, as Magistrate Frank W. Walker from Owen Sound proclaimed from the bench in an assault trial arising from a dispute with a relief foreman, that any man could stay off relief if only he 'were possessed of the sterling qualities of independent Canadian citizenship.'[27]

In good times women had marked their competence as homemakers by their ability deftly to manage life on the cusp between market and non-market production, to choose what they would make and what they would buy so as to turn their resources to the best possible purposes. They had been able to stretch the cash at their command by choosing what, when, and where to buy and in what quantities. Relief was paid, not in cash, but in 'closed' vouchers, redeemable only at specified stores, for specified goods, at pre-established prices. The Welfare Board claimed that the voucher system protected women and children, that in other jurisdictions 'men receiving cash spent it on beer and other non-essentials instead of buying food and clothing for their families,' but excluding cash from the domestic exchequer of those on relief compromised women's control, authority, and autonomy in significant ways. There were no weekend bargains for those on relief. And whereas cash purchases formerly had complemented household production, women now had to plan that production around the constraints imposed by the limited range of goods available with relief vouchers.[28]

By January 1933 fifty-four heads of families and 187 dependants, one in thirteen of the town's 3,000 inhabitants, were on relief. Those who stayed off relief, who manifested the 'independent Canadian citizenship' Magistrate Walker so admired, were building up formidable obligations. Having to apply for relief, to register formally as a public dependant, was the last straw, but most family men recalled their tenuous hold on subsistence in those times as a complex of heartening and shaming interdependence, only partially denominated in cash and contract. 'I was never on relief but ... ' most began. After the 'but' there followed a rendering of heterogeneous accounts woven in memory as of one piece. Two-thirds of Knechtel employees were in arrears in their municipal taxes in 1933, all those with six children or more at least one full year behind. Woodworkers were relying on their representatives on council to limit tax sales to vacant lots and negotiate modest instalment plans for owner-occupiers in default to the town. Many men remembered accounts with local coal dealers and grocers that lingered for two and three years unpaid. The credits and debts here are not intelligible if viewed from the perspective of the market economy alone. They were not so much calculations as dispositions lodged in community and family values. A family should not be turned out of house and home. A family man should not be pressed to leave town to work away. A man with many children should have the most work. A grown son should not claim a place at his mother's table when there was not enough food to go around. A merchant should not press for his bills to be paid when his neighbours' children were in need. These dispositions were not binding obligations, but they were grave and highly gendered elements in the distributional conscience of the community.

CONCLUSION

There is no doubt that, within the market economy, men's claims to jobs, and the hourly rates those jobs paid, were defined by their maleness, in distinction from the fewer and different jobs and the lower wages which were due to women. In factory production, in industrial capitalism, the sex-typing of occupations and the rates of remuneration set for waged work gave all men rights on the basis that some men had families to support. The resilience of this pattern is undeniable, but it is not a state of affairs that can be explained by reference only to the needs of owners to support the next generation of workers entering into their collective employ. Single fellows were given the same entitlements as family men, and family men's wage rates were not proportional to the numbers of dependants in the households they headed. Men who were owners and men who were workers forged common cause around the breadwinner wage and the sexual division of the waged labour force on the basis not of the logic of capital but a more broadly constituted logic about the fit social distribution of resources and power.

That logic governed not only the market, but the distribution of authority and other entitlements within social existence generally. The distinctions among men, between single fellows and family men and among family men, although absent from wage relations, were insistently present in both public and private life, among both co-workers and family members. Fine distinctions were drawn in eligibility for municipal office and municipal support between males who were family men and males who were not. Life outside the market was integral to definitions of independent citizenship and understandings of manly identity. They hedged sons' claims upon their mothers and fathers; fathers' claims upon their co-workers; families' claims upon the state in certain seasons of the year. All this activity outside the market economy, all these ways to produce the stuff of a livelihood, the threads of shame and guilt, obligation and entitlement, which tied together a way of life, cannot be distilled to compensations, silent servants of capitalist intentions. They were made in more of life than that and were too frequently, as in the case of Hanover, the very grounds upon which challenges to capitalist relations were lodged.

■ Chapter Ten

Union men

THE CRISIS OF THE 1930S IN THE FURNITURE INDUSTRY

Like a creaking roller-coaster hastily constructed for a summer fair, business conditions in the Canadian furniture industry careened unsteadily between depths and heights through the inter-war years. After hard times in the early 1920s, productive capacity in the sector grew rapidly. There were 238 furniture-making firms in Canada on the eve of the First World War, 367 in 1929. In the eleven years between 1918 and 1929 capital invested in the industry increased by 84 per cent from $22.7 to $41.8 million. By comparison with manufacturers generally, furniture makers fared well in the late 1920s, but with the onset of the depression in 1929 their fortunes declined more deeply, and through the 1930s their production levels remained relatively lower, their recovery slower than in secondary industry as a whole.[1]

Patterns beyond the community level are crucially important in explaining the different plights of Hanover and Paris through the inter-war years. The knit-goods and furniture sectors were radically different in their industrial structures. Whereas Penmans and a handful of other firms dominated their market through a tightly managed oligopoly, selling essential articles of clothing which through wear needed regularly to be replaced, Knechtel was but one of hundreds of firms, producing goods purchased with discretionary income and durable enough to be passed down from generation to generation. The liberal authors of the Royal Commission on Price Spreads hopefully noted 'a relative freedom from monopolistic development' in furniture, by comparison with other industries that had come under their purview, but they turned quickly to the bleak corollary of this freedom. The furniture industry, as 'a completely disorganized body of producers,' privately financed and dominated by no one group of companies, had experienced price declines greater than 'in any other important industry.' As John Ross Shaw, the former president of Canada Furniture Company, himself unemployed since 1932, acknowledged before the Price Spreads commissioners in 1935, 'possibly we built too many' of these small companies. But mid-western Ontario had been sustained by farming and the woods, and 'when wheat-growing was killed and went West,' communities 'had nothing to do but go into manufacturing in an effort to preserve their towns and villages,' into the furniture industry 'naturally, as a matter of course.'[2]

There was no unity in the circumstances of Canadian capitalists during the depression. The small private companies that composed the furniture industry in the counties of Wellington, Huron, Grey, and Bruce were no match for the retail mass buyers of Toronto. As department stores undercut the prices of retailers specializing in furniture, small sellers and producers alike stared into the bare face of market power. 'Hard-boiled' representatives from the department stores canvassed manufacturers for bids on lines they intended to sell below cost, 'holding out an order for standard lines at regular prices as an inducement.' An independent retailer, after consulting the Eaton's catalogue, dared not place orders with manufacturers unless he could meet Eaton's prices, knowing all the while that he would 'lose his hide' at the prevailing prices whether or not he tried to sell furniture. Manufacturers agreed to sell at a loss, 'hard pressed to turn' their growing 'inventories into cash,' 'to keep the steam in their factory and the sprinkler system from freezing up,' 'to keep their men employed so that they should have their bread and butter.' The predicaments of furniture manufacturers and retail mass buyers were as different as chalk and cheese. The department stores held the upper hand in the wholesale market for goods. They also had purchase in the market for finance capital, where the small private companies in the furniture sector found themselves absolutely without hope. As year by year furniture manufacturers exhausted their working capital by selling below cost, having been refused credit by the banks and other institutional lenders, the department stores consolidated the forces with

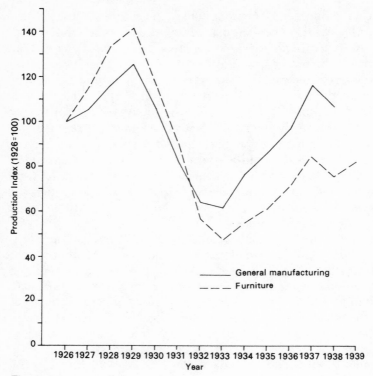

Figure 9
Production, general manufacturing, and the furniture industry, 1926–39

which to weather hard times, even forcing producers to finance retail inventories by delaying longer and longer in settling outstanding accounts.[3]

Furniture manufacturers' first collective response to the crisis of the 1930s was the same one they had tried in the depression following the First World War. They turned to price fixing. At a meeting in the Walper House in Kitchener on 4 August 1933 the Furniture Manufacturers Association appointed industrial engineer C.V. Fessenden as 'enforcer' of a 'cooperatively-set, uniform price level capable of quick and simultaneous adjustment.'[4] In this initiative they received support from both likely and unlikely quarters. E.H. Lane, an American manufacturer who 'not only survived the depression but emerged enlarged and with a national reputation' by selling his mass-produced cedar chests to young women as a symbol of love 'nearly as universal as the diamond ring,' wrote candidly to Karl Knechtel, son of J.S., noting that Canadian goods often were priced lower than furniture sold south of the border, 'although all the elements that go into them come from down here. There is absolutely no sound reason or excuse for this. Frankly, if I were running that business, I would, in some manner, get my main competitors under an agreement on the inside finish so you would have legal excuse for talking with them about prices.' So indirect an instrument was not necessary in Canada. Even Harry M. Cassidy, a professor of social work and leading Ontario social democrat, supported the furniture price code when it was widely publicized in the spring of 1934, arguing that in furniture as in the clothing industry which he had previously studied, 'competition may be the death of trade instead of the life of it.' The problem, however, quickly overwhelmed this voluntary solution. Within months the 'disorderly body of producers' who manufactured furniture in Canada found themselves beset once again by 'chislers' within their ranks.[5]

Like knit-goods manufacturers, Ontario furniture makers would have had difficulty meeting external competition without tariff protection. The centre of the u.s. industry had moved from Grand Rapids, Michigan, south into states where, even after National Recovery Administration codes were in force, wage rates were lower than those paid in Ontario. These southern plants were closer to remaining North American stands of furniture hardwoods, particularly fashionable walnut, oak, and gum woods unavailable in commercial quantities in Canada. All American furniture manufacturers paid less for glass, mirrors, finishes, and hardware than did their Canadian counterparts, and they reaped scale economies through longer production runs for a larger market. Between 1926 and 1930 the value of American imports into the Canadian market trebled, to over $3 million. In response, in 1930 the Bennett government raised tariffs on furniture from their traditional percentage levels, which had been high enough to protect Canadians from Michigan but not southern producers, to over 40 per cent. This protection was effective and through the early 1930s imports declined to pre-1926 levels. But the Canada-United States trade agreement which went into effect in January 1936 set furniture tariffs lower than they had been since the promulgation of the National Policy, at 27.5 per cent, and imports immediately began to rise. The volumes of American furniture entering Canada were not enormous, but laid down in carload lots into the hands of mass buyers they worsened the already dire predicament of furniture makers in the market. Recognizing the

disparity of market power in the sector, the Tariff Board in 1937 recommended a rise in the rate of protection to nearer 34 per cent for two years but emphasized that this concession was in the nature of temporary relief 'rather than a final view of the amount of protection required by the industry.' Not only did the lower level of industrial concentration in their sector reduce the market power of furniture manufacturers by comparison with the select fraternity of knit-goods manufacturers, but 'disorganization' weakened their relative influence with the Tariff Board and cabinet as well.[6]

Knechtel fortunes mirrored those of the industry as a whole. Net profits had averaged over 5 per cent on capital employed through the 1920s, but in 1930 the firm slipped into the red and remained there through the rest of the decade. By 1936 Knechtel factories in Walkerton and Southampton and their Winnipeg warehouse were idle, empty, and up for sale. Production had ceased in the desk factory as well, and what manufacturing took place was concentrated in the main Hanover plant. To cover $100,000 liabilities in direct advances and discounted trade paper the Bank of Montreal in 1935 demanded and received mortgages on some Knechtel property, floating charges on others, and a debenture as collateral security for twice the sum owed. Just before Christmas in 1932 Daniel Knechtel wrote to his friend John Leypoldt, minister at Erin Avenue Baptist Church in Cleveland, deeply troubled that his straitened finances meant he could no longer fulfil the charitable obligations of a Christian man and especially concerned to keep his wife from knowledge of his diminished circumstances: 'I feel the Depression very much now as I get no Dividends from the Furniture Co now for 2 years ... As many workmen cannot pay even half rents and had heavy losses in stocks so that I am a poor man now ... I owe at present 45,000.00 so now for 2 years I could pay nothing for missions or charity which I allways done with pleasure, my losses are so heavy. I give you in strict

---

Knechtel manufactured Lane cedar chests on licence from the u.s. firm. These items continued to sell relatively well during the depression, marketed as a symbol of love and domestic stability. As the text from this Lane publicity package reads: 'What a gift for a sweetheart, daughter, wife, mother or sister the Lane Cedar Chest is! For centuries the Hope Chest has been the very cradle of romance ... And why not? Will it not contain her wedding trousseau and those belongings so dear to the heart of every young girl? ... For mother, it provides a safe place for her downy woolens and fur-trimmed things.'

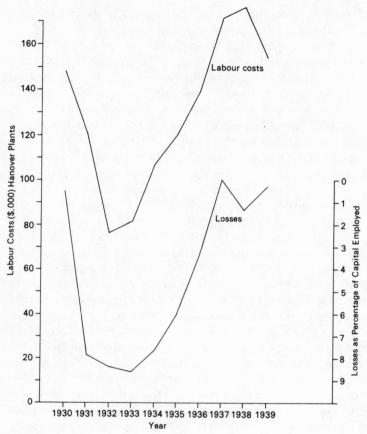

Figure 10
Knechtel labour costs and losses on capital employed, 1930–9

confidence my trouble and don't tell my wife this.' He did share his
troubles with his male kin, and in 1933, for the first time since before the
First World War, Dan Knechtel's name appeared on the payroll of the
firm he had passed to his son. Until the year before he died he received
monthly the amount paid members of the female office staff. J.S. himself
stood down from the firm in 1930, replaced by his son Karl as managing
director. As J.S. had faced more difficult industry conditions than had
beset his father, so too did Karl. By 1939 the firm's capital was severely
impaired, eroded to half of the 1929 levels, and it was necessary to write
down the value of each Knechtel common share from $25 to $7.[7]

UNION MEN

The workers of Hanover had two clear advantages over the workers of Paris as they attempted to change the power relations within their community: the greater resources for undertaking public action which tradition and experience embodied in their manliness and thus accrued to them through their gender; and the comparative weakness of their capitalist adversaries, who by their divisions and conflicting strategies showed owners' power to be not forbidding and inevitable, but an array of contending alternatives subject to pressure and change.

Leadership conventions from the pietistic and craft origins of the community had contained strong voluntaristic and collective elements and had been broadly inclusive among men. From the earliest days of the town, working-class men had served as leaders in local churches and sporting leagues. They had dominated the community's renowned band and its fire department and regularly held municipal office. They were thus experienced with formal organizations, with running meetings, raising funds, and effecting change through institutional means, in ways that women, excluded from municipal and church office, were less likely to be. The craft tradition in woodworking, though hierarchical, gave men claims to authority based on their skill and the obligation to exercise judgment in the workplace. Union organizations with experience in the trade were available to offer organizing advice. The agricultural roots of many woodworkers remained strong, and the forming producers' co-operatives and the farm-based political movement consolidating locally in the 1920s provided ready alternative organizational support when the male factory workers of Hanover became disillusioned with the Brotherhood of Carpenters and Joiners after 1923.

Whereas in Paris Penmans' presence and Penmans' way of conducting its affairs seemed as fixed and enduring as the steep valley sides that hemmed in the town, in Hanover the employer side in labour-management negotiations was heterogeneous and changeable. By 1930 the dozen chair-making, upholstering, and case-goods concerns present in town at the turn of the century had dwindled to four. The original Knechtel family company ran a desk plant manufacturing office equipment, including filing cabinets and barristers' bookcases made under licence using mass production methods, and the main plant, where tables, chests of drawers, bedsteads, and cabinets were made in short runs for the medium-priced market. Knechtel Kabinet Kreations, founded by Daniel's Roman Catholic cousin Jerome, made mixed wood and metal kitchen furniture including the flat-to-the-wall 'hoosier' cabinets popular at the time. Peppler, the firm formed the year after Henry Peppler parted company with the Knechtels in 1911, was producing case goods for the high end of the market. Jared Spiesz continued to make chairs and modestly priced wares. Despite bosses' declamations to the contrary, skilled workers who were discontented or discharged moved readily between the firms, particularly between the Knechtel main plant and Peppler.[8] Male family members were dispersed among the firms, and a work action at one plant did not leave the whole work force without wages at one stroke. Jared Spiez was the hard-liner among local employers, willing to lock out his workers on the slimmest provocation and head out of town for vacations of indefinite length. Knechtel and Peppler were warier of losing their more skilled employees and of failing, because of strike actions, to meet delivery dates when contracts were scarce.

None of this is to say that the working men of Hanover held the upper hand in town during the 1930s, but by their gender and by the structure of the industry in which they were employed, they held a stronger hand against a weaker adversary during that decade than did the mill families of Paris. In retrospect they recalled the 1930s as 'the struggle time' when 'by striking every week' if they had to, they had consolidated their position with their employers into a regularized pattern of collective bargaining. They shaped a union structure in which they were represented at all levels, which they kept closely responsive to local needs, and by their organized presence proudly claimed their community as a 'union town.'

The 'struggle time' began formally in the fall of 1933. Sometime in August, as Thomas Reis, an early member of this first union of the 1930s remembers it, the men began to get together. 'Why we got so strong,' future leaders such as Clarence Helwig claimed, was that the union 'originated right in town here. We were working for 13 cents an hour. Anything was better than that. We stuck together just beautiful.' By September there was national press coverage of a strike among furniture workers in Stratford, organized by the Chesterfield and Furniture Workers' Industrial Union, affiliated with the Workers' Unity League. League organizers have been noted for the 'speed, secrecy and fervour' with which they 'signed up workers at Stratford's seven small furniture factories and took them out on strike.'[9] This is not the picture which emerges in Hanover. Again, as Thomas Reis recalls, 'We started to organize a union. These two guys were down in Stratford and some-body phoned down and asked them to come up, which they did. That time, some of the departments were working overtime at nights – to eight, half past eight, nine o'clock – and then we went to a certain hall and had a meeting.' Years later Fred Collins, the Toronto-based League organizer who came to speak at the hall the men had rented for the meeting, remained a hero among unionists in town. R.E. Hallman, the local union's recording secretary, writing to Norman Dowd of the All-Canadian Congress of Labour in 1940, noted, 'in our fight we had no one to help us financially, but we had a great fighter leading us in Fred Collins.'[10] In 1985 Alan Lang, a skilled cabinet-maker, remembered Collins, a Glaswegian former policeman in this way, 'He could talk. I don't know what accent it was, it wasn't English anyway. He was very friendly. He did his job.' Men working for Agnes Macphail, the UFO, and the CCF insisted that Collins and the industrial union had credentials where it counted. Of Isidore Minster, the other Workers' Unity League organizer regularly in town, Reis affirmed, 'We didn't choose the union as communist. All I'm saying is that he was a communist and he was a Jew and we didn't have anything against him. He stood a hundred per cent behind us.' Jacqueline Dowd Hall and her colleagues found that within southern U.S. textile communities outside organizers at this time are remembered as troubleshooters, rather than as instigators. The distinction is an important one, and apposite in Hanover as well. A later mayor of the town called Collins 'a misleading person, a rabble-rouser who wasn't necessary in a town like Hanover,' but the more common recollection is of a gifted man working in common cause with the local community.[11]

By 20 September Collins must have felt some urgency about respond-ing to his Hanover invitation. Unfinished radio cabinets were being loaded on trucks in Stratford bound for Knechtel.[12] The next night Collins and a group of men and women from Stratford addressed the several hundred Hanover residents crowded into Speers Hall. Seated in the front row so as to follow the speeches closely was Daniel Knechtel, hard of hearing in his ninety-first year, his cloth cap in his lap, his face intent with concentration. When Collins asked if anyone wanted to speak, Knechtel rose to outline 'the difficulties facing local manu-facturers' and doubt 'the wisdom of bringing in organizers from Stratford and Toronto to stir up trouble.' There were boos and hisses in the hall. When Collins insisted on Knechtel's right to a fair hearing, Knechtel finished his speech and remained to see 110 men come forward to join the union that night, shaking his head and muttering in discomfort. The next week more Stratford workers attended another meeting in Hanover, and several Hanover men went to Stratford to observe the strike for themselves. Elmore Philpott, a leader of the CCF, addressed the riding association at week end. He spoke in support of local unionists, decrying unfounded reports in the national press that Knechtel had been silenced by his workers, agreeing that the 'capitalist system was dying.' Although he warned them to be wary of 'agitators' and emphasized that strikes ought not to be men's first resort, he agreed, considering their predicament, that 'the only way to deal with some people was with a club.'[13]

The first president of the Furniture Workers' Industrial Union in Hanover was Sam Gateman, a sixty-year-old teamster at Knechtel. Gateman himself had not been hard hit by the depression. He rarely worked less than fifty hours weekly in 1933 and took home just under $800 in pay for the year. As a municipal councillor, the chairman of the town streets committee co-ordinating relief work on local improvements, and a long-time trustee of the local band, his presence marked the continuity of the industrial union with established workingmen's organizations in town and the continuing labour interest in community politics.[14] In 1934 Gateman was succeeded as president by William H. Fischer, a forty-one-year old Knechtel upholsterer. Fischer had been active in community organizations in the early 1920s, a member of the choir at the Evangelical Lutheran church, 'an ardent poultry fancier,' and secretary of the Hanover Poultry Associaton. He had worked at both Morlocks and Meades, the two factories in town manufacturing upholstered furniture, and had been a foreman in the latter firm until 1925. When he left with his young family in that year to establish himself in business as an upholsterer in Detroit, his departure was marked by formal presentations of gifts and declarations of best wishes. In the summer of 1932 Fischer, his wife, and two daughters were back in Hanover, four of ten persons sharing his father's house. For the first four months of 1933 he had almost no work at all; by year end he had earned a total of $541 at Knechtel.[15] His reputation in town was as 'a good worker and a family man.' In the union he was regarded as a good organizer: 'He was above-board and honest and his decisions weren't outrageous. He was fair with the firm as well as with the union.' F.R. Oliver, the local MLA, wrote on 3 August 1934 to Arthur Roebuck, attorney-general of the province, describing Fisher as 'a level-headed chap, certainly not the firebrand type,' a leader who, like Gateman, had broad credibility and deep roots in the community.[16]

On 1 August 1934 William Fischer was dismissed from Knechtel's employ. The firm had not recognized the union, but since the fall of 1933 an agreement, by which Knechtel managers promised not to cut wages or return to piece-work without prior notification, had been in place with a shop committee of union members, among them Peter Stalker and Serph Gingrich. On 16 July a letter over Fischer's signature was sent to all furniture workers in town, urging them to maintain their memberships and pay up their dues, 'that we may know where we stand for this autumn's event.' The union claimed that this allusion concerned an impending return to piece-rates. The company interpreted the passage as the threat of a strike at the height of the fall season, which would compromise Christmas orders already in place, and the firm's ability to compete for further contracts. They fired Fischer for threatening agitation which would compromise the prospects of the firm. As Thomas Reis remembers the day, 'When we got out at night, at four-thirty, five o'clock, he was standing outside and he said to us, "Boys, I'm fired." Some of us guys told him. "Don't worry, we'll look after you."' The next morning, and for two weeks thereafter, none of the 125 employees at the Knechtel main plant reported for work. As the local newspaper reported, 'it was a rather unusual strike, not caused by a demand for better pay or better hours, but simply as a protest against alleged discriminations.' F.R. Oliver described it as about 'organisation, the rights, nature and extent thereof.' Gordon Peck, a Peppler tenoner and president of the union in the late forties, described it as the beginning of the struggle for recognition, 'going on strike three times a week if we had to, showing them we meant business, that we wouldn't back down, that when we said something we were going to stand behind it.' Fred Collins addressed a meeting in Victoria Park, which the Toronto press described as 'attended largely by women and youths.' Once again, the editor of the *Post*, who had protested other newspaper stories that Dan Knechtel had been shouted down the September before, attempted to correct outside reports that cast the union in a bad light, insisting that 'this is, of course, quite contrary to the facts, as there was a large attendance and many workers were there, as well as a good attendance of women and others.' Agnes Macphail, the local MP, retained her close connections and sympathies with Hanover furniture workers even after differences between the UFO and the CCF led her to stand down from the provincial council of the CCF in March 1934. She visited the strikers in their committee rooms, 'urged them to stick together' and made 'a substantial contribution to the strike fund.' Fischer, in addition to being president of the union, was vice-president of her local riding association, now formally separated from the CCF and renamed the UFO-Labour Association. Under their auspices, Macphail planned to contest the riding of Grey-Bruce in the next federal election. Before officials from the Department of Labour had reached town, J.A. Patterson, a local conveyancer, had succeeded in arbitrating the dispute, securing Fischer's reinstatement and an agreement that there would be no strike before 1 January 1935, so long as there were no wage cuts nor a return to piece rates.[17]

The union was strengthened, rather than weakened, by the strike. Through the next winter their support in the community was consolidated. Their February carnival at the town rink was widely attended. The broom-ball game, featuring one side dressed as women and the other as men, was a particular hit, and at the end of the day the festivities had yielded a tidy profit.[18] The Furniture Workers' Industrial Union had strong and admired local leadership, had kept closely in touch with local priorities, and was attuned to the pace at which local men wished to make change. Collins and his colleagues from the Workers' Unity League remained respected among working people in the community.

In 1935 the Workers' Unity League was disbanded upon directions from the Comintern. The decision was impelled by an urgent need in Europe for a genuinely unified left in the struggle against fascism. In Canada members of industrial unions organized under the umbrella of the league, and their staff were urged to join affiliates of the Trades and Labor Congress and the All-Canadian Congress of Labour. Collins joined the United Brotherhood of Carpenters and Joiners (UBCJ), and by early 1936 the furniture workers of Hanover were reconstituted as local 1002 of the UBCJ. This alliance was approached with considerable trepidation. On the west coast woods workers, formerly affiliated with the Lumber and Sawmill Workers, whom the Carpenters were willing to allow only fraternal non-voting memberships in their union, struck out again on their own within the year. In Grey and Bruce, furniture workers from industrial unions, though granted full membership in the UBCJ, tarried but a little while longer in the company of mainstream wage-oriented unionists.[19]

The Carpenters had been long absent from the furniture towns of southwestern Ontario, but after the Furniture Workers' Industrial Union had established a presence in Stratford, Hanover, and several surrounding towns, the Carpenters' organizers again appeared. Marsh by this time had left the union to become deputy minister of the Ontario Department of Labour and was replaced by Andrew Cooper as general representative of the UBCJ. Martell had stayed on, now as chief executive board member. In 1934 and early 1935 Martell and Cooper were about in Chesley, a few miles north of Hanover, and in Kincardine on the nearby Lake Huron shore, collecting signatures and hoping to form locals. Even after he had joined the Department of Labour, Marsh on occasion went along to address Carpenters' meetings and consistently urged workers who wrote to him in his capacity as deputy minister to consider joining the Carpenters rather than the industrial unions.[20]

Hanover's history with the Carpenters was, of course, unhappy, and Martell and Marsh, by their presence, provided unpleasant reminders of the UBCJ confusions of speed-up with job satisfaction and their lack of support for locally initiated work actions. For quite different reasons, Cooper soon proved himself no ornament to the Carpenters' cause among Hanover working men.

Until the League disbanded, the men of Hanover saw no reason to reconsider their 1920s rejection of American Federation of Labor unionism. Collins's critique of the AFL, offered at a meeting during the Fischer strike of 1934, was for them no hypothetical abstraction, but a reasonable summary of their own experience a decade before. They agreed with Collins's claim 'that the American Federation of Labor allowed workers very little voice in the management of their own affairs.' They knew that they had been left high and dry when in the 1920s they had struck 'without consent from headquarters,' and that in 1934 they had closed the Knechtel plant first, notified League organizers after the fact, and still be able to count upon the League to support their local initiatives. Remembering how Martel and Marsh had insisted they accept productivity-enhancing engineering schemes implemented by management, Hanover woodworkers recognized themselves in Collins's 'history of the American Federation of Labor's continued betrayal of workers' interests.'[21]

While their differences with Marsh and Martell concerned men's rights, as men and craftworkers in the workplace Hanover unionists' views of Andrew Cooper distilled more explicitly to matters of sexual conduct, to the private morality required of men who represented themselves in the community as leaders or counsellors of other men. In the spring of 1935 as the move from the Furniture Workers' Industrial Union to the Brotherhood of Carpenters and Joiners was coming under discussion, men from Hanover went to Chesley to attend a Carpenters' meeting Cooper had convened. Chesley was a smaller centre than Hanover, and though the workers had the support of local clergy, the town was dominated by one employer, Krug Brothers. The Krugs were absolutely intolerant of labour representation. Garnering support in such a setting required deftness and discretion. As Thomas Reis remembers, 'We had a nice meeting up there, but the dog-gone fool was living with another woman in the hotel.' The day of the demonstration, after Cooper had spoken to the crowd, he was arrested in his hotel room with a woman not his wife and charged with false registration under section 14 of the Hotels Act. Reis was livid. 'He was two-faced and a dog-gone fool. We told him to get the hell out of town and never come back.' News of Cooper's conviction and $100 fine on this morality offence appeared at top centre on the front page of the Hanover *Post*, under the erroneous headline 'WUL organizer in court.' Local union men, left to mop up the damages done their collective reputation, were understandably apprehensive when the prospect of rejoining the Carpenters entailed having Cooper formally associated with the furniture workers' cause not only in Chesley, but also in their own town. During the months after the direction to disband the League, Hanover workers hesitated, forestalling leaving their industrial union for the Carpenters much longer than their fellow unionists in other furniture centres.[22]

Through 1935, usually with William Fischer in the chair, Agnes Macphail and Workers' Unity League organizers continued to share the platform at meetings of the local Farm-Labour Club. They also shared concerns about the unemployment insurance proposals being considered in the federal parliament, and hopes that some industry-wide wage scale, akin to the United States NRA codes, might stabilize conditions in the furniture industry. In September there was another strike at Knechtel, again provoked by a dismissal without just cause, again arbitrated by community leaders before Department of Labour officials reached town. By March 1936 the merger with the Brotherhood of Carpenters and Joiners was formally completed at a meeting held in Hanover and attended by furniture workers' representatives of both League and TLC unions from Stratford, Kitchener, Listowel, Kincardine, Chesley, Owen Sound, and Ingersoll. By this time an industry-wide wage scale for the province, excluding Toronto, was in place.[23]

On 18 April 1935 the Industrial Standards Act came into effect in Ontario. This legislation, which drew its inspiration primarily from the United States National Industrial Recovery Act of 1933 and collective labour agreement extension acts passed in 1934 in Quebec and for the cotton manufacturing industry in England, permitted representatives of employers and employees to petition for a conference chaired by an official of the Department of Labour at which a schedule of hours and wages, applicable to a defined portion of the province, would be formulated.[24] The Canadian Manufacturers' Association opposed the Act as an instrument that would abridge managerial rights,[25] but the Ontario Furniture Manufacturers, whose own plans to break the 'tyranny by the minority' of chisellers in their trade through price fixing had failed, were willing to accept codes if they would standardize labour costs in the sector. As James Ferguson, a former Knechtel manager, now with McLagan at Stratford and chairman of the manufacturers' legal committee told Arthur Roebuck, the minister of labour, in December 1934, 'The majority of the members of our industry are heartily in agreement with your plan, in fact from what you have said now you would almost think you had been listening in at our meetings.' Chastened by the failure of voluntarism in their group, furniture manufacturers pressed for a vigorous measure of compulsion once codes were in place in their industry. 'We have tried to do something in a voluntary way,' Ferguson reported, 'but it has always fallen to pieces because it is voluntary. Sometimes it works well but most of the time it does not, and we have passed through five years of times when it does not work.'[26] Early promises were for an act with considerable force. Both Roebuck as minister and Marsh as deputy-minister of labour had stated publicly that employers who failed to comply with the codes would be 'driven out of business.'[27] But neither Premier Mitchell Hepburn nor Roebuck's cabinet colleagues would tolerate so major a departure from the voluntaristic traditions governing labour relations in the province. As Bora Laskin later observed, the act as passed could not be effective 'unless there [were] employer and employee collectivities to provide the substratum of support needed,'[28] exactly the conditions wanting among the 'disorderly body of producers' in the furniture trade. While manufacturers generally were comforted by the weakened enforcement mechanisms in the final legislation, both employers and employees in the furniture industry, still hoping for 'strict supervision and penalties,' noted with regret that Roebuck and Marsh apparently had 'been talking off their own bat' and that Premier Hepburn appeared 'not very much in sympathy with any attempt at regulation of industry.' In Ontario codes were developed in only two manufacturing sectors, the two Harry Cassidy had highlighted, garment making and furniture.[29]

Implementation of the Industrial Standards Act got off to a slow start. Roebuck had resigned as minister of labour in October 1934 and his successor, David Croll, was in Europe during the summer of 1935. Questioned in Croll's absence about enforcement, A.W. Crawford, chairman of the Minimum Wage Board and charged with initiating prosecutions, replied 'All this is a question of viewpoint, whether you are a member of an [Industrial Standards Act] advisory board or of the permanent government staff. The trouble in brief is that we have no staff to carry on this work.' Soon the grounds for trouble expanded. Hostile 'to the encroachment of regulatory power on their traditional jurisdiction,' the courts construed the act narrowly and ruled that several schedules exceeded the powers specified in the legislation.[30]

The first furniture code, to govern the period 1 September 1935 to 1 July 1936, arose from conferences at which only Brotherhood of Carpenters and Joiners representatives were present on the employee side. J.S. Knechtel, Norman Peppler, and Jared Spiez from Hanover were among the employers, but no Hanover labour men, still unwilling to make common cause with the Carpenters, attended.[31] Larger manufacturers initially honoured the code,[32] but after nine months' experience they had all but given up on the act. They could not take comfort from Croll's March 1936 account before the legislature of the government's predisposition: 'We have felt that if we are to make the Act a success we must look to the contracting parties for a measure of co-operation in enforcement. We don't like sledge-hammer legislation. We don't like to enforce a social statute with a squad of policemen. If policemen are needed to insure observance by a majority of those in the industry concerned, then the Act is a failure and we can only scrap it and consider that its introduction was premature.'[33] In June 1936, bent under the weight of increasing American competition as a result of the lower tariff in place since 1 January, and also by the advantages non-compliance with the code had given renegades within their own ranks, the furniture manufacturers changed their position on the act, and endorsed Canadian Manufacturers' Association opposition to government intervention in industry. Representatives of forty-two firms whose output constituted more than 75 per cent of production in the industry informed Croll that it was now their belief 'that as there are too many free lance competitors or those having decided wage advantages, there should be less government interference with business,' more opportunities for all manufacturers to interpret the industry code according to their own lights.[34]

By a 'gentlemen's agreement' the first code was extended through July 1936, but from early August 1936 until March 1937 there was no code in the furniture industry. During this period workers in Hanover and Stratford reckoned they lost whatever gains they had made under the earlier agreement. Employers, citing rising Quebec competition and the declining tariff, were unwilling to grant rates as high as those specified in the previous code and insisted that the skill classifications, which low-waged firms had ignored, be replaced by a single minimum wage.[35] The Carpenters, now representing all furniture workers in the province, refused to consider either wage cuts or an end to classification. During six conferences spread over ten months, no progress was made. In mid-February of 1937 the employees' side declared that they had 'been toyed with long enough' and demanded that negotiations be concluded by 1 March.[36] No agreement having been reached, on 1 March 1,200 unionized workers, the employees of thirteen firms in ten southwestern Ontario communities, struck.

They were out for a week – in Hanover, 500 men, at a cost in lost wages of $1,300 a day. The *Post* reported 'orderliness and good spirit' on the lines, since 'there were no local grievances in Hanover, nor in any of the other towns where the men were on strike.' The grievances were against employers in non-unionized communities such as Chesley and Durham. The work action persuaded employer representatives to sign a new code, which specified both average minimum and hourly rates by skill, but these gains were pyrrhic. As a condition for employer agreement, there were still no effective enforcement mechanisms, or procedures for uniform classification by skill. In the end the Carpenters' strike against unionized employers probably profited most their real adversaries, the 'chisellers,' whose non-union factories continued in regular production throughout the dispute.[37]

There were four more strikes in Hanover during 1937, three against the town's 'chiseller,' Jared Spiesz. In the first of these, O.C. Jennette of the Department of Labour 'tried to impress upon Mr. Spiesz the childishness of his attitude,' in refusing to allow his employees to wear union buttons. During the second, a twenty-day lock-out in April with Spiesz absent on an 'extended tour of the south,' the most William Fischer, on behalf of the Carpenters, could secure was a frail non-discrimination clause and a six months' trial for an elected shop committee.[38] On 1 October Spiesz's seventy-five men were out on strike again; their employer left town on holiday again; this time the dispute concerned two men who had refused to join the union. After five weeks, the town council, conveyancer Paterson, and Department of Labour representatives prevailed upon the two nay-sayers to become members

of the union, and the men went back to work.[39] The Peppler strike in
April was more typical of those town unionists later associated with the
1930s, a three-and-a-half-day walk-out of ninety-two workers to get
higher wages for several older employees and more satisfactory skill
classifications for the rest. 'The code was alright, it was something to
work on,' Alan Lang remembered. 'It helped,' said Gordon Peck, a
tenoner who had left Knechtels for Pepplers and had participated in the
negotiations, but 'we still had to make a standard. The union had to
bring up a standard or else they [management] would never do it. Even
the government couldn't force them to do it ... We got nowheres until
we started to put our own force, to enforce our own standards.'[40]

The experience of 1937 had emphasized the reality of the Industrial
Standards Act, as a weak prescription which would gain force only by
concerted local action. The diversity of town employers' reactions to
union activity, revealed in particularly strong contrast during the
simultaneous April strikes at Peppler and Spiesz, reinforced town
woodworkers' conviction that they needed strong local control in the
formulation of strategy if they were to gain recognition for their shop
committees and effective employer acceptance of closed shops. If the
government was unwilling to intervene strongly to enforce workplace
standards, a union closely tied to the most senior officials in the
provincial Department of Labour was unlikely to be of much help. The
problem with the Carpenters, Clarence Helwig remembered, was that
their 'leaders sold us out. We moved right away from them. We got into
a union where we could have representatives from our own town.'

As a first step, the furniture workers of Hanover formed themselves
into a congress local of the All-Canadian Congress of Labour (ACCL)in
the autumn of 1938 as Local 3, National Union of Furniture Workers.
Aaron Mosher, president of the ACCL, agreed to appoint William Fischer
as a special organizer for the new union, at a monthly salary of $100 plus
expenses, subscribed jointly from local dues and congress funds. There
was one more strike in Hanover in the late 1930s, against Pepplers for
seven days in October 1938, which successfully forced a recalcitrant
finisher to renew his union membership.[41] By the spring of 1939 there
were National Union of Furniture Workers' locals in the four principal
northern woodworking centres of Hanover, Owen Sound, Listowel,
and Kincardine, with William Ford of Hanover, a Knechtel tenoner,
born in town in 1908 and in the firm's employ since 1923,[42] serving as
president. In November 1945 these congress locals formed the nucleus
of a new National Union of Furniture Workers and Allied Crafts, of

which Ford remained president, with sixteen locals throughout south-western and central Ontario and as far east as Montreal. By this time the ACCL, reconstituted as the Canadian Congress of Labour, included not only the railway unions, which had been the backbone of the national union movement in the inter-war years, but a number of CIO industrial unions, among them mine workers, electrical workers, and the International Woodworkers of America. Keeping furniture workers organized remained difficult in the presence of persistent employer discrimination against union members, but as Felix Eggiman of Owen Sound wrote to Pat Conroy of the CCL in 1944, 'the aim for which we in this district have been working, not only recently but for many years ... [is] to some day have not a Furniture Workers Union but a Woodworkers National Union.' In May 1947 this aim was accomplished. The National Union of Furniture Workers merged with the International Woodworkers of America (IWA), and the woodworkers of Hanover, after twenty-eight years' struggle inside and outside craft, industrial, and national unions, settled down to what they later called 'the steady time,' as Local 486 of the IWA. The IWA did not organize the furniture towns of Ontario, as has been lately affirmed; the furniture workers of the southwest came into the IWA in 1947, organized and by choice. [43]

The path thereafter was not strewn with roses. The furniture workers of Ontario had made common cause with a union deeply divided in British Columbia between CCF supporters and men more closely identified with the woodworkers' period as members of the Workers' Unity League, all the while being pressed by the International, through the instrument of the Taft-Hartley Act, to rout the communists from their midst. The view from Local 486 on these divisions is not plain. The members lately had refused a check-off in support of the CCF, but the reasons for this decision remain obscure. The clearest statement – and it is none too clear – on the communist question comes from R.E. Hallman, a highly skilled lathe and router operator and set-up man at Knechtel, born in Hanover in 1905 and from 1921 an employee of the firm, [44] who, since the 1938 breach with the Carpenters, had been recording secretary of succeeding Hanover locals. In June 1947, Hallman wrote, on IWA letterhead, to Mackenzie King concerning the proposed National Labour Code:

At this time we hear much about Communism ... We believe that more consideration should be given to the thoughts of men like Mr Cyrus Eaton ... when he said 'To avoid extinction, capitalists would have to change their attitude to and methods of dealing with labour.' We also believe that such bills as proposed by Hartley-Taft and Bill 29 in British Columbia should not be considered ...

Primarily our organization is a true labour organization and we cannot boast one Communist, but we realize that larger centres probably have. We believe that the proper way to curb this is by proper conditions within the country so that the wind will be taken from these people's sails.[45]

Perhaps Hallman was trying to chart a middle course where there was none to be found, but there is a continuity between this statement, his 1940 praise to Norman Dowd of the ACCL of Fred Collins's leadership , and the widely held view in the community that communist organizers should be judged by their acts, and by these they had been shown to be four-square behind the working man.

Moving to the IWA did not remove Hanover workers from harsh union disciplines imposed by the forming industrial relations system in their own province. In the summer of 1947 Local 486 struck for ten weeks against the three unionized local firms for a 10-cent increase, two weeks' vacation, and nine statutory holidays with pay. They were forced back to work at depleted resources by the end of the summer, to await an arbitrator's ruling which specified a 5-cent increase and six statutory holidays – the employers' offer before the strike began. The 5-cent outcome sounds familiar, recollecting the result of arbitration in Paris in 1949, but there are two differences of moment to be marked. The woodworkers of Hanover were being paid rates that amply exceeded those prevailing in textiles, and they had a union, recognized, certified, and maintaining a closed shop, through which they could safeguard the most vulnerable of their members, particularly older and disabled workers. They also had grievance procedures and the collective will to strike, if need be, to protect fellow employees from arbitrary discipline or dismissal.[46]

CONCLUSION

In what ways did sex and gender matter in the development of Hanover as a union town, in the patterns of 'the struggle time' and the transition to 'the steady time' in labour relations in the community? How did the maleness of the wage-earners in the furniture industry, and the particular ways in which they understood their own masculinity and defended prerogatives claimed as rights of men, influence their aims, their instruments, their modes of working together as union men? These are not questions to be weighed but to be woven, not to be calibrated in a scale of priority against class, community, ethnicity, and religious faith, but to be understood as part of a texture. They cannot be teased apart into separate analytical threads without causing the fabric of the social experience to disintegrate but must be analysed as a web of interdependence, densely felted into a single whole.

The way in which manliness mattered in Hanover begins with the relationship between wood and soil, in the upper Rhine, in Waterloo, and finally in Bruce and Grey, in the authority men shared as agricultural proprietors and craftsmen of recognized skill. In this authority they were distinguished by gender from women who did not share land title, whose proficiencies were private and unremarked. These ties among men created a fellowship of producers in the district which in the inter-war years emerged as a strong farm-labour political movement and supported the particular form that class-based action took in town, when the union men of Hanover parted company from mainstream unionism in 1921, 1933, and 1938.

That the furniture workers should have come formally together in an organization lodged in their common predicament as wage-earners and have made that organization function well, if not always successfully, to defend their common interests is also integrally a matter of gender. Their experience in church and voluntary organization and in municipal politics prepared them for making change through institutional means and established broad ties of loyalty and amicable interest across class lines in the town. There was no ambiguity, either among furniture workers themselves or in the community of which they were so completely a part, about their rights to be wage-earners. That as wage-earners they were also breadwinners, responsible as family men, took them some considerable away through gender across class, to a broad community consensus about their rights as wage-earners as well. That there were men in town who as capitalists behaved in childish ways, that as union men woodworkers condemned class allies who breached codes of manly respectability – both these realities forged solidarities in gender that brought the town together in their cause, proffering resources to mediate disputes, to name and condemn destructive behaviour on both sides of the class divide.

That there were unions to turn to, and then to choose among, is less an accident by trade, more a pattern by gender, formed in the uncontested right and necessity of men to labour for a wage, to arbitrate the quality of their work and defended their quality of life at work. That they were men together, with common obligations to kin, common standards of dignity and self-worth in their common gender, made their solidarity more resolute, the appeal to brotherhood more fitting and certain, and the obligations of and to those among them chosen to lead clearer and more compelling than would have been the case had all these understandings of their social existence been cast in two separate and distinct social experiences of manliness and womanliness in gender.

■ Conclusion

This book has been a long lingering amid the particularities of daily life in Paris and Hanover, listening to talk exchanged across kitchen tables, parsing payrolls and ledgers of plants now empty or gone. There have been only fleeting visits to the corridors of power as they are conventionally construed, only glimpses of the tall buildings and bright lights that are the totems of the modern world. European excursions have been closely scripted and confined. Perhaps by now you are feeling some of the restlessness of small-town youth, wondering whether Woolf might have been mistaken, whether it might not be 'that life exists more fully in what is commonly thought big than in what is commonly thought small.'

Times in these two small places were eventful enough; within these narrow precincts there were characters of some complexity; wise and worldly observers; rhetoricians with the power to stir. The present hoards of mundane paper are sufficiently ample to refeature the habits of the past. Perhaps then, it is not smallness per se that is the problem, but that Paris and Hanover are exiguous exceptions. There was much more complexity in the texture than might have been expected. Could there be other places more authentic and less anomalous than these, in particular places where the market ordered more of daily life and gender intruded less, where class and gender relations were more systematic and predictable, where meanings were more straightforward and settled?

Perhaps. It is true that statistically Paris appears to be an oddity, but Hanover, by the conventional demographers' measures, looks ordinary enough. If these are to be templates for a 'women's town' and a 'men's town' they meet at least the minimal criterion of being, by the end of the period considered here, quite different from one another.

By 1950 the woodworkers of Hanover were breadwinners. Through the authority they had asserted as craftsmen, the self-sufficiency they sustained through rural connections and handyman skills, and the confidence claimed through gender, they had established themselves as persons of account in their town. Their representatives were present to articulate their interest in municipal politics. Their assent was required if a community consensus was to be formed. Their union hall was conspicuous on main street, a busy hub of social, service, and organizing activity. Their children graduated from the local high school and carried off their share of prizes on commencement day.

In Paris the standing of textile workers was more compromised. Mill families had come to town and stayed because there were jobs for women and young people at Penmans when there were not jobs for them elsewhere. They had adapted the forms of their households and forged networks of exchange among neighbours and kin to accommodate lifelong female wage work. Within the mill community these shared obligations, celebrations, and lore secured a sense of competence and self-esteem. But the inappropriateness, the anomaly, and ambiguity of their circumstances was, in certain ways, impossible to escape. Even in the town where they had lived for decades, where their pay packets were the mainstay of municipal commerce, there were many who believed that it was haplessness or moral failing which had brought mill families to their peculiar predicament. Their clubbing together to get by, their reliance upon the wages of mothers and daughters in the absence of a well-paid and regularly employed male breadwinner, were read by their fellow citizens as signs of improvidence or imprudence rather than of ingenuity, practicality, and thrift. Neither functionally nor ideologically were they fully citizens of the town. They were more considered than consulted in the public affairs of the municipality. Their children rarely finished high school and Penmans graduation awards were carried off by young men and women from other parts of the community and the countryside nearby.

Focusing upon the differences between the two towns initially is clarifying. But the interpretive promise of this research lies elsewhere, in attending to the internal diversity so starkly apparent within each setting. Hanover and Paris existed in different relations to mainstream ideologies concerning gender, class, and ethnicity, but in neither place were the social practices of workplace and intimate life unitary or stable in either time or space. The referents by which class, gender, and ethnic identities were understood, and solidarities in ethnicity, gender and class were formed, were changeable and often interchanged. The processes by which these meanings were made and the institutions through which they were articulated were neither singular nor settled. The mainstream ideological categories of that time were present, but as taut threads shot through the ordinariness of daily life, frequently distinguishable from the pattern itself. On the other hand, the categories of social theory from our own time often seem presumptive, caught in a logical artifice of their own, as cables strung over the texture sorting but also shadowing its intricacy. The advantages of presuming less about the connectedness and disconnectedness of ideology and social practice, about the constituting elements and processes of gender, class, and ethnicity and the relationship of these identities to the exercise of power, seem to be the most compelling opportunities arising from research such as this. Putting questions that tolerate specificity and diversity as answers is not to deny the existence of hierarchy or politics. It is rather a way to begin to craft explanations that more fully comprehend both the access to power and the grounds upon which this access, successfully and unsuccessfully, has been challenged. Let us consider some examples from the cases at hand.

Emigration is generally considered as a gendered process, beginning for men with a solitary experiment in distant lands, for women with a long interlude between two worlds waiting for word that it is safe to follow. For men the journey has seemed a response to international differentials in the labour market, for women a way to begin or to consolidate a married life. Emigration usually is seen to cast men in active and women in adaptive roles, men being part of a structured system, women living out the consequences of a subjective choice.[1]

Yet single female emigrants, such as those who travelled from the east midlands to Paris, have not been uncommon historically. And most working-class women understood that marriage, either before or after emigration, would not end their experience with waged work. Thus female emigrants have had their eye on the job market, both short and long term. In Canada even young women recruited for their domestic skills often remained for many years in the labour force before marriage. In the twentieth century the Penmans migrants were not alone in undertaking emigration as a flight from marriage rather than a strategy to pursue it, a way either to evade or to escape conjugality.[2]

As emigration is a sex-selective process experienced differently by women and men, so too is it part of a wider social existence in which gender is perceptible only as it is confounded by time, class, and place. Emigration can be the product of sex imbalances; it also forms them, both in the old country and in the new.[3] As large emigrant flows alter the economies at both source and destination, they also change the demography and create communities, of which Paris was only one, in which same-sex bonds are especially important. Sometimes this heightened homosociability is an unintended and unwanted consequence of the move. In other instances it may be an integral part of the decision to emigrate for both the emigrants and the non-emigrating kin.[4] For the mill families of Paris emigration offered a release from domestic tensions as well as an escape from economic deprivation. For these skilled, wage-earning women, anomalies in both the factory and the family circle, the recruiter who promised a 'Golden Land'[5] in Canada suggested new lives in more than a material sense.

Gender is an ever present connection in both economic and social existence. When few women generally were members of the waged labour force, when fewer still went out to work in factories, and almost none continued in waged work after she was a wife, owners and managers in the textile industry could not proceed about their business without taking mainstream gender ideology into account. In sectors employing men, gender relations also were part of the lobbying over priorities in the national political economy and deeply were embedded in politics of labour relations. But in textiles generally, and in the particular case of the Penmans Paris mills considered here, the gender of the work force presented both obstacles and opportunities which managers resolved by representing a broad range of their actions though a particular imagery, the patriarchal imagery of protection.

The factory paternalism common in the early years of the industry, the welfare capitalism practised by many textile firms through the first half of the twentieth century, and the national tariff which has been the mainstay of the sector from the start, different as they were in context and compass, shared this common protecting imagery. As the nation ensured the life of the industry through the tariff, textile employers influenced the lives and livelihoods of their workers through paternalist and welfare capitalist management schemes.

The gender of their work force placed textile manufacturers in an anomalous and weakened position in bidding for prized tariff protection. While the argument for a national interest in the creation of manufacturing jobs for male breadwinners was favourably received, at least in urban central Canada, the social benefits accruing from the protection of jobs that supported female-headed households, or households where adults and adolescents contributed jointly to the family income, were more difficult to defend in any part of the nation. Indeed, the contrary proposition, that a policy that encouraged female factory employment fostered a social evil, was more consistent with contemporary ideology concerning women's domestic roles.

If the atypicality, the apprehended pathology, of female factory work complicated and compromised the position of textile manufacturers in the policy debate concerning tariff protection, those same gendered ascriptions strengthened their hand when dealing with the women they employed. The manly responsibility, grounded in patriarchal relations, to safeguard womanly virtue gave a dutiful face to the class-based imperative of male managers to discipline and control female workers. And because opportunities for dependable, lifelong female employment were unaccustomed and uncommon, women felt especially constrained in their relations with the firms that offered them work to see their jobs as gifts and as individual accommodations. The advantage to Penmans and other mill owners of employing women, which obtruded so inconveniently into discussions concerning the tariff and seemed to set the textile interest against the national interest, paled for women workers in mill communities, who preferred the social burden of being unconventional to the economic calamity of being unemployed.

There were customary exclusions in the discourse of protection. Given the prevailing power imbalance between the parties, it was accepted as fitting that the needs of the protected and the duties of the protector be made explicit, formally and publicly stated. The needs of the protector and the duties of the protected were no less integral, no less essential to the functioning of the relationship, but they usually remained implicit and unstated, because of their customary silence made more notable when they were given voice. Seeking out those unspoken duties, of the manufacturer's accepting protection from the state, of the worker schooled to think of her job as a gift, makes the politics of the protecting relationship clearer, the ways in which needs are muted or amplifed by access to power more apparent. The textile tariff was such a bargain, a balance between shelter and responsibility, which the federal Liberal party, in both the 1880s and the 1930s, found it politic to reappraise in plain and public view. During each of the three Penmans strikes, and by the many more individuated acts of resistance which occurred during the years between 1907 and 1949, mill workers acted out another reappraisal, underscoring the ways in which the managers of the firm were dependent upon the skills of those they claimed to favour by their offer of regular work.

In studies of the sexual division of labour, it is contemporary theory that has cloaked the shifting mutuality and antipathy of gender relations and the relations of production. Sexual division has been an obvious and enduring characteristic of workplaces. Gender roles, household forms, and community welfare have been made and remade by changing access to paid work. But while the theoretical literature on gender segregation in the labour force is rich, economists and feminist theorists have been interested in sexual divisions as general features of the economic or sex/gender system rather than as boundaries between tasks forged in defined contexts by particular clashes of interest. Whether in specifying the social groups that benefited by gender division, the systematic relationships that generated the boundaries, or the traits upon which lines of partition were drawn, most analysts have dealt with gender division as a characteristic of the work force as a whole.[6]

While sexual segregation is a long-standing pattern in aggregate labour force statistics, at the disaggregated level where women and men have looked for and tried to hold onto jobs, the picture is rather different. Sexual division in the labour force is the sum of the sex labelling of specific tasks. As the comparison of knitters in Ontario and the east midlands makes clear, the same jobs have been assigned to different genders at different times in the same place and in different places at the same time.

What is germane to the analysis of domestic, workplace, and town politics, is both the particular local array of entitlement by gender to specific jobs with known rewards and detriments and the changes in these entitlements. In contrast with sexual segmentation as a character-istic of the economy as a whole, the processes by which jobs have been assigned by gender have not been much studied.[7]

There is an important opportunity here. As the comparative case study of knitters suggests, the interactions between class and gender emerge most clearly in contests over the sex labels of jobs. In studies of entitlement to particular jobs the processes that theorists have isolated are forced to keep the same awkward company they do in real life. By looking at the ways gender and class merge and refract to create a diversity of contending interests and influences, we may solve the riddle of why 'a job that is clearly and exclusively women's work in one factory, town or region may be just as exclusively men's work in another factory, town or region.'[8] Perhaps, in the bargain, we shall see the social power to dominate and exclude full face, emerging from behind the conceptual masks our categorical theories have imposed.

Of course the influence of the sex labelling of jobs on the shop floor does not stop at the factory gate or remain settled in its implications over time. In many Canadian resource towns, mining, forestry, and pulp and paper companies have established a work force by recruiting families and large numbers of single men to isolated locations. As these towns have matured and single men have married, the surplus of women who might wish waged employment has often become acute.[9] In Paris this same pattern developed, but its gender configuration was reversed.

The social implications of the prevailing twentieth-century pattern privileging men in the work force are familiar: the struggle for a male breadwinner wage, the reinforcement of social patterns that cast women as consumers rather than as producers in the market economy, and the persistent poverty of female-headed households. When women workers constituted the stable majority of the labour force, skilled, crucially situated in the production process, difficult to recruit and to replace, and jobs for men were in short supply, the social implications of industrial work have been different.

In Paris men took on the characteristics of dispensability and irregularity in employment that dual labour market theorists have commonly associated with the secondary sector and with women.[10] Those who stayed on in irregular work, who commuted to jobs elsewhere, or who were among the male minority with secure local employment, were members of households where the family income was collectively amassed, not won by a male breadwinner. Similarly, in these households, domestic labour was derived from several sources rather than delegated to a single homemaker. These circumstances evoked some changes in thinking about women's and men's roles and in the practice of domestic gender divisions, but the influence of patriarchal ideology continued to cast women as the primary custodians of kin. In Paris, mill families coped by generally accepting mainstream prescriptions about what was manly and womanly work within the home. To accommodate lifelong female wage work they rather remade the boundary between the household and the market by purchasing goods and services conventionally created within the home. They also reconstrued the borders of the household itself, clubbing together as female kin, sharing houseroom, trading domestic labour, and determining by their own logic of mutual advantage who ought to go to the mill and who might better stay at home.

The organizing drive of the post-war years was an unsuccessful attempt to move beyond these private adaptations and communal accommodations and through the public remedies offered by formal union institutions to change the relationship of mill workers with their employer. This initiative put accustomed social relations in town fundamentally in question. The strike that followed in early 1949 cast townspeople in roles they had never rehearsed and never intended to play. The words *mother*, *sister*, *friend* and *neighbour*, *boss* and *foreman*, *constable* and *court* were emptied of their conventional meanings, found to entail obligations, demand behaviours, and convey values not previously acknowledged or understood. The strike is remembered as a time when the whole town was transformed into an alien territory, where all events were like those on a stage, grotesque, harshly shadowed, played towards extremes. Those remembering are accepting of a dissonant undercurrent in their narrative; they tell their story as if they had lived their lives out of bounds in those months, and yet as if an implacable force had informed and ordained their every act. They pause longest to consider the roles of woman and neighbour; in identities drawn from gender and community the strike magnified difference and played upon the conflicting possibilities of release and restraint.

In many settings, womanly militance might seem an oxymoron, and labour activism among small-town women an impossibility. But the history and traditions of Paris were rich in the resources from which effective collective action might be crafted. For many in the community waged work in the mill was accepted as the sustaining continuity in an adult woman's life. Long-standing kin and neighbourhood networks extended the collectivity of interested parties to any workplace dispute far beyond the limited numbers on the Penmans payroll. The paternalistic practices for which the firm was renowned, the company-owned housing, the recreational association, the annual lakeside outings, the discretionary pension plan, all elaborated beyond the wage relationship the common interests Penmans employees shared. But these collective sensibilities were the stuff from which both dogged loyalty and determined opposition were made.

The strike also prompted an invasion – of senior executives, labour organizers, representatives of national manufacturers associations and trade union federations who came to manage the dispute; of state apparatus crafted beyond the local level, police, judges and lawyers who arrived to contain and ajudicate; of journalists and photographers who descended in moments of most acute conflict to interpret and display the event in ways their distant audiences had come to expect. In Paris, this commanding, externalizing attention was disorienting, intimidating, and prone to call into question local confidence in local ways. The dispute became an unequal dialogue between mill families and the mainstream culture, compromising the local resources from which change might have been made, without offering an alternative which was comprehensible in town.

Women hosiery workers came to Paris drawn by Penmans' advertisments and recruiters, but also by the glimpse of a social possibility, hoping the promise of lifelong female wage work might sustain the unconventionality that by predilection and happenstance had become their lot. The woodworkers of Hanover came into the valley of the Saugeen seeking a place to live a manly convention, illusory in practice but long honoured in tradition. The central ambiguity of social life in Paris was about gender, most starkly arrayed in the disparity between who actually earned wages in town and mainstream understandings about womanly work. In Hanover as factory industry grew, the awkward alliance, which had by turns both nurtured and disabled wage-earning men, was between the workshop and the soil, between land work and craft work. It was not the gender of the agricultural proprietor or the artisan working in wood that was unresolved. Both were masculine from time out of mind, cast beyond time in the pietistic and anabaptist communities from which they had come by the example of the carpenter of Nazareth. The question was how landwork and craftwork, potentially both mutually sustaining and mutually destructive, would settle together in the same social space, how the farmer without markets and the artisan without land would appraise one another as they stood eye to eye on a village corner.

The town flourished, its prosperity nourished by the near stands of fine timber and the skilled mechanics, carpenters, and finishers drawn to Hanover as a German-speaking community. When gender identity became problematical in town, as it did during First World War, it was not with occupation that the masculinity of the men in town rested uneasily, but with German origins and anabaptist beliefs. Ethnicity and religious faith were ambiguous and subject to conflicting readings – a man could be too mighty a warrior, or too Christlike a believer. The declaration of war against Germany in 1914 placed the loyalty of the town in question, set the authority men drew from their faith and their craft against the external mainstream demands that manliness be proved by military service. The test of gender against German-ness was arduous, but one around which the community made a separate, saving peace, which had salutory economic effects for the local employers and the municipality, anchoring many craftsmen ever more firmly in town.

In the years after 1918 the grounds upon which to claim manliness were shifting in Hanover. Unlike the locally distinctive crisis of the war, the dilemmas of 1919 and the 1920s in town were probably shared in many industrial communities large and small. Frequently, at least since occupations have been called choices and accomplishments rather than estates, it is work that has made the man, and it is in relationships in the workplace and the qualities of working life that masculine identities have been located. This manliness made by work has not been unitary or fixed but cross-cut into contending and complementary possibilities by class and age, fashion and belief, and the changing priorities of production and reproduction.

While the wartime crisis drew the men of Hanover together, the struggles of the succeeding decade set them apart and against one another. The founder of the leading firm in town passed control of the enterprise to his son, who bent, faltered, and called in industrial engineers, finding his father's mantle too heavy and unsuited to him or his times. The town's craftsmen lost a part of themselves when the old man's ways were set aside and sought new means to defend their worth as men. The union to which they turned would not help them on their own terms and attempted to persuade them to see themselves in different ways. The class lines in the community were not redrawn, but the bases upon which the owners justified their actions as leaders of men were transformed. At the same time both the criteria by which manly work was to be judged and the qualities in workplace relations against which men tested their masculine identities changed.

Like Topsy, it seemed that the nineteenth-century industries of Hanover had just 'growed,' nourished by the rich stands of timber nearby and the skills and ambition of men who had not found a place in the less ample surrounding agricultural lands. The cabinet-makers' and chair-makers' workshops and the small local flannel mill, built with capital subscribed by farmers with fleece to sell, made products for the community from materials country neighbours brought to town. That the woodworkers' shops grew to substantial factories and the flannel mill failed was, of course, a matter not of local endowments but of a national bargain which made Canadian furniture a protected good and

Canadian wool an imperial pawn to placate a wool-producing Mother Country. Until 1900, however, none of this growing, and not growing, was considered much within the municipal competence. Prosperity came to town, it seemed, either as a gift from providence or as a favour conferred in a political economy governed from away.

The fire that levelled the Knechtel main factory just before Christmas in 1900 forced the citizens of Hanover to rethink the question of how a community's fortunes were made. The tradition of municipal incentives to attract industrial employers was by this time long established in other central Canadian centres. With the plant went its payroll; the cooling ashes gave the power imbalance among men and women in town an acrid physical presence. The owners of the plant realized they were at liberty to rebuild elsewhere and found they could command large favours should they deign to do so. The community generally was left to contemplate the bleak dimensions of its dependence. Men who had been employed at Knechtel would have to seek other work, competing down wages in town. No one would reward them handsomely to abandon their Hanover property. Retired farmers who had subscribed the town's bond issues considered the frailty of the paper assets they had traded for their land. Men together discovered themselves men apart. After a torchlight parade, led by the town band and enlivened by the antics of small boys, Hanover ratepayers voted to pay the most privileged men in their community not to exploit the advantage the fire had given them over all those others with whom they only lately had seemed to share the same social space.[11]

This debate over bonusing explored the hierarchy of privilege within the community as a matter between men. The divisions that emerged were in the capital market and the labour market, territory which in turn-of-the-century Hanover was men's terrain. The only females who figured in the debate were poor women and widows, by happenstance tied to the market through the paying boarders they would lose should the plant not be rebuilt. The power the possession of capital bequeathed had been made palpable by the fire and made recognizable the hierarchy of class interest in town.

Yet in time the same policy instrument, municipal bonusing, was used to create women's, or more strictly speaking, girls' wage jobs in town. In this case, municipal intervention was not invoked to mediate diverging class interests, but to regulate sexuality, conservatively to manage the transition of daughters into wives. Waged work in town promised girls some money of their own, and parents some measure of supervision over their daughters' early experience with sexuality and their choice of spouse. For the town the initiative was akin to frugal housewifery, a way to use more intensively resources already to hand within the community.

The divisions of labour within the mills of Paris revealed most about the ways in which the contention and mutuality among class and gender interests fashioned biddable and contingent sex labels for jobs. Close study of shop-floor conventions and workplace satisfactions in Hanover makes a quite different point about gender identity and wage labour. Within a single nominal gender, a diversity of understandings can exist about what being of that gender appropriately means. At Knechtel, within the four storeys of one factory, boys learned to be men through quite distinct processes. To become masters of their work, they were called upon to acquire different interpersonal skills. In the machine room boys advanced through clientage and deference; in the cabinet shop by autonomous deliberating observation. Some work made its practitioner manly by its danger, its demands upon physical strength and mechanical facility. Other tasks were manly for the aesthetic sensibility, the deft hand skill, and the patient economy of effort they required. There was no doubt in town that wage work was both men's to do and part of the measure of a man's worth. The ideological consensus was complete: females could not excel in the manly domain of woodworking. Still there was no unanimity in the qualities, habits, and accomplishments by which manliness was marked. As a matter of both practice and claim, manliness was not one. Masculinity, as it was recognized and experienced in wage work, was not a unity but a severalty in its social existence.

In the early 1920s American Federation of Labor representatives failed to convince Hanover furniture workers to think of their jobs in an instrumental fashion, sacrificing control for pace and quality for higher wages and trading off the intrinsic meanings and values to be found in the work for cash. Local men rejected the notion that the worth of their factory work could be distilled to the wage. Neither did they rely upon factory work alone to meet the material needs of the households they headed. As waged work grew more scarce and undependable in the hard years of 1921–3, the local labour organizations made common cause with area farmers, founding a co-operative store, gaining rights to local woodlots where they could cut cordwood for fuel. Both their resistance to the idea that the value of a woodworker's job was extrinsic and their collective response to lean times, turning their local union organization to creating non-waged ways of securing a livelihood, are clear signs that the city-based AFL organizers too narrowly construed what work was and meant to these men. Marsh, Martel, and the other men from the United Brotherhood of Carpenters and Joiners were not alone in their views.

Much twentieth-century class analysis, and the socialist feminist elaboration of class analysis to include domestic labour, rests on assumptions closer to those espoused by Marsh and Martel than to those lived by working people. In this case, the union organizers left town irritatedly labelling their Hanover members backward, too attached to outmoded craft and agricultural values to understand the reality of their work lives in the modern world, deluded 'farmers' hiding in a backwater town from the realities of their place in the capitalist system. Subsequent social theory, framed to see men's relationships to their work through their identities either in gender or in class, would tend towards a similar result, casting such men outside the analysis, either as local anomalies or as quaint vestiges of an unresolved pre-industrial past. But it is worth considering whether the inadequacies are in the workers or in the theories of work, whether the 'narrowness' of conception may be in the observers rather than the observed.

About the same time as the furniture workers of Hanover were rejecting the concept of the breadwinner wage, the British feminist Eleanor Rathbone wrote a powerful critique of the same concept. Only poverty and misery could result, she argued, from a system with tied 'families of all sizes and stages of development to the the Procrustean bed' of a single adult male wage. Retrospectively it is clear that men could not, and did not, support their families on the proceeds of a single, waged job. Peter Stearns has called the male breadwinner concept a 'half-fiction.' Michele Barrett and Mary McIntosh have called it a myth. They are surely right that the concept does not serve 'as an accurate description of the means by which the working class has been supported and reproduced.' It is not only, as Patrice Grevet has noted, that 'the needs of wage-earner's dependants are unrecognized and unrecognizable' in this part of the fable about the capitalist wage system. The predicament of the family man also is camouflaged in the fiction. If we are to understand the domain in which the men called breadwinners lived, we must historicize male power, not only in waged work but, as men carried their identifications as single fellows and family men, in a more holistic way than we have heretofore, attempting to understand what manliness entails, including how it comes to be weakened, and how, with whose help and why it comes to be reasserted. 'Like the women,' Margaret Stacey reminds us, 'men win some and lose some. We need to know more about what they are up to and how they do it' – up to and also its converse, up against.[12]

Contemporary theories of work insist that as, by a 'great transformation,' productive activity became concentrated in industrial workplaces, the generalized and customary patterns of work and exchange in household and communal production also were remade to complement and mirror the industrial mode, that there was one, single, dominating mode of production. If this assumption holds true, it would be only sensible and appropriate to think of all productive activity in categories derived from the market economy and to conceptualize all work in terms of its relationship to the market. Yet as recent detailed cross-cultural research has shown, the nature and location of production and exchange continues to move, both away from and towards the money economy as the characteristics of those engaged in work and the technology of production change. The Hanover experience of the inter-war period and after suggests a similar pattern, cross-currents of movement among household-, community-, and factory-based work rather than one great linear transformation towards industrial production.[13]

If neither breadwinners nor domestic workers were ever so thoroughly or continuously and completely proletarianized as existing theories of work assume; if they were never known, never exercised authority only through their connection to the market economy; taking the history of class relations as the key against which the history of all work relations and identities are understood and theorizing 'exchange and labour *in the money economy* ... in advance of all other kinds of exchange and labour' only amplifies this distortion throughout the whole world of work. It seems far better, as R.W. Connell suggests, to try to think of social production as a totality, placing waged work from the start 'in the full context of the housework, child-rearing, education, household maintenance, building and gardening and informal neighbourhood exchange of services ... that in fact make up the greater part of *total social labour* even in advanced capitalist societies.'[14]

Even working men who were thoroughly proletarianized were never only proletarians but were men, husbands, fathers, and sons, not in auxiliary but in integral aspects of their being. We are burdened in trying to understand what work means within a way of life by a history of analytical dualisms – capitalist and non-capitalist production, waged and non-waged labour, public and private life, masculine and feminine roles – which line up in orderly opposition as two sides waiting for the beginning of a cavalry charge. The language sets class and gender relations apart; the theory acknowledges that they interact; but we have so long thought of them as separate, bound by their distinctive capitalist and patriarchal codes and allegiances, that it is difficult even to find words to say that they have one life, that they do not interact (whether in a hostile or harmonious fashion) thus to exercise some external influence upon one another, that they are not autonomous, obeying fastidious diplomatic protocols – but rather that they are one, each utterly unable to distinguish the internal politics of one from the other, perfectly willing to meddle in their most intimate affairs and as insiders admirably situated to do so with greatest force and utmost discretion.[15]

Work is a word that, so long as it is unmodified, still travels freely across the conceptual frontiers dividing domestic from market relations, capitalist from patriarchal domains. Thus reflecting upon what we mean by work and what it means to work may be a way to see past the partitions in our analytical apparatus to the living space beyond. This is not, of course, an untried project. Reclaiming the wholeness of the world of work was a central goal in the domestic labour debate.[16] The problem is that even recent studies focused on work 'hidden in the household' have been couched in terms derived from the analysis of capitalist relations, thereby definitionally filtering the phenomena in view of those aspects that do not appear functional in capitalist production. The unity forged in the world of work is thus located in its relation to and service of a historically specific model of labour in an advanced capitalist state. The incongruities, the inefficiencies, the lunatic incompatibilities between a system crafted only to birth, rear, and sustain industrial workers and the actual workings of many conjugal households led by family men in industrial societies – these are marginalized, so that it seems almost creditable to claim that 'if the basis for the present family household form had not existed when capitalism emerged, it would have had to be invented.'[17] We thus 'overlook the intermediate forms of enterprise where women [are] so often located,' and present '"production" as what the family *used* to do in its glorious past – but now does no more,'[18] at best by conceptual inadvertance dismissing as vestiges social forms that are both vital and enduring.

There can be no doubt that families are part of an hierarchical social system. Analysing them primarily in terms of their relation to capital often has led logically enough to the assumption that what is good for the male breadwinner/wage-earner, that his success in industrial struggles, is of benefit to the family as a whole. This is certainly the point Marsh and Martel made as they organized among the furniture workers of Hanover. Jane Humphries, in particular, has made the same argument in a scholarly way.[19] Yet something vitally important is being lost by concluding that the family is one, and that one is the male breadwinner. There is clearly something more to the family man than the imagery of economic man can comprehend, something more complicated governing his relations with the others in his household, both female and male, than his relation to the market alone can explain.

Similarly, union practices and the effectiveness of union organizations relied upon connections and understandings framed beyond the point of production. Small southern Ontario communities have not been commonly regarded as union strongholds. Owners and managers of city manufacturing concerns, counting upon the greater individualism and inexperience with industrial work of small-town residents, fortified in these beliefs by municipal Boards of Trade, have located in communities at a distance from large urban centres to escape the demands of organized labour. 'Run-away' shops – in the 1930s garment-making and food-processing firms, more recently tire and automobile manufacturers – have run away to small towns. Labour organizers have embarked upon union drives among manufacturing employees in small centres infrequently and warily, seeing smallness as insufficiency rather than opportunity, sceptical or uninformed about the resources with which collective action could be crafted in such communities. Paris conformed to these expectations inferred from scale. Hanover did not.

After an interlude in the late 1920s, Hanover was once again a union town by the fall of 1933, and it remained so, resiliently, for the next fifty years. Not only were the woodworkers of Hanover union minded. They espoused a philosophy of collective action that was broadly political rather than narrowly wage oriented in its goals. They described themselves as organizing rather than being organized, and as choosing with whom to ally among the national and international unions representing woodworkers, giving as well as receiving leadership on both the provincial and the national labour scene.

The sense in which the union men of Hanover were political is problematic. The histories of the labour movement in Ontario in the 1930s and 1940s generally have been written from the top down and have given great moment to the struggles between communists and social democrats for control.[20] While there is no denying the force and clarity with which the lines were drawn between supporters of the Canadian Communist party and the Co-operative Commonwealth Federation in international unions and the national umbrella organizations (the Trades and Labor Congress and the All-Canadian Congress of Labour) with which they were allied, it is not clear, at least in Hanover, that distinctions among socialists were parsed so finely at the local level. Admiration for the communist organizers who had worked in town remained deep in the community decades after the Workers' Unity League had been disbanded. Local men worked closely with men from the League at the same time as they were serving on the executive of the UFO-CCF riding association which repeatedly sent Agnes Macphail to represent the district in the federal and provincial houses. What they demanded from organizers who arrived from outside and from local men who took on salaried positions as organizers representing national union bodies was a close attention to the local roots of class-based militance, to the local concerns which, because they transcended distinctions between waged and non-waged work and between workplace and family concerns, gave collective action in the community deeper meaning than class solidarity alone and gave it a broader constituency, a power that was both compelling and enduring because it came closer to politicizing the fullness of everyday life.

The moral of these stories is not that gender was made in the history of women's industrial employment and that class conditioned the industrial history of men. Men, like women, were gendered subjects. Both women and men were formed and constrained in class relations. Never did class and gender, either singly or in conjunction, map the whole of social existence; both personally and collectively, understandings and obligations were also framed in religious faith, ethnicity, and nationality. None of these roles was assumed sequentially. A man was not by day a worker and by night a man, Saturdays a husband and Sundays a Baptist. Women who were mothers were mothers at the mill and at home, at the laundry line, and on the picket line. The market appraisal of their skills influenced their working conditions, and their emigration decisions, and their sexual experience. The simultaneity of these ways of being was inescapable, and from this simultaneity followed heterogeneity. Neither manliness, nor womanliness, worker nor boss, native nor newcomer was a unitary condition; each comprehended diverse possibilities and practices. Sometimes within the tight grip of a triumphant ideological prescription, sometimes out of hand and incidentally free from its grasp, both power and oppression were framed in this unsettled and unsettling contention, always more, often very different, in the whole than they might appear to be by parts.

■ Note on method

In 1981 I began surveying southern Ontario in search of industrial towns of roughly similar size and duration of manufacturing activity whose labour forces differed substantially by sex. Among many comparable groups considered, Paris and Hanover were chosen because each could be documented through (1) a weekly newspaper, (2) a relatively complete set of business records for the town's principal employer, (3) municipal assessment rolls that included reasonably detailed householder data, (4) a trade journal for the town's major industry, and (5) sufficient federal and provincial government paper to track the process of state interventions relevant to the health of the local economy. Among the materials I had decided were prerequisites for the study the most difficult to locate proved to be business records that included name-specific employee data either in the form of payrolls or personnel files, complete board of directors' minute books, regular appraisal reports on plant equipment, and good financing and costing accounts and industrial relations files. Penmans and Knechtel records were accessible, substantially intact, and complete in the plants. Knechtel went bankrupt in 1983, and after a fire that put their records at risk, the documents from their vault were donated to the Queen's University Archives. A smaller collection of catalogues and photographs remains at the Hanover Public Library. When Penmans closed their last Paris plant in 1985, their historical collection was moved to the firm's new building in Cambridge, Ontario. The Penmans records previously donated to the Paris Historical Society, including the assisted passage ledgers for the British emigrants, remain with the society.

Between the spring of 1982 and fall 1985 I lived for approximately eight months each in Paris and Hanover. After experimenting with boarding, I took up less personal accommodation, in Paris at a conference centre and in Hanover at a motel owned by recent migrants, so as to avoid becoming identified with any one group in town. In each place I began by working in the plant for four months then moved on to the town hall. I spoke regularly with townspeople throughout my stay, particularly while I was entering data (my portable computer was a good conversation opener in the early 1980s) and also on the street, in lunchrooms, and at community social gatherings. I began formal interviewing only after the documentary research was almost complete.

WORK FORCE DATA BASE

Penmans: The work force for each of Penmans mills in Paris was reconstructed for 1936, the year the Royal Commission on the Textile Industry held hearings in town, and 1948-9, the prelude and period of the strike, on the basis of the personnel cards maintained for each employee for the duration of his or her employment with firm. All Penmans wage books have been lost in floods, save two, those for February 1933 and 1934, provided by management to the Royal Commission on the Textile Industry and now in the Royal Commission on Price Spreads collection (RG 33/18 111) at the National Archives, which by their provenance give cause for caution. The personnel cards, however, in addition to providing name, address, birthdate, sex, and marital status for each worker, provide a relatively complete employment history, noting the successive departments in which each employee worked, the dates at which each term of employment began and ended, and the particular reasons why each period of work terminated, including a wide range of personal and health considerations, workplace conflicts and dissatisfactions, short time at the mill, and participation in the strike of 1949. Usually these records were treated as four sets, those for the hosiery mill on the Nith River, and for the underwear, sweater, and spinning mills several blocks and a bridge away on the Grand, in each of 1936 and 1948.

I then attempted to locate each employee in the municipal assessments rolls. The Paris assessments provide the name and age of each household resident; age, religion, and occupation of the household head; data on household tenure, the size of lot, value of land and buildings, taxes paid and in arrears, household size, households per dwelling, number of persons residing in the dwelling, males resident aged twenty-one to sixty and children aged five to sixteen and five to twenty-one. From these data additional variables were constructed to record household structure, the relative age of husbands and wives, and the presence or absence of children under five. In 1936, 73 per cent of female and 88 per cent of male employees, and in 1948 66 per cent of female and 72 per cent of male employees for whom personnel cards existed were found in the tax rolls.

Additionally I created a one-in-ten sample of all household heads for 1936 and 1948 and collected sex, occupation, tenure, household size, real property valuation, and arrears information for each. The extant payrolls were used to analyse hours of work, modes of payment, and earnings by sex and task for each employee in the four mills.

The work force of the Knechtel main plant was reconstructed for 1923, 1928, 1933, and 1938 using payroll ledgers. From the payrolls it was possible to collect information upon the hours worked and earnings for each employee in each of twenty-four annual pay periods and the bonuses earned in each pay period for 1923 and to calculate total hours worked and total earnings for each employee for each year. I also recorded the hourly rates paid in January and December of each year. The payrolls were organized by department, the foreman's being the first name listed for each department. Using personnel cards prepared in 1940 and 1942 in connection with wartime registration, the occupational lists prepared between 1936 and 1939 under the terms of the Industrial Standards Act, and with help from former employees in identifying foremen, a departmental designation was developed for each employee for each of the four years and a reliable occupational designation for 1938. The household data added from the assessments were the same as for Paris, except that in Hanover lot size in acres was regularly available as well as a notation as to whether the property was part farm, and that in Hanover no information was supplied as to the ages of children in the household. A one-in-ten sample of all householders was created for 1923, 1928, and 1938, and a full listing of householders for 1933 using the same variables used for Paris. The percentage of names listed on the payrolls, subsequently located in the assessment rolls, was 70 per cent for 1923, 63 per cent for 1928, 77 per cent for 1933, and 63 per cent for 1938, somewhat lower than for Paris, probably because the payrolls included all those who worked for even a few hours during the year, short-term workers from whom Penmans might not, in similar circumstances, have created cards.

INTERVIEWS AND TRANSCRIPTS

I recruited men and women to interview in Paris through the help of the Paris Historical Society and in Hanover with the assistance of Local 486 of the International Woodworkers of America. In the summer of 1984 the Paris Historical Society created a storefront museum of Penmans memorabilia on Grand River Street and included a description of my work and a book in which former employees willing to participate in the project might leave their names. Retired Hanover woodworkers played cards regularly in the afternoon at their union hall and during breaks in their games agreed to later interviews and suggested others in town I might contact.

I spoke with each person informally first, sometimes by telephone, usually at her or his doorstep, to describe the project and the interview and request help. I promised that their names would not be used in the book and that I would not present their stories in such a way that they might be identified by context. Most interviews took place about a week later, during which time those who agreed to talk with me had time to cast their minds back over the several decades and consider what they wished and did not wish to speak about. At the start of each interview I showed them the consent form I would ask them to sign after we had finished our discussion and promised I would leave the tape of our conversation behind with them if at that time they wished to withhold their consent. I also reiterated the suggestion I made in our first conversation: that they should feel free not to answer any of my questions and to reply that they did not know or did not remember in these instances if this made them more comfortable. I interviewed five couples, each spouse individually but while the other was in the room. The rest I spoke with alone, although frequently other members of the household were about the house and called upon by the person being interviewed for help on certain questions. Often the formal interview was but a small part of our entire conversation, but I agreed not to use any information passed on to me over cups and glasses after the tape recorder was off. The interviews were not closed structured, but I worked from a questionnaire which included sections on personal and family history, work history, married life, housing, community life, and union activity.

Full transcripts of thirty-six Paris and twenty-four Hanover interviews were created, those for which the information was sufficiently dense and the tape quality adequate to justify a dictatypist's time. Tapes of the untranscribed interviews will be deposited along with the transcriptions and transcribed tapes and the interview schedule at the Queen's University Archives, but only the transcribed interviews have been cited. The citations are by pseudonym assigned to each person interviewed and noted on the transcripts, for Paris with the reference PIHP, for Hanover HIHP, referring, respectively, to Paris and Hanover Industrial History Project.

For Paris I used two other collections of interviews, those housed at the Nottingham Local Studies Library, including duplicates from the Essex Oral History Project east midlands interviews, cited as NLSL, and those conducted in the late 1970s as part of a Local Initiatives Project in Paris. Transcriptions of these interviews are in the Paris Public Library Historical Perspectives collection and are cited as HP and by name. The tape of the untranscribed interview with Martin Hogan is with the records of this project at the Paris town hall.

■ Notes

The following abbreviations are used in the notes:

AO	Archives of Ontario
CTJ	*Canadian Textile Journal*
CWFM	*Canadian Woodworker and Furniture Manufacturer*
HIHP	Hanover Industrial History Project
HP	*Historical Perspectives*
HTJ	*Hosiery Trade Journal*
ISA	Industrial Standards Act
IWA	International Woodworkers of America
KP	Knechtel Papers
LRO	Leicestershire Record Office
NAC	National Archives of Canada
NLSL	Nottingham Local Studies Library
NUHKW	National Union of Hosiery and Knitwear Workers
PHS	Paris Historical Society
PIHP	Paris Industrial History Project
UTWA	United Textile Workers of America

INTRODUCTION

1 Connell, *Gender and Power*, 138; see similarly Lorna Weir, 'Socialist Feminism and the Politics of Sexuality,' in Heather Jon Maroney and Meg Luxton, eds, *Feminism and Political Economy* (Toronto 1987) 75–6.
2 Poovey, *Uneven Developments*, 18–19

3 Hartmann, 'Capitalism, Patriarchy and Job Segregation by Sex,' 230
4 There is an excellent discussion of the ways in which patriarchy has been specified or remained unspecified in relation to modes of production such as capitalism in Fox, 'Conceptualizing "Patriarchy."'
5 Elsa Barkley Brown, 'Womanist Consciousness: Maggie Lena Walker and the Independent Order of Saint Luke,' *Signs* 14: 3 (Spring 1989) 612; and Brown, 632, citing Vernon Dixon, 'Two Approaches to Black-White Relations,' in Vernon J. Dixon and Badi G. Foster, eds, *Beyond Black or White* (Boston 1971) 25–6
6 Adamson, Briskin, and McPhail, *Feminist Organizing*, 109
7 Poovey, *Uneven Developments*; Scott, *Gender and the Politics of History*; Riley, *'Am I That Name?'*; Connell, *Gender and Power*
8 Poovey, *Uneven Developments*, 80
9 Scott, 'Deconstructing Equality,' 37
10 Poovey, 'Feminism and Deconstruction,' 58
11 Scott, 'Deconstructing Equality,' 35
12 Poovey makes this point compellingly in her introduction; *Uneven Developments*, 3.
13 Virginia Woolf, 'Modern Fiction,' in *Collected Essays*, vol. 2 (London 1966), 107

CHAPTER ONE Gender, culture, and labour recruitment

1 Smith, *Forks of the Grand*, 1, 64; 'Industry in Ontario Urban Centres, 1871: Towns of the Middle Grand Valley,' data bank from 1871 manuscript census compiled by Elizabeth and Gerald Bloomfield. The Penmans wage bill in 1871 was $13,000 for seventy-five employees. Adams and Hackland's wage bill in 1871 was $10,800. It is likely, thus, that the census report that they employed only eight workers is in error. If average wages in the two mills were similar, Adams and Hackland's wage bill would have supported sixty-two workers. Young, *Brant*, 474–7. Douglas Reville, citing an 1875 account, suggests that Penmans employed 125 in that year. Reville, *History of Brant* 11, 417
2 In 1871 the population of Paris was 2,640, and there were 132 knitting-mill employees. In 1881 the population of Paris was 3,173. In 1883 the Rev. A.M. Young reported that the Paris Manufacturing Company employed 150 manufacturing knit goods, Adams and Hackland employed 200, and Penmans 400. 'Industries of Ontario, 1871: Towns of the Middle Grand Valley' (Bloomfield data bank). Young, *Brant*, 474–8. Smith, *Forks of the Grand*, 1 64. When Penmans employees struck in 1907, the

Department of Labour reported 1,000 employees out, 850 of them women. The population of the town in 1901 was 3,229; in 1911 it was 4,098; in 1921 it was 4,368. *Census of Canada 1931*, vol. 2, table 8

3 Dublin, *Women at Work*, 10, 41

4 Knowles, 'Beyond Domesticity,' 47, 54, 119–20

5 Ibid., appendix 3, 175–6, based upon the *Annual Report of the Commission of Agriculture and the Arts for the Province of Ontario*, 1883, 54–6 and *Annual Report of the Bureau of Industries for the Province of Ontario*, 1888, 93, 150

6 Knowles scoured the manuscript census for South Dumfries, the farming township surrounding Paris, in the years 1871 and 1881, looking for the names of young women who a decade later were factory workers in town. Altogether over the period she found only twenty. Many may have come and gone from farm to town between census years or been unrecorded or misrecorded in the count. Even multiplied manyfold, however, such a stream of female hands from the countryside would not have met the requirements of the three large mills, making hosiery, sweaters, and underwear, which Penmans ran in Paris by 1891. Knowles, 'Beyond Domesticity,' 56, 61. On the effects of mechanization upon the demand for agricultural labour see Parr, 'Hired Men,' 97–8.

7 Saxonhouse and Wright, 'Two Forms of Cheap Labour'; Saxonhouse, 'Country Girls'; Tsurumi, 'Female Textile Workers'; Dublin, *Women at Work*; Hall et al., *Like a Family*; Cuthbert-Brandt, '"Weaving It Together"'

8 Knowles, 'Beyond Domesticity,' 83, 122

9 There were numerous local newspaper reports on midlands emigrants to Paris in the 1880s. See *Paris (Ont.) Star*, 8 Feb. 1934; 25 April 1935; 25 July 1936.

10 Fawcett Library, British Women's Emigration Association, vol. III, 'Factory Scheme Subcommittee,' Jan.–Nov. 1904; 'History of the Factory Workers' Fund,' *Imperial Colonist*, Oct. 1905; Nov. 1906; July 1909; May 1910; Nov. 1911, 404; Dec. 1919, 424

11 *HTJ*, June 1907, 223. The *Leicester Mercury* through the spring of 1908 ran a specific advertising section called 'Emigration' directly following the 'Hosiery Hands Wanted' listings. I am grateful to Dr Ian Keil, Department of Economic History, University of Loughborough, for arranging for me to have access to the department's collection of Leicestershire newspapers. See also *HTJ*, April 1910, 137.

12 *Imperial Colonist*, July 1904, 75; Sept. 1904; May 1910; *HTJ*, April 1910, 137, 158; *CTJ*, Jan. 1917, 3; Gurnham, *Trade Union Movement*, 112; NLSL Oral History Collection, Interview A19, a male knitter born in 1919. I am grateful to Judy Kingscott, oral history coordinator, for assistance in using this

collection. The quote from the Penmans technical expert is in Paris Industrial History Project, Charles Harrison, 11. On the 'instinctual knowledge' of midlands hosiery workers see *HTJ*, April 1936, 42. Of the female immigrants from whom data on earnings were available, 147 of 267 were earning high enough wages from the day they began work in Canada to repay their fares at the maximum rate. Penmans Imported Help Books, 3 vols, Paris Historical Society (hereafter PHS)

13 *HTJ*, June 1907, 223; April 1910, 137, 158; May 1910, 206

14 Ibid., July 1910, 302; Aug. 1910, 350. The party from Derbyshire and Nottingham was detained and then deported because the Penmans agent had not arrived with sufficient funds to meet the £5 in hand requirement for entry of each non-agricultural immigrant.

15 UK, *Working Party*, 9. *HTJ*, May 1909, 202; April 1910, 136. For statistics on 1920s unemployment in the industry see *HTJ*, March 1928, 94, following the Hosiery Trade Enquiry; *HTJ*, May 1926, 96 and June 1926, 46; LRO, NUHKW, Leicester DE 1655/2/7, Secretary's half-yearly report, S. Bassford, 9 May 1925; DE 1655/2/8, Secretary's half-yearly report, H. Moulden, July 1928; Hinckley DE 1655/3/3, 1 February 1921; Loughborough DE 1655/7/1, 27 Aug. 1923, 30 Aug. 1928; NLSL Oral History Collection, interview A19, 9–10; F.A. Wells describes a recovery in the industry after 1924, *Hosiery and Knitwear*, 169, but he bases his discussion on production figures. Union officials were reporting on declines in employment that accompanied technological change. Technological change in the hosiery is discussed in more detail in chapter three. See also Bradley, 'Technological Change.' On overseas tariffs see 'British Hosiery Trades Future,' *HTJ*, July 1926, 34; LRO, NUHKW, DE 1655/2/7, 9 May 1925.

16 H.W. Hill, a midlands hosiery expert who visited Canada frequently, reported a 50 per cent wage differential in 1908; *HTJ*, March 1908, 122. George Wooler, a midlands emigrant to Paris in 1910, reported the same spread during an extended visit home in 1923; *Paris (Ont.) Star*, 15 Aug. 1923.

17 On seasonality in the Nottingham trade see Wells, 'Nottingham Industries,' 34. Jeremy Crump made the same point for Leicester in his paper 'Leisure and Non-work in Leicester,' given at History Workshop 16, Nov. 1984 in Leicester. The promise of 'steady' work was prominent in publicity directed towards female industrial emigrants from early in the century. See *Imperial Colonist*, Sept. 1904, 101, and Nov. 1906. The quote linking seasonality and the unemployment insurance act is from NLSL, Oral History Collection, transcript A17a, Reginald Smith.

18 For accounts of peripatetic, skilled emigrants see Charles Harrison, Ida Glass, PIHP; for agricultural immigrants, Ida Pelton, Jean Hubbard, Elwood Bain and May Phillips, Doris Ashley, Lottie Keen, PIHP; *Paris (Ont.) Star*, 23 Aug. 1922. On skilled male workers see Charles Harrison, Thomas Blaney, Horace Timpson, PIHP.

19 Registers for the assisted emigration are incomplete. The Paris Historical Society has 'Imported Help Books' for thirteen of the twenty years in which recruitment is known to have taken place, including the First World War, but excluding 1907–8 and 1919–23. The indexes in these registers list 442 names, but the volumes are in poor condition, and only 378 collection sheets recording biweekly repayments remain. From oral evidence, it seems reasonable to assume that at least as many immigrants arrived in the seven years for which records are gone as in those thirteen for which the registers remain, hence the estimate of approximately 700. The statistics that follow are based on the 378 immigrants for whom repayment schedules exist in the Paris Historical Society collection.

20 Names in the registers appear in two forms, initials and last name alone, or full Christian name and surname preceded by 'Miss' or 'Mrs.' All those listed by initial only were assumed to be men, a convention that biases the test against the assumption that most assisted emigrants were women, as several identified by initial were later discovered in the personnel files to be female. By this convention, 285 of the 378 emigrants for whom repayment schedules exist were assumed to be female; 227 of these were identified as 'Miss' rather than 'Mrs,' or 80 per cent of the 285.

21 PHS, Imported Help Books. Ticket vouchers and copies of several contracts are interleaved with the registers. The sum extended and the date the loan was made appear on each repayment schedule.

22 One hundred (27.1 per cent) of the 369 immigrants for whom clear schedules exist defaulted before the full debt was repaid.

23 Corrigan 'Feudal Relics,' 450, citing Karl Marx, *Capital*, 1 (London 1967) 641

24 Newbury, 'Imperial Workplace' 226

25 Penmans imported help: repayment or default on loans by earnings levels

Earnings level*	Repaid	Defaulted	Total
Low	100	82	182
(row %)	(54.9)	(45.0)	(52)
(col %)	(40)	(82)	

Continued on next page

High	150	18	168
(row %)	(89.2)	(10.7)	(48)
(col %)	(60)	(18)	
Total	250	100	350
(%)	(71.4)	(28.6)	

*Low earnings levels were those of less than $6 per week. High levels were $6 per week or more. Those earning more than $6 repaid twice as much per week on their passage debts as those earning less.

26 PHS, Imported Help Books. Clara Fox, emigrated 30 March 1910, had the balance of her debt collected by Mr Isaacs at the Canadian Hotel, Paris. Miss G. Eley, emigrated Jan. 1912, repaid her passage through her employer at the New Royal Hotel. The T. Eaton Company, Toronto, docked the wages of Mrs Morley, emigrated from Ilkeston, July 1912, at the rate of $3 per month. The Ellis Company, Hamilton, collected Penmans loan from Mrs Pemberton, emigrated Oct. 1910, for a year after she left Paris.

27 PHS, Imported Help Books, F.A. Morris, 32; Mrs Albert Smith, 186. The work history data come from the personnel cards in the Penmans Archives, Cambridge, Ontario. I am grateful to Mr Fred Bemrose and Mr Gordon Parsons for helping me to locate and use these records. Erickson, 'Why,' 35. Among female emigrants who left and later returned to Paris see: PHS, Imported Help Books, May Barker, emigrated Sept. 1913, left Paris Dec. 1914, returned and balance paid Sept. 1919; Lily Russell, emigrated Aug. 1912, left Paris May 1913 for Hamilton, returned Dec. 1914, debt discharged June 1915. Olive Cavan, Alice Russell, PIHP

28 See Taylor, 'Effect of Marriage.'

29 UK, Royal Commission on Labour, testimony of B.C. Wates, president, Leicester Chamber of Commerce questioned by A.J. Mundella, 533, and James Holmes, Midlands Counties Hosiery Federation, questioned by Mundella, 541

30 Note the Essex Oral History interview with Mrs Randall, born 1910, whose mother, a knitter, did not work after marriage. Randall herself, however, was employed as a winder and knitter throughout her married life. NLSL, Essex tape no. 157. See also NLSL, Oral History Collection, A53, interview with Mrs Fretwell, born Shaw 1883, an overlocker and mender. The Jersey Wage Books, 1924–6 for Samuel Davis and Sons, Hinckley, show more than a third of employees as married, LRO DE 2544/30. The J. Lewin and Company records, 1865–1937, in the LRO also include wage books. The

1946 Board of Trade, *Working Party on the Hosiery Report*, found that 'the hosiery industry retains a large proportion of its women employees after marriage. This applies more particularly to the long established centres of Leicester and Hinckley,' 95.

31 Leicester Trades, minutes of 17 May 1919, LRO, NUHKW, DE 1655 2/7; Hinckley minutes on meeting of the Hosiery Federation on the married woman question, 22 June 1921, LRO, NUHKW, DE 1655 3/3. On the devices through which a Nottingham chevenner's husband who was irregularly employed maintained his familial standing as breadwinner see Thompson, *Edwardian Childhoods*, 69, 71, 74.

32 The best discussion of this process of negotiation and resolution is Eisenstein, *Give Us Bread*, especially 47–52.

33 Gittins, *Fair Sex*; Gittins, 'Marital Status'; Connelly and MacDonald, 'Women's Work'; Ross and Rapp, 'Sex and Society,' 56, 68, 117

34 Mary Cavan, Anne Hedley, Maud Chappell, Betty Shaw, Frances Randall, PIHP; *Paris (Ont.) Star*, 17 Dec. 1936; PHS, Imported Help Books: Olive Adcock, emigrated 30 March 1910; Mrs Fanny Adcock, Doris Adcock, Albert Adcock, emigrated 17 Oct. 1910; Violet Kelford and Gladys Kelford paying for Rupert Kelford, emigrated 19 July 1912. Annie, Eunice, and Lillian Woods repaid the debt of their father, Thomas Woods, emigrated 20 Sept. 1912.

35 Edith Elliott, Ida Pelton, May Phillips, PIHP. Paris Public Library, *Historical Perspectives*, Hilda Sharp Scott

36 *Paris (Ont.) Star*, 13 Jan. 1926, advertisement signed S.G.W. Horsley; 17 April 1930, letter from Bert Raynes

37 Lillian Watson, Frances Randall, PIHP. The statistics are for the Penmans work force as a whole rather than the immigrant group separately. Forty-seven of the 170 women located in the tax rolls in 1936 were living in single-headed households. Thirty of these households included children.

38 The Addison suicide is reported in the *Paris (Ont.) Star* 14 April 1920. The obituary for Susan Baldwin appeared on 30 May 1935 and the correction on 6 June 1935. For instances of women's households as centres for community social activities see *Paris (Ont.) Star*, 12 Sept. 1923, Lily Cotton and her sisters; 26 Dec. 1923 and 10 Aug. 1927, the Misses Barlow; obituary for Alexandrine Patterson, 6 April 1933. Ida Glass, PIHP. The activities of the Maids and Daughters of England and the Paris Pleasure Club were regularly reported in the local paper through the 1920s. Of the ninety-four single women located in the personnel files as employed in 1936, twenty-six, or 27.7 per cent were older than age thirty-six.

39 PHS, Imported Help Books. Only twenty-six of the 227 single women for whom passage repayment schedules remain were married before their debts to the firm were extinguished. Of the 168 women traced in the personnel records as employed in 1936, sixty-eight were married.

40 Westwood, *All Day*, 111–19. The characterization of the costumes as pornographic is on 117; the interpretation of the brides' rites on 118–19.

41 *Paris (Ont.) Star*, 29 April 1937; see similarly 31 Aug. 1939, 8 Aug. 1935, 2 March 1927. In the latter report Mrs Bert Raynes, soon to be denounced as a bigamist, was the bridegroom.

42 Edith Elliott, PIHP

CHAPTER TWO The politics of protection

1 *Globe* (Toronto), 10 June 1882; Smith, *Forks of the Grand*, I, 259–61

2 *Brant Review*, special edition, 19 June 1882

3 Cohen, *Women's Work, Markets and Economic Development*, chaps. 3 and 4

4 Young, *Brant*, 476

5 *Brant Review*, 19 June 1882

6 Young, *Brant*, 477; *Brant Review*, 14 Nov. 1885

7 See Knowles, 'Beyond Domesticity,' 43–4: Smith, *Forks of the Grand*, I, 64, and his '1949 Strike,' 28. On the central school see *Paris Review*, 14 Feb. 1907; on the welfare hampers see *Paris (Ont.) Star*, 16 Dec. 1937.

8 *Paris Review*, 14 Feb. 1907; Smith, '1949 Strike,' chap. 5

9 The Minute books in the Penmans Archives begin at the date of the take-over, and there are few business records at all remaining for the Penmans Manufacturing Company. All the references to Penmans' debt load as a result of the expansion of the 1890s are retrospective, frequently attached to accounts of Sir Charles Blair Gordon's role in the merger movement. See, for example, Penmans Archives, Cambridge, Ont., Minutebooks, vol. 4, 25 Sept. 1939; Charles Harrison, PIHP.

10 Royal Commission on the Textile Industry (1938) 179; Reid, 'Industrial Paternalism,' 581–2

11 Penmans Archives, Minutebooks, vol. 2, 20 Nov. 1912. The explanation accompanying the request that John Penman vacate his office at this date was that the space was required for other purposes. By this time his Mercury mills had become a considerable competitive force in the Canadian knit-goods market.

12 *CTJ*, June 1916 156–7 and a series of articles in the *CTJ*, 10 Dec. 1926, 1235–6; 17 Feb. 1927, 141–2; 5 May 1927, 397–8

13 Penmans Archives, Minutebooks, vol. 3, 25 April 1921; 19 Sept. 1921; 23 April 1923; *Paris (Ont.) Star*, 11 July 1929; 2 Dec. 1948

14 Smith, '1949 Strike,' 29–30
15 Horace Timpson, Ellwood Bain, Lottie Keen, May Phillips, Florence Lewis, PIHP
16 Penmans Archives, Deed of Trust and Mortgage from Penmans Limited to the Royal Trust Company, 1906, describes the holdings of the firm in detail.
17 *Paris (Ont.) Star*, 17 Nov. 1920, 24 Nov. 1920, 14 March 1929, 10 Oct. 1929, 1 Aug. 1932, 9 March 1933, 14 June 1934
18 *Paris (Ont.) Star*, 3 July 1930. The candidate was John Harold, a local woodworker. He believed the allegations had affected his fortunes as Liberal candidate for Brant in 1917.
19 Horace Timpson, PIHP, 27. On the two sides of deference in a U.S. textile town, see Beatty, 'Textile Labor.'
20 *CTJ*, 3 Aug. 1920, 410–11; Charles Harrison, PIHP
21 On employers' formulation of recruitment strategies to create exceptions to local conventions about labour force participation see Erickson, 'Why,' 35; Perrot, 'Three Ages,' 160.
22 Saxonhouse and Wright, 'Two Forms of Cheap Labor'; McHugh, 'Family Labor System'; Phillips, 'Southern Textile Mill Villages'; Lown, 'Gender and Class'
23 Joyce, 'Labour, Capital and Compromise' 70–1
24 Ida Pelton, Henry Kelly, Jean Hubbard, PIHP
25 Penmans Archives, Minutebooks, vol. 2, 19 April 1916, 16 Oct. 1916
26 PHS Archives, 'What Penmans Offer You,' 1923
27 *Paris (Ont.) Star*, 4 May 1921, 9 Jan. 1924, 2 July 1924, 15 Oct. 1924, 11 May 1927, 23 Jan. 1930, 4 Feb. 1937, 1 April 1943
28 *Paris (Ont.) Star*, 12 May 1920; 26 March 1924; 6 May 1925
29 *Paris (Ont.) Star*, 18 April 1923, 31 Jan. 1929, 19 July 1934
30 Lown, 'Not So Much a Factory,' 40; Tsurumi, 'Female Textile Workers'; Dublin, *Women at Work*
31 *Paris (Ont.) Star*, 26 March 1924
32 *Paris (Ont.) Star*, 2 Feb. 1921, 31 Jan. 1929
33 Penmans Archives, General Transfer Ledger, 9, 1922
34 Lillian Wilson, PIHP
35 *CTJ*, 3 Aug. 1920, 412–13, 416
36 *CTJ*, Dec. 1917, 312–13. The subtitle of this article reads, 'It is not based on philanthropy, but on sound business principles.'
37 *Paris (Ont.) Star*, 31 March 1920, 2 June 1920, 12 Jan. 1921, 13 April 1921. The final disposition of housing built in Paris under the Ontario Housing Act of 1919 is recorded in the Minutebooks of the Paris Housing Commission, 1938–43, Paris Town Hall.

38 Penmans Archives, Minutebooks, vol. 3, 21 April 1922, 23 April 1923.
   Edith Elliott, Jean Hubbard, Kathleen Jenner, and Paul Nelles, PIHP

39 Penmans Archives, Minutebooks, vol. 2, 28 May 1919; Penmans Benefit
   Society, Minutebook, 1910–1918 in the PHS Archives. The society foun-
   dered in the last years of the war when its 428 members voted against
   the doubling of fees, a move that C.B. Robinson, secretary-treasurer of
   Penmans, said would be necessary to cover current claims on the
   fund.

40 Penmans Archives, Minutebooks, vols 3, 4, 5. Charles Harrison, PIHP. On
   the obligations attendant on the granting of pensions see Royal Commission on the Textile Industry, testimony of witnesses in Paris, testimony
   of James Granton, NAC, RG 33 20, vol. 5, 9696.

41 *Paris (Ont.) Star*, 28 April 1920, 18 Aug. 1920, 31 Oct. 1923, 9 July 1924, 13
   Aug. 1924, 28 Dec. 1927. Sam Howell, Charles Harrison, PIHP

42 *Paris Star-Transcript*, 16 Oct. 1907, 23 Oct. 1907; NAC, Labour, Strikes and
   Lockouts, RG 27 295/3010; *Brantford Expositor*, 14–19 Oct. 1907

43 NAC, Labour, Strikes and Lockouts, RG 27 327 22(11); *Brantford Expositor*, 8,
   15, 18, 22, and 27 Feb. 1922; *Ottawa Citizen* 16 Feb. 1922. The reference
   to the union is in the *Expositor*, 18 Feb. 1922.

44 The date on capacity are from the background files of the 1938 Turgeon
   commission on textiles, NAC, RG 33 20 35. On the success of the firm and
   its place in the industry see *CTJ*, 10 Feb. 1927, 109–10, 131–2; 27 Oct. 1927,
   941.

45 Penmans employment of equipment and labour, 1926–35

	(1) No. knitting machines	(2) Operations as % of capacity	(3) No. factory workers
1926	1,681	115	
1927	1,709	95.7	
1928	1,769	99.6	
1929	1,827	97.6	724
1930	1,899	84.2	696
1931	1,926	84.0	684
1932	1,946	85.4	690
1933	1,961	81.1	714
1934	1,986	95.5	
1935	2,011	93.4	

(1) and (2) Royal Commission on the Textile Industry, background papers, NAC, RG 33 20 35
(3) Canada, Royal Commission on Price Spreads, *Report* 2931.
Indices of industry activity in the knit-goods sector are in Price
Spreads, *Report*, 2913.

46 Charles Harrison, Edith and John Elliott, Jean Hubbard, Ida Pelton, May
Phillips, Elma Jones, Frances Randall, PIHP. For a similar pattern of
personalistic relationships around flexible work schedules see Frankel,
'Southern Textile Women,' 46–7.
47 Reports on Turgeon royal commission hearings in Paris, *Brantford Expositor*, 16 Oct. 1936; Ellwood Bain, Ida Glass, Frank Boyle, PIHP; Royal
Commission on the Textile Industry, NAC, RG 33 20, vol. 5, 9676
48 Ida Glass, Clarence Cobbett, Charles Harrison, PIHP
49 Background paper on the financial history of Penmans prepared for the
Royal Commission on the Textile Industry, NAC RG 33/20, vol. 61; Cross-
examination of C.B. Robinson based on the background paper, during the
Paris hearings of the commission, NAC, RG 33/20, vol. 5, 9516–62; Johnston
and Ward, Montreal, 'Monthly Market Letter,' May 1927, in Advisory
Board on the Tariff, NAC, RG 36 11, vol. 24, 42–13
50 Erickson, *British Industrialists*; Gurnham, *Trade Union Movement*; UK, *Working Party*; Taylor, *Significant Post-War Changes*; Taylor, *Full Fashioned
Hosiery Worker*
51 Canada, Royal Commission on the Textile Industry, *Report*, 53–4; and
Royal Commission on Price Spreads, *Report*, 2924–7
52 Royal Commission on the Textile Industry, background papers, NAC, RG
33/20 vols 19 and 35; Canadian Woollen and Knitgoods Manufacturers'
Association exhibit, NAC, RG 33/20 19, exhibits 707–19, and the testimony
by H.W. Lundy in Paris, 16 Oct. 1936, NAC, RG 33/20 5, 9704–55
53 Canada, Royal Commission on Price Spreads, Report, 2849
54 Canadian Manufacturers' Association, General Minutebook, 1886–99,
'Knit-Goods Section,' 206–9, NAC, MG 28, I, 230; Tariff Enquiry and
Commission, submission by the knit-goods delegation, NAC, RG 36 8, vol.
3, 3355–65
55 Mahon, *Politics of Industrial Restructuring*, 20; Williams, *Not for Export*,
chaps. 2 and 3
56 Canada, Royal Commission on the Textile Industry, *Report*, 66, 85, 266–9
57 Representation by the knit-goods delegation before the Tariff Enquiry and
Commission, 1896, NAC, RG 36 8, vol. 3, 3356; Richard Thomson quoted
in summary of tariff commission evidence, NAC, RG 36 17, vol. 10, 272;
submission by H.V. Andrews to the Advisory Tariff Board concerning
reference 42, NAC, RG 36 11, vol. 24, 29 June 1927; digest of second hearing
on woollen knit-goods, reference 42, 27–29 June 1927, testimony by
Henry Barrett, NAC, RG 36 11, vol. 23, file 42–3; Knitted outerwear memorandum, 15 June 1927, reference 42, NAC, RG 36/11, vol. 22, file 42A
58 *CTJ*, 13 Feb. 1925 155–8; 3 Dec. 1926, 1209; 17 Nov. 1927, 1009–10; 12 Feb.
1932; 'Woolen tariff schedule, Canada, brief presented to the Hon. Mr.

Robb, Minister of Finance, 1 February 1927,' reference 42, Advisory Board
on Tariff and Taxation, 20–2, reprinted in *CTJ*, 10 Feb. 1927; Canada,
Royal Commission on the Textile Industry, *Report*, 194

59 Harold Wilson, in an analysis of conditions in the Canadian industry prepared in connection with reference 42, 16 May 1927, Advisory Board on
Tariffs and Taxation, NAC, RG 33/11, vol. 25, 42–21

60 Royal Commission on the Textile Industry, *Report*, 6, 117, 127, 205

61 F.R. Scott to A.S. Whiteley, Secretary, Royal Commission on the Textile
Industry, 10 Oct. 1936, NAC, RG 33/20, vol. 66, file 'Professor F.R. Scott'

62 Royal Commission on the Textile Industry, *Report*, 205–6

63 Ibid., 190–1

64 Mahon, *Politics of Industrial Restructuring*

CHAPTER THREE When is knitting women's work?

1 Smith, *Industrial Archaeology*, 27; Church, *Economic and Social Change* 259,
262; Erickson, *British Industrialists*, 94, 176–8. The Canadian factory
hosiery industry began, as did the English, in the 1850s; Penmans, the
leading Canadian firm, dates from 1868. For a fine historical discussion
of the sexual division of labour in the French knitting industry see Helen
Harden Chenut, 'Changements techniques et métiers à maille: la division
sexuelle des techniques dans la bonneterie troyenne, 1860–1939,' in
Jean-Claude Rabier, ed., *Travail et travailleurs dans l'industrie textile* (Paris
1986).

2 An exception to this pattern is Valerie Kincade Oppeheimer 'Sex Labelling
of Jobs'; Alexander, *Women's Work*, 22; F.A. Wells, the modern authority
on the hosiery trade, notes the power of prefactory custom in factories in
the 1890s, in Wells, *British Hosiery Trade*, 190.

3 I am grateful to Dr Stanley Chapman of the University of Nottingham for
pointing out these early examples to me and sending me evidence for
one active knitting centre. In the framework village of Ruddington there
were twelve female framework knitters in 1841, twenty-nine in 1851
and fourteen in 1861. Roughly 5 per cent of all frame workers were female
in this village in these years. Census Enumerators Returns, 1841–61

4 These patterns are charted by Osterud, 'Gender Divisions' and Rose,
'Gender Segregation.'

5 William Felkin, the best source on nineteenth-century knitting technology,
describes the circular, known also as the griswold, as a ladies' machine.
Felkin, *History*, 496. F.A. Wells describes the differentials in adaptation to
steam power. Wells, *Hosiery and Knitwear*, 174. On the dominance of

women-run circulars in the early factory stage, see Gurnham, *History*, 34; Erickson, *British Industrialists*, 181; Felkin, *History*, 507, 543–4 and Wells, *Hosiery and Knitwear*, 156.

6 Felkin, *History*, 498; Wells, *Hosiery and Knitwear*, 156; UK, Royal Commission on Labour, 549, *British Parliamentary Papers* [hereafter Labour Commission 1892]; *Knitters' Circular and Monthly Record*, May 1895, 2; *HTJ*, Jan. 1900, 7, and July 1905, 243; Taylor, 'Effect of Marriage' 50

7 Hinckley, 10 Nov. 1920, LRO, NUHKW, DE 1655 3/3; *HTJ*, June 1914; UK Royal Commission on Labour, c. 6795-III, pt 3, 579; Leicester, 21 Oct. 1922, LRO, NUHKW, DE 1655 2/7; Gurnham, *History*, 55, 108; *HTJ*, Sept. 1919, 500, and May 1926, 80; Osterud, 'Gender Divisions,' 64; on the influence of local factors on gender divisions in the Scottish hosiery industry, see Gulvin, *Scottish Hosiery*, 81, 114; The post-Second World War Working Party on the Hosiery saw labour availability as central in the reshaping of gender divisions in knitting. UK, *Working Party*, 38–9. For similar patterns in the woven-textile industry, see Lazonick, 'Industrial Relations,' 239, 249; and Saxonhouse and Wright, 'Two Forms of Cheap Labor.'

8 See, for example, *HTJ*, June 1905, 199, and Sept. 1918, 434–6; advertisements noting the affinity of the new circulars to unskilled female labour appeared in almost every issue.

9 *HTJ*, Jan. 1900, 7; June 1902, 167; Jan. 1907, 7; April 1910, 138; Jan. 1919, 80

10 Gurnham's *History* is the best study of the hosiery unions; see especially chaps 3, 4, and 5. See also Wells, *British Hosiery Trade* 239–40. The active role of unions in shaping gender divisions in the workplace is discussed in Milkman, 'Organizing the sexual division of labor,' 101, and in Rubery 'Structured Labour Markets,' 244.

11 UK, Royal Commission on Labour, c. 6795-IX, 49–50; Wells, *British Hosiery Trade*, 239; Gurnham, *History*, 105–6; John Benson 'Work,' in Benson, ed., *Working-Class in England*, 78–9

12 LRO, NUHKW, DE 1655: Nottingham, 4/1, 5 June 1915; Leicester trades, 2/7, 22 Feb. 1918, 1 March 1919; Nottingham hosiery finishers, 5/1, 27 Dept. 1921, 28 July 1927; Leicester 2/7, 17 Aug. 1920

13 *HTJ*, Sept. 1919, 524. LRO, NUHKW, DE 1655: Leicester trades, 2/7, 24 June 1919; Nottingham, 4/1, 28 Aug. 1915, 5 Feb. 1916, 4 March 1916. A contemporary analysis of the use of this 'unsymmetrical pressure' by male unionists in Edgeworth, 'Equal Pay,' 438.

14 LRO, NUHKW, DE 1655: Hinckley, 3/3, 10 Nov. 1920; Loughborough, 7/1 15 May 1925, 20 June 1925, 17 Oct. 1925

15 UK, Royal Commission on Labour, c. 6795-III, XXXVI pt 3, 577. LRO, NUHKW, DE 1655: Leicester trades, 2/7, 30 Jan. 1918, 22 Feb. 1919, 2 March 1921, 14 March 1922; Nottingham, 4/2, 26 Oct. 1919

16 *HTJ*, June 1921, 498; LRO, NUHKW, DE 1655: Ilkeston, 6/2, 23 Aug. 1920; Nottingham, 4/2, 27 Nov. 1920; Leicester, 2/7, 24 Nov. 1926; *HTJ*, Aug. 1927, 104

17 'Union Official's Attack on the Shift System,' and editorial response, *HTJ*, Dec. 1937; on 'Changing Methods in the Hosiery Trade,' see the 1939 article by William Davis of the University College, Nottingham, in the *Hawick Express*, in Hosiery Clipping Files 1919–39, NLSL. See similarly Armstrong, 'If It's Only Women,' 32.

18 In 1919 John Chamberlain argued that this aspect of job composition 'cannot be settled in the offhand manner which is sometimes used by machine builders. The number of machines workable by one operator often depends more upon the operator than the machines, and due allowance must be made for the type, sex and efficiency of the operator.' 'Production of Standard Knit Goods,' *HTJ*, Jan. 1919. On agreements under the Joint Industrial Council see Wells, *British Hosiery Trade*, 241. Hinckley, 3/2, 19 May 1920, LRO, NUHKW, DE 1655; *HTJ*, March 1927, 64; July 1927, 54; UK *Working Party*, 33. The oddest intervention on this question is John Chamberlain, 'Future,' *HTJ*, May 1926, which argues that British knitters were less efficient than American knitters on seamless hose machines because more British operators were women. Seamless hose machines were run by both men and women in the United States as well. They were more productive because American operators ran more heads than either men or women did under the midlands collective agreements. Baker, *Technology*, 137–9; UK, *Working Party*, 34

19 *HTJ*, Nov. 1906, 409; Jan. 1907, 7; Fawcett, 'Equal Pay,' 4

20 Armstrong, 'If It's Only Women,' 30; the lending analogy is from Cockburn, *Brothers*, 160.

21 *HTJ*, March 1939, 56; NLSL, Oral History Collection, Transcript A15 11

22 Wells, *British Hosiery Trade*, 231; NLSL, Oral History Collection, Transcript A15, 19–20; Bradley, 'Technological Change'

23 Erickson, *British Industrialists*, 124; NLSL, Oral History Collection, Transcript A19, 15 and Transcript A3d, 38

24 On the effects of yarn quality on knitting see *HTJ*, May 1937, 44. The same arguments are made for the Canadian case by Roscoe Hill, 'Problems of Production and Quality,' *CTJ*, 4 Dec. 1942, 29. On the interdependence between the yarn and knitting rooms see Irene Cobbett, 13; Henry Kelly, 7, PIHP.

25 Smith, *Forks of the Grand* II, 205–7; PHS, Penmans Immigrant Registers, nos 1, 2, and 3

26 1930 Appraisal, Penmans Ltd by Canadian Appraisal Company.
Penmans Archives, reconstruction of the Penmans labour force from
personnel and plant records. Numbers of circular knitters: 1936, male
thirty-seven, female twenty-five; 1948, male forty-five, female twenty-one.
In 1948, 48 per cent of knitters on American circulars and 28 per cent of
knitters on British circulars were women. On burson knitting see Frank
Boyle, 5–7, 22, PIHP; on knitting foremen see Charles Harrison, Sam Howell,
Clarence Cobbett, PIHP.

27 Irene Cobbett, 7, 8, 10, 13; Alice Russell, 7; Charles Harrison, 30; Horace
Timpson, 8, 11, PIHP

28 *CTJ*, Jan. 1916, 12; 30 April 1918, 161; *CTJ*, 2 March 1939, 20; UK, *Working
Party*, 199, noted this feature of the Canadian industry.

29 *CTJ*, 24 April 1942, 36, 38

30 *CTJ*, 21 Sept. 1934, 26

31 Testimony of James Granton, Paris Hearings, Royal Commission on the
Textile Industry, *Report*, 1938

32 Penmans Payrolls, Feb. 1934 found in NAC, Royal Commission on Price
Spreads, RG 33/18, vol. 111, earnings by sex by task, earnings/hours
worked by sex by task. Henry Kelly, 6; Irene Cobbett, 9, 16; Alice Russell,
18–20; Horace Timpson, 23; Sam Howell, 29, PIHP. Paris testimony,
Royal Commission on the Textile Industry, NAC, RG 33/20, vol. 5, Norman
Taylor 9631–42, Leslie Smith 9656, 9666, Phyllis Wilson 9669. There is a
compelling description of the gendered construction of workers' relationship to machines, based on the Australian appliance industry, in Game
and Pringle, *Gender at Work*, 36.

33 PHS, *What Penmans Offer You*, 8

34 Annie Hedley, 11; Irene Cobbett, 5, 6, 12–15; Alice Russell, 5, 8, 10–12, 16;
Horace Timpson, 13; Sam Howell, 27; Paul Nelles, 11, PIHP

35 *CTJ*, 3 March 1939, 20, 34–5; 24 April 1942, 35–6; UK, *Working Party*, 34,
200. Charles Harrison, 7; Horace Timpson, 8–9, 13; Irene Cobbett, 12;
Alice Russell, 5, PIHP

36 The recruitment of young male knitters is evident in the declining relative
age and length of work histories of men between these two years. In
1936 women knitters had worked an average of 14.9 years (n = 30); men,
23.4 years (n = 43). In 1948 women knitters had worked an average of
16.7 years (n = 36); men, 18.1 (n = 56). In 1936 41 per cent of knitters were
women (n = 73), while only 36 per cent were women in 1948 (n = 88).

37 Charles Harrison, 7; Paul Nelles, 5, 6, 11, 13; Horace Timpson, 9, 10, 17;
Clarence Cobbett, 22, PIHP

CHAPTER FOUR Domesticity and mill families

1 On this pattern in the United States, see Aldrich and Albelda, 'Determinants.'
2 The average length of service among male Penmans employees in 1936 was twenty-six-and-a-half years; in 1948 it was eighteen years. One-fifth of the men employed in 1936 had been hired before 1913; 40 per cent had joined the firm between 1914 and 1928, and 30 per cent of the 1948 male employees had started at Penmans more than twenty years previously (n[1936] = 210; n[1948] = 301). Although many men did not return to the mill after wartime service, still in 1948 31.3 per cent of male hosiery mill workers and 27.2 per cent of yarn, sweater, and underwear mill workers had started work at Penmans more than twenty years previously.
3 Lottie Keen, Charles Harrison, Stella Beechey, Anne Hedley, Frances Randall, James Baker, Ellwood Bain, Alice Russell, Robert Fletcher, Thomas Blaney, Paul Nelles and Ida Pelton, PIHP; Hilda Sharp Scott and Martin Hogan, HP
4 Paris (Ont.) Star, 17 and 24 Nov. 1920, 26 Sept. 1929. Gordon Madden and Martin Hogan, HP, and Charles Harrison, PIHP. In 1933 Penmans employed 797 in Paris, and the Wincey Mill employed eighty-three. See Manual of the Textile Industry (Montreal 1935).
5 Clarence Cobbett, Ida Glass, Charles Harrison, Stella Beechey, Jean Hubbard, May Phillips, Ida Pelton, Ila Graham, Florence Lewis, Robert Fletcher, PIHP; and Hilda Scott Sharp, HP
6 Saxonhouse and Wright, 'Two Forms of Cheap Labor,' 8, note the precariousness of this balance. See also Barron and Norris, 'Sexual Divisions,' 47–69.
7 Olive Cavan, Frances Randall, Florence Lewis, Mildred Hopper, Ila Graham, Stella Beechey, Betty Shaw, Jean Elliott, Ann Eames, Maud Sharpe, and Irene Cobben, PIHP
8 This pattern holds true for the Canadian hosiery and knit-goods industry as a whole in 1931, where women comprised 59.6 per cent of the labour force but 63 per cent of employees under fifteen and under nineteen. See Canada, Royal Commission into the Textile Industry, Report, 149. In 1936, all mills, female age start work, n = 231; female age start work by year started work, sweater and underwear mills, n = 55. In 1948, of women employed in the hosiery mill 161 had begun in the years 1939–48, 19 per cent at fifteen or younger, 41 per cent at nineteen or younger. In the sweater and underwear mills, where many seamers were required, young girls continued to be employed in large numbers throughout the

period. One-third of the women who started work in these plants before 1914 were fifteen or younger; one-half of those who started work in the decade following 1929 were of this age. Alice Russell, Ida Pelton, Mildred Hopper, and Edith Elliott, PIHP

9 See *Paris (Ont.) Star*, 14 June 1922, 10 Aug. and 14 Dec. 1921; and Ida Pelton, PIHP.

10 Paul Nelles, PIHP. Among 1936 employees 39 per cent of women and 24 per cent of men had begun work in the mills at fifteen or younger.

Ages work begun, by sex, 1936 and 1948

		Flats		Hosiery	
		Women	Men	Women	Men
1936	X	22.11	28.65	21.10	22.51
	s.d.	10.36	12.04	8.9	9.2
	n	42	88	158	113
1948	X	27.8	33.6	26.10	22.23
	s.d.	12.4	15.6	12.65	10.62
	n	144	148	237	152

At 95 per cent confidence, the differences in the means are significant in 1936 and 1948 for workers in the yarn, sweater, and underwear mills. The 1936 difference is not significant at the hosiery mills; women employed in the hosiery mills in 1948 started work at a significantly later age than men. At the hosiery mill, women who started work in the years before 1939 were younger than men, but many younger males of pre-enlistment age were recruited in large numbers to replace men leaving for military service in the Second World War. Enlistments were less numerous in the yarn, sweater, and underwear mills, where men in 1936 were an average of seven years older. In 1936 the mean birth year of employees in the yarn, sweater, and underwear mills was 1894, n = 89; the mean birth year of employees in the hosiery mill was 1901, n = 113.

11 Hilden, 'Class and Gender,' 369; Canada, Royal Commission on the Textile Industry, *Report*, 149; Florence Lewis, PIHP

12 Jean Hubbard, Paul Nelles, James Baker, Frances Randall and Thomas Blaney, PIHP; for advice on how to minimize 'annoying, expensive' labour turnover by making exceptions to rules for female employees, *CTJ*, 26 June 1925, 593–4

13 The relationship between male monitoring of female employees and housing forms is discussed in Lown, 'Gender and Class,' 318–21; Saxonhouse

and Wright, 'Two Forms of Cheap Labour'; and Tsurumi, 'Female Textile Workers.'

14 *Paris (Ont.) Star*, 12 May 1920, 2 Feb., 2 March and 4 May 1921, 10 May 1922, 18 April 1923, 9 Jan., 26 March and 2 July 1924, 6 May 1925, 12 May 1926, 11 May 1927, 31 Jan. 1929, 23 Jan. 1930, 5 Feb. 1931, 8 Feb., 15 March, 4 Oct. 1934, 7 Feb. and 14 Nov. 1935, 4 Feb. 1937, 5 Oct. 1939

15 Hilda Sharp Scott, *HP*; Lillian Wilson and Mildred Hopper, PIHP

16 In 1936 all mills tenancy: men, boarding 10.3 per cent, tenants 3.4 per cent, owning 10.3 per cent, n = 58; women, boarding 3.2 per cent, tenants 10.7 per cent, owning 9.6 per cent, n = 93. In 1948 all mills tenancy: men, boarding 11.5 per cent, tenants 3.8 per cent, owning 7.6 per cent, n = 52; women, boarding 5.9 per cent, tenants 13.4 per cent, owning 20.8 per cent n = 67.

17 *Paris (Ont.) Star*, 26 Dec. 1923, 23 Feb. and 10 Aug. 1927, 6 April 1933, 30 May, and 6 June 1935

18 In 1936 all mills: 27.6 per cent of single women were over age thirty-six, n = 94; 20.6 per cent of single men were over age thirty-six, n = 58; proportion of unmarried workers living in parental home, women 76.3 per cent, n = 93; men 77.5 per cent, n = 58. In 1948, all mills: 45 per cent of single women were over thirty, n = 68; 26.4 per cent of single men were over thirty, n = 53; proportion of unmarried workers living in parental home, women 59 per cent, n = 67, men 76.9 per cent, n = 52.

19 In 1936, all mills: proportion of workers living in parental home when older than thirty-six, women 17.6 per cent, n = 68; men 8.3 per cent, n = 108. In 1948, all mills: proportion of workers living in parental home when older than thirty, women 19 per cent, n = 47; men 9.6, n = 42

20 In 1936, all mills: 27.6 per cent of female workers lived in single-headed households; 63.8 per cent of these households included children, n = 170. In 1948, all mills: 26.17 per cent of female workers lived in single-headed households. Of these households 47 per cent included children, n = 256. *Paris (Ont.) Star*, 17 Dec. 1936, obituary for Rebecca Fisher; Irene Cobbett, Maud Sharpe, Olive Cavan, and Lillian Wilson (describing her husband's mother), PIHP

21 The exception is Hilda Sharp Scott, *HP*, who describes in detail her male kinsmen's decisions to leave town.

22 Proportion of workers living in parental home in single-headed households, women 18.9 per cent, n = 74, men 22.4 per cent, n = 49, all mills in 1936. In 1948, all mills, women 22 per cent, n = 45, men 17 per cent, n = 42

23 *Paris (Ont.) Star*, 21 July 1932; Jean Hubbard, Charles Harrison, PIHP

24 Hilda Sharp Scott, HP. In 1936 all mills, proportion single among workers over age thirty-six, women 38 per cent, n = 68; men 11.7 per cent, n = 102. Although the proportion of older women remaining unmarried had decreased by 1948, the ratio of older single women to men remained great, reduced from four to one in 1936 to two to one in 1948. In 1948 all mills: proportion single among workers over thirty, women 18 per cent, n = 165, men 9 per cent, n = 155

25 Gittins, 'Inside and Outside Marriage,' 32, and her more recent 'Marital Status, Work and Kinship,' 253

26 *Paris (Ont.) Star*, 20 Aug. 1924, 17 Feb. 1926, 20 July 1927, 6 April 1933, 1 Nov. 1934, 30 May 1935

27 The Hamilton example is from Jane Synge, 'Parents and Children in the Working Class,' typescript, 40 and 50, part of a larger study in progress of family and community in this nearby city.

28 Aldrich and Albelda, 'Determinants,' find a similar pattern in their study of textile, silk, and glass workers in the United States. See also Gittins, 'Marital Status, Work and Kinship,' 264.

29 Stella Beechey, Jean Hubbard PIHP; see also Beverly W. Jones, 'Race, Sex and Class,' 449.

30 Synge, 'Parents and Children,' 73. For the Paris study twenty-four married women were interviewed, seven of whom were wed at age twenty-two. Gittins found female factory workers in inter-war Britain married on the average at age twenty-four. *Fair Sex*, 85. Anne Hedley, Ila Graham, Elma Jones, PIHP; Hilda Sharp Scott HP; *Paris (Ont.) Star*, 12 May 1932 and 30 Sept. 1937

31 Lillian Watson, Maud Sharp, Irene Cobben, Frank Boyle, Mildred Hopper, PIHP; Gittins, *Fair Sex*, chap. 5. In 1936, eighteen of the sixty women whose husband's age was known were older than their spouses. By 1948 only twenty-two wives were older that the 160 husbands whose age was known, 14 per cent. Improved transportation provided access to more areas in the search for a spouse and may have made it easier to conform to mainstream prescriptions that husbands be older than wives.

32 Luxton, *More Than a Labour of Love*, 33; *Paris (Ont.) Star*, 27 Oct. 1920, 26 Dec. 1923, 12 Oct. 1933. William Labron and Elizabeth McKay, who had both come to Paris from Almonte after the Penmans mill there closed, married simply in Paris in October 1933. *Paris (Ont.) Star*, 12 Oct. 1933. See also ibid., 19 Nov. 1931 and 27 Aug. 1936. The only cases of women stopping work immediately upon marriage were those of Olive Cavan and Frances Randall, both of whom married Lancashire spinners. Both Jill Liddington and Jill Norris, *One Hand Tied behind Us* (London 1978) and

Elizabeth Roberts, *A Woman's Place: An Oral History of Working-Class Women,* *1890–1940* (Oxford 1984), have observed that work after marriage was much less common among women in spinning than weaving towns.

33 Proportion of Penmans women employees married, by birth year, 1936 and 1948

		>1919	1910–19	1900–9	<1900
1936	%	13	23	71	53
	n	15	64	21	68
1948	%	59	74	76	47
	n	93	58	38	69

One-quarter of the women who worked in the hosiery mill in 1936 gave 'home duties' as their reason for terminating their first period of employment at the mill, 15 per cent cited 'to be married,' and 28 per cent worked steadily until they retired, n = 101. In 1948, 20 per cent cited home duties as their reason for leaving Penmans for the first time, 7 per cent cited 'to be married,' and 9 per cent worked steadily until retirement, n = 187.

34 Fraundorf, 'Labor Force Participation,' 416; Cookingham, 'Working after Child-Bearing'; Rotella, 'Women's Labor Force Participation'; Klaczynska, 'Why Women Work'; and Liddington, 'Working-Class Women'

35 In 1936, in all mills: average age of female employees thirty, n = 200; married, 40.4 per cent, n = 168; in 1948 average age of female employees 33.8, n = 390; married, 62 per cent, n = 258. The Paris assessment rolls list adult household members by name, and both the number of children aged five to twenty-one and the total number of persons in the household. Children under five were assumed to be those unaccounted for. Of the sixty eight married women employed in the mills in 1936 for whom good household data were found, 40 per cent by this inference had children under age five. In 1948 26 per cent of the 168 married women linked with the tax rolls had children under five living at home.

36 Maud Sharp, Lillian Wilson, Irene Corbett, Olive Cavan, and Mildred Hopper PIHP. In 1936 average number of children aged five to twenty-one in households of married female mill workers: hosiery 1.16 (n = 48), yarn, sweater, and underwear 1.08 (n = 18); in 1948 the average number of children age five to twenty-one in households of married female employees was 0.8. Textile workers' households, however, were larger than others in Paris and larger than the average household in Ontario

towns of similar size. In Paris in 1936, in a 10 per cent sample of household heads, mean household size was 3.7, n = 118. In Ontario towns in 1931, with populations from 1,000 to 30,000, the mean household size was 4.16, and the average number of children per household was 1.86. See *Census of Canada 1931, Canadian Family*, 12: 37, 169.

37 Gittins, *Fair Sex*, chap. 5; May Phillips, Lillian Wilson, Olive Cavan, Alice Russell, Stella Beechey, and Florence Lewis, PIHP

38 In 1936 three-quarters of male employees worked for the firm in one continuous period of employment; another 20 per cent returned after one period away, usually occasioned by wartime military service (n = 211). The majority of women, 60 per cent, also has uninterrupted work terms; another 20 per cent left the firm once and returned; the last 20 per cent worked between three and seven different periods at the mill. Length of service: hosiery women, n = 176, hosiery men, n = 119; yarn, sweater, and underwear women, n = 55, men, n = 91. Similarly in 1948, 72 per cent of men and 53 per cent of women worked for the firm in one continuous term; 24 per cent of women and only 6.7 per cent of men worked between three and seven different intervals, n(men) = 296, n(women) = 390. See Becker, *Economics of Discrimination*; Brian Chiplin and Peter Sloan, *Tackling Discrimination in the Workplace: An Analysis of Sex Discrimination in Britain* (Cambridge 1976); Paul Phillips and Erin Phillips, *Women and Work* (Toronto 1983) 65–8; Armstrong and Armstrong, *Double Ghetto*, 141–5; Morley Gunderson and Frank Reid, *Sex Discrimination in Employment* (Ottawa 1983).

39 Sam Howell, John Elliot, and Charles Harrison, PIHP. Saxonhouse and Wright, 'Two Forms of Cheap Labor,' 31; and Goldin, 'Work and Wages,' 87. The same preference for piece-work among married, knitted-goods employees has also been found in post-war Britain. See Brown, Kirby and Taylor, 'Employment of Married Women,' 24.

40 Elma Jones, Jean Hubbard, Anne Hedley, Doris Ashley, May Phillips, Ida Pelton, Thomas Blaney, Ann Eames, Florence Lewis, PIHP

41 Kathleen Jenner, Jean Hubbard, Alice Russell, Betty Shaw, Mildred Hopper, Doris Ashley, and Ann Eames, PIHP. See Connelly and MacDonald, 'Women's Work,' 58.

42 Alice Russell and Jean Hubbard, PIHP. The *Paris (Ont.) Star* listed ads from commercial laundry services and town women offering laundry services, all targeted at mill workers. See 14 and 28 April 1920, 15 March 1921, 25 June 1924, 19 Aug. and 9 Oct. 1925, 31 March 1926, 17 Oct. 1929, 16 Jan., 15 May, 26 June, and 30 Nov. 1930, 31 Dec. 1931, 14 April and 3 Nov. 1932.

43 Hilda Sharp Scott, HP; Ida Pelton, Stella Beechey, John Elliott, Kathleen Jenner and Alice Russell, PIHP

44 Anne Hedley, Ann Eames, Ida Pelton, Stella Beechey and Edith Elliott, PIHP. Note the greater difficulty the women of post-war maritime fishing communities had arranging such exchanges when they relied upon their spouses for help in household labour. Connelly and MacDonald, 'Women's Work,' 64–5. However, there was a similar pattern (to that demonstrated in Paris) of balancing work between the market and household economy according to the needs of the household. Ibid., 58–61.

CHAPTER FIVE Womanly militance, neighbourly wrath

1 Lists of strikers and non-strikers prepared from the formal interviews and informal discussions with townspeople during my eight months in town were accurate without exception, when compared with the personnel records of the firm.

2 Smith, '1949 Strike'

3 'History of UTWA organization,' Parent-Rowley Collection, NAC, MG 31 B19 1/15, and Leo Roback, 'The Canadian Textile Industry, an Economic Review, 8 November 1949,' Parent-Rowley Collection, NAC, MG 31 B19 5/5. In the knit-goods sector profit increases outpaced wage increases in the decade after 1939 by 300 per cent. While cotton mill workers held their ground by comparison with all manufacturing employees, and workers in woollen and rayon plants made gains, the relative position of hosiery and knit-goods workers grew markedly worse between 1945 and 1949. For the pattern of agreements in a typical woven-goods plant, Bates and Innes at Carleton Place in the Ottawa Valley, see Parent-Rowley Collection NAC, MG 31 B19 9/3–5; the York Knitting, Woodstock, Ontario, contracts for 1945–51 are in the same collection, NAC MG 31 B19 10/6.

4 The union filed cards for 303 of Penmans Paris employees. The company union contested the 1947 certification claim; Penmans lawyers had the question referred to the National Labour Relations Board arguing the petition concerned employees in both Quebec and Ontario. By the time the issue was returned to provincial jurisdiction and the cards were checked, in the early new year, the union was ruled to represent only 265 of the 600 employees declared eligible in the plant. Jerry Regan to Kent Rowley, 25 March 1946, in Madeleine Parent, private collection; lists of members signed as of 27 April 1946, and factory notices from the works council, Parent-Rowley Collection, NAC, MG 31 B19 11/5. On reaction in the yarn mill to the earlier attempt to organize a spinners' union, see Frances Ran-

dall, PIHP; on the loss of momentum in the summer of 1946, Rowley to Regan, 19 July 1946, and Regan to Rowley, 4 Aug. 1946, in Madeleine Parent, private collection; on company union flyers Parent-Rowley Collection, NAC, MG 31, B19 2/13; on report of a company union meeting, *Paris (Ont.) Star*, 12 Sept. 1946; on the first certification attempt, Parent-Rowley Collection, NAC, MG 31 B19 2/10, 11/5, 17/2; and on Canadian Labour Congress, Madeleine Parent to J.A. Sullivan 4 Dec. 1946, NAC, MG 28 I 103, 8.

5 Charles Alexander to Kent Rowley, 23 March 1947, NAC, MG 31 2b19 2/10; UTWA, *Canadian District News*, 9 May 1947, NAC, MG 28 I 103, 8

6 Brockbank, Hogan, and Smith were interviewed on this topic for a local history project conducted in Paris in the 1970s. Transcripts of the Smith and Brockbank interviews are in the Paris Public Library in the *Historical Perspectives* collection. The tape of the Hogan interview, which was not transcribed, is with the records of the project at the Paris town hall; see also Smith, '1949 Strike,' 37.

7 *Paris (Ont.) Star*, 25 March 1949; *Brantford Expositor*, 3 April 1949

8 For a 'History of the Negotiations' from the union perspective, correspondence concerning the constitution of the conciliation board, union, and company submissions to the conciliation board and the majority report see NAC, MG 31 B19 11/6; the petition for conciliation and both the majority and minority reports are in Labour Department Conciliation Services Branch, Company and Strike files, AO, RG 7 V-1-b 31, 1948, P–S. The report on Penmans response to the conciliation is in *Brantford Expositor* 25 Nov. 1949.

9 W.E. Stewart to Drummond Wren, 27 Oct. 1948, NAC MG 31 B19 11/6

10 The size of the Penmans payroll has been inferred from the personnel records of the firm which list by day, month, and year the periods of employment for each worker. The wage books themselves were lost in a flood. The personnel records show the cause for each interruption of employment and explicitly identify the strikers. These records are in the Penmans Archives, Cambridge, Ontario. There is only one, undated, membership list in the UTWA files for 1948, NAC, MG 31 B19 11/7. It includes 433 names, nineteen fewer than the number of cards filed in the March 1948 petition for certification. The hourly rated payroll would be larger than the bargaining unit by the number of supervisors, who were preponderantly male; many male maintenance workers crossed the line by agreement with the strike committee and thus do not appear in the personnel records as strikers, although they supported the work action. Both these factors would tend to understate the proportion of men who supported the strike.

11 The household structures of 256 of the women who worked in Penmans four Paris mills were determined by linking the personnel records in the Penmans Archives with the municipal assessment rolls in the Town Hall. Twenty-six per cent of these women, sixty-seven of the 256, lived in female-headed households. Irene Cobbett, who lived with her widowed mother and sisters, describes the evening visits from 'union men,' PIHP.

12 For example, in the largest mill, the hosiery mill, in 1948 the average age of women workers was thirty-two, the average age for women strikers thirty-six; the average male striker was thirty years old, the average male waged employee was twenty-nine. At the same mill, 45 per cent of male strikers and 29 per cent of male employees were single; 18 per cent of women strikers and 8 per cent of women employees were widows; 64 per cent of women strikers and 55 per cent of women employees were wives.

13 On the activism of wives and widows see Turbin, 'Beyond Conventional Wisdom,' 59–61; Tilly, 'Paths of Proletarianization,' 415–17 and Cameron, 'Bread and Roses.' The quote is from Sam Howell, but see also Horace Timpson for a description of the same pattern, both in PIHP. On Florence Miller see *Brantford Expositor*, 28 Feb. 1949; the *Expositor* lists her age as sixty-eight, but the town assessment rolls show her age as sixty-two.

14 On dignity and honour as a foundation for female militance in other settings, see Kessler-Harris, 'Problems of Coalition-Building,' 119 and Frankel, 'Southern Textile Women,' 52; Betty Shaw, Florence Lewis, Robert Fletcher, Charles Harrison, PIHP; Smith, '1949 Strike,' 20–1, 40.

15 Betty Shaw, Mildred Hopper, PIHP

16 Lottie Keen, Mildred Hopper, Betty Shaw, Florence Lewis, Clarence Cobbett, Thomas Blaney, Robert Fletcher, PIHP

17 The quotation is from a letter to Helen Murphy, the secretary of Local 153, signed 6 Dec. 1948 by ten senior employees of the firm, five fixers and two experienced knitters among them: eight men and two women withdrew their membership from the union. NAC, MG 31 B19 2/10.

18 Note the similar pattern observed in Santos, 'Community and communism,' 247–9; Betty Shaw, Lottie Keen, Irene Cobbett, Paul Nelles, Ida Pelton, PIHP.

19 The quotes are from Alice Smith and Charles Harrison, PIHP; see similarly Betty Shaw, Horace Timpson, PIHP.

20 *Brantford Expositor*, 22 Feb. 1949, 24 Feb. 1949, 1 March 1949

21 Smith, '1949 Strike,' 22; Florence Lewis, Robert Fletcher, PIHP

22 Charles Harrison, PIHP; *Brantford Expositor*, 22 Feb. 1949, 5 March 1949, 12 March 1949; Lawrence Brockbank, *HP*; tape of untranscribed interview with Martin Hogan, Paris town hall, *HP*

23 The strike vote was taken on 22 Nov. 1948. *Brantford Expositor*, 23 Nov. 1948. By this time the voluntary, irrevocable check-off was a common feature of UTWA contracts in Ontario. See NAC, MG 31 B19 5f3. In the wake of the strike vote, however, ten key members of the local resigned, angry to be 'facing a possible cessation of our livelihood.' Leslie Stewart, Clarence Naylor, D. Naylor, James Stewart, Clifford Naylor, Nel Warren, M. McBride, Ruth Teasdall, George Arthrell, A.T. Hurn to Helen Murphy, 6 Dec. 1948, NAC, MG 31 B19 2/10. For the statement that the strike was primarily about union security see: for the union side, the letter from Eugene Stratton, a brillant fixer from the hosiery mill, *Brantford Expositor*, 16 March 1949; and for the management side, D.L.G. Jones, solicitor for Penmans, *Brantford Expositor*, 25 Jan. 1949.

24 Charles Harrison, Frances Randall, Horace Timpson, Thomas Blaney, PIHP; Martin Hogan, tape of interview for *Historical Perspectives*, in Paris town hall; on the resignation letter of the ten senior workers in the wake of the strike vote see notes 18 and 24, above.

25 On womanliness, respectability, and community see Ross, ' "Not the Sort," ' 39 (emphasis in original). Kessler-Harris, 'Independence and Virtue,' 3–9. Jameson, 'Imperfect Unions,' 171–2. Jones, 'Race, Sex and Class,' 449; the quote concerning the merchant's wife is from Smith, '1949 Strike,' 65.

26 *Brantford Expositor*, 3 and 9 March 1949

27 *Globe and Mail*, 20 Jan. 1949; William J. Haggett, Clerk and Treasurer, Town of Paris to Helen Murphy, secretary, Local 153, UTWA, 21 Dec. 1948, NAC, MG 31 B19 11/6, refers to a letter to council from Penmans dated 20 Dec. 1948 requesting Ontario Provincial Police intervention.

28 *Toronto Star*, 21 Jan. 1949

29 *Brantford Expositor*, 22 Jan. 1949

30 On the relationship between the wider women's culture of Lawrence, Mass., and activism in that community see Cameron, 'Bread and Roses.'

31 On Mrs H., the wife of the shipping-room boss, see James Baker, PIHP; the Barrett case was reported in both the *Paris (Ont.) Star* and the *Globe and Mail*, 3 Feb. 1949; on day care see, for example, *Toronto Star* and *Globe and Mail*, 21 Jan. 1949.

32 In the hosiery mill 37 per cent of the female employees and 36 per cent of the female employees in the sweater, yarn, and underwear mills owned their own houses in 1948. Hilda Scott, *HP*. The notation 'could not get a boarding house' was recorded on the personnel cards of strike breakers. Penmans Archives. Mrs Clem Smith's actions are reported in *Brantford Expositor*, 22 Feb. 1949; the quote concerning giving houseroom to scabs

was reported in the *Globe and Mail*, 22 Feb. 1949. Mrs Smith was supported by a woman on the street outside her house, who told reporters the strike breakers should 'go back where they came from.' The soup kitchens, as they were called, were described in many of the interviews. See especially Robert Fletcher and Florence Lewis, PIHP.

33 Grieco and Whipp, 'Women and the Workplace,' 120–1; Lamphere, 'Bringing the Family to Work,' 521, 539; Santos, 'Community and Communism,' passim

34 Jean Hubbard's mother-in-law was Florence Lewis's neighbour. See the respective renderings of their dispute in Florence Lewis and Jean Hubbard, PIHP.

35 *Toronto Star, Globe and Mail,* and *Brantford Expositor,* 21 Jan. 1949; *Paris (Ont.) Star,* 27 Jan. 1949

36 Both Alexander's statement and the council's depiction of the strike as a 'family quarrel' are in *Brantford Expositor,* 8 Feb. 1949.

37 Charles Alexander to Val Bjarnason, 1 March 1947, NAC, MG 31 B19 2/10; Smith, '1949 Strike,' 60; *Toronto Star,* 20 Jan. 1949

38 This dilemma is described compellingly in both contemporary and historical studies. See Hall, 'Disorderly Women'; Karen Mason, 'Feeling the Pinch: the Kalamazoo Corsetmakers' Strike of 1912,' in Groneman and Norton, eds, *To Toil,* 145, 147, 150; Costello, 'Working Women's Consciousness,' 291, 299; Strom, 'Challenging "Woman's Place,"' 360, 364, 370; and Nash, 'Resistance as protest,' 261, 270.

39 Mildred Hopper, Lottie Keen, May Phillips, Frances Randall, PIHP

40 *Brantford Expositor,* 14 March 1949

41 *Toronto Star,* 20 Jan. 1949; *Brantford Expositor,* 21 Jan. 1949

42 *Brantford Expositor,* 26 Jan. 1949; Clara Farr, *HP*; Smith, '1949 Strike,' 55

43 Ida Glass, PIHP; *Paris (Ont.) Star,* 17 March 1949; *Brantford Expositor,* 25 Feb. 1949; *Toronto Star,* 24 Feb. 1949

44 *Brantford Expositor,* 3 and 4 Feb. 1949; Strikes and Lockouts clippings file, NAC, RG 27 467; UTWA notes on court sessions, NAC, MG 31 B19 2/11

45 *Brantford Expositor,* 11 and 16 Feb. 1949; personnel record, Elizabeth May Cardy, Penmans Archives

46 *Brantford Expositor,* 7 Feb. 1948

47 UTWA legal files concerning the Penmans strike NAC, MG 31 B19 11/7

48 *Brantford Expositor,* 8, 9, 15 Feb. 1949

49 *Brantford Expositor,* 16 Feb. 1949

50 Memorandum of settlement, re Penmans Limited, Paris, Ontario and the United Textile Workers of America, 9 April 1949, NAC, MG 31 B19 11/2; *Brantford Expositor,* 9 and 11 April 1949

51 *Toronto Star* and *Globe and Mail*, 11 April 1949

52 NAC, MG 31 B19 11/7

53 Proceedings of the 1949 UTWA convention, NAC, MG 31 B19 5/5; Charles
Alexander opposed the settlement and gave his reasons in the *Brantford
Expositor*, 26 April 1949. The phrase 'picked the wrong union' is from
Lottie Keen, PIHP, but see also Jean Hubbard, Betty Shaw, May Phillips,
PIHP.

CHAPTER SIX As Christ the carpenter

1 Walker, *Germany and the Emigration*, 1–15; Miletus L. Flaningham, 'The
Rural Economy of Northeastern France and the Bavarian Palatinate,
1815 to 1830,' *Agricultural History* 24 (1950), 166–70

2 Walker, *Germany and Emigration*, 48–69; Diefendorf, *Businessmen and
Politics*, 313, 326; Walker, *German Home Towns*, chap. 10; Braun, 'Impact of
Cottage Industry'

3 Lehmann *German Canadians*, 18, 64; Epp, *Mennonites*, chap. 2; Bassler,
'Inundation,' 95

4 Lehmann, *German Canadians* 68; Epp, *Mennonites*, 62–3

5 Lehmann, *German-Canadians*, 71–3; Leibbrandt *Little Paradise*, 29, 66;
English and McLaughlin *Kitchener* 18, 21. The quote is from Lehmann,
German Canadians, 72.

6 Bassler, '"Inundation,"' 103; Walker, *Germany and Emigration*, 69–80;
Walker, *German Home Towns*, 352–58; Gladys Heintz, 'German Immigration
into Upper Canada and Ontario from 1873 to the Present Day,' MA thesis,
Queen's University, 1938, 101; Kalbfleisch, *History*, 34

7 Walker, *German Home Towns*, 334–5; Inoki 'Aspects,' 105–33, 245; Walker,
German Emigration, 153–192

8 Leibbrandt, *Little Paradise*, 66–8; Theobald Spetz, *The Catholic Church in
Waterloo County* (np 1916), 107; Lehmann, *German Canadians*, 73–83,
418, 419; Robertson *History*, 47, 63, 286; Hahn, *Home*, 9

9 Edith M. Knechtel, *The Knechtels: Descendents of Daniel Knechtel* (Alton, Ont.
1975); Wool Boot Company Ledger, 1887, Knechtel family notes transcribed from Family Register at Jacob Knechtel's house, Rosthern Saskatchewan 1910 QUA, KP 7; *Hanover Post*, 27 Dec. 1900; 2 June 1932;
23 Jan. 1936

10 Knechtel, *The Knechtels*, 8; Cooper 'Growth and Development'; Owen
Sound Herald, *The Herald's Magazine of Industry* (Owen Sound 1911), 51;
Hanover Post, 27 Dec. 1900; 31 Jan. 1924

11 *Hanover Post*, obituaries: W. Fleischer, 5 May 1898; Harry Wisler, 11 March

1920; Samuel Fellman, 11 Nov. 1926; Adam Sieling, 20 Nov. 1930; Chris Thedorf, 26 May 1932; Henry Peppler, 19 Nov. 1936; Andrew Hamel, 17 March 1938; Hahn, *Home*, 189, 211; *Our Rise from the Ashes*, QUA, KP 5; 'Historical file,' biography of Bernhard Urstadt, QUA, KP 5; Davidson, *New History*, 100

12 *Hanover Post*, obituaries: George Huber, 30 Nov. 1933; Gottlieb Stadtlander, 16 April 1936; Henry J. Manto 17 Aug. 1933. Serph Gingrich, Thomas Reis, Thomas Schaus, Jacob Krueger, Ed Wilson, HIHP

13 Christie, 'Furniture Industry,' 20–5, 36; the materials orientation of the North American furniture industry in the late nineteenth century was general. See Oliver, *Development and Structure*; John Christie, 'Knechtel's –Forests and Furniture,' *Your Forests* 10:3 (Winter 1977), 26, 34; *Hanover Post*, 9 Dec. 1897, 2 Dec. and 15 July 1897, 21 Nov. 1899, 3 Nov. 1898, 8 May 1924.

14 Christie, 'Furniture Industry,' 20, 32; After 1900 local lumber supplies were not sufficient to Hanover manufacturers' needs. From 1899 to 1911 Knechtel harvested timber limits around Stokes Bay on the Bruce Peninsula, but in a dozen years these resources were exhausted. Increasingly the firm came to rely on American woods, which were more dependable in supply and quality and more easily worked than harder northern timber. William Sherwood Fox, *The Bruce Beckons* (Toronto 1952), 192–9

15 Talbott, 'Philadelphia Furniture Industry,' 26–9; note the examples in McIntyre, 'From Workship'; Bird, 'Friedrich Ploether,' and 'John P. Klempp.'

16 *Hanover Post*, 27 Dec. 1900, 1 May 1899, 23 Jan. 1936; Christie, 'Knechtel's,' 25–9

17 Chandler, *Visible Hand*, 242, 248; Pye, *Nature and Art*, 37; McIntyre, 'Arms across the Border,' 61

18 This point is well argued in Hounshell, *American System*, 126–51; see also Talbott, 'Philadelphia Furniture,' 139; Ettema, 'Technological Innovation,' 198, 206. Jennifer Trant is misled to conclude that factory production was more standardized than craft production, because she compares factory goods with cabinet makers' production for their own families rather than for the market. 'The Victorian Furniture Industry in Grey and Bruce Counties, Ontario,' MA thesis, Department of Art, Queen's University, 1987

19 Ettema, 'Technological Innovation,' 201, 204; McIntyre, 'From Workshop,' 31; Hallock, 'Woodworking Machinery,' 102

20 Richards, *Treatise*, 47, 56, 282; Earl, 'Craftsmen and Machines,' 308, 311,

321; Hallock, 'Woodworking Machinery,' 59, 91, 93. In the light of this technical research, I do not think that Forster is correct to assume that new machines, especially carving machines, were more efficient than the older technology at the turn of the century, or in his suggestion that the use of less-mechanized equipment was allowed by the tariff. Forster, 'Finding the Right Size,' 162

21 Koltun *Cabinetmaker's Art*, 148, 172. The claim that Victorian furniture design was formed by the capacities of new woodworking machines is effectively refuted in Ettema, 'Technological Innovation,' 198, 206.

22 *Hanover Post*, 27 Dec. 1900, 4 April 1918, 25 April 1901

23 *Hanover Post*, 4 April and 2 May 1901; *Statutes of Ontario* 1901, ch. 54, 'An act respecting the village of Hanover'; Directors' Minutebook, 18 Feb. 1902, QUA, KP

24 Minutebooks 1904–1911, QUA, KP

25 *Census of Canada, 1931* vol. 2, 3, 11; 1901, vol. 3, xxvii; 1911, vol. 3, 114; sales per year QUA, KP 4, 8, 10; Christie, 'Furniture Industry,' 12; Cooper, 'Growth'

26 QUA, KP 5, 32 and Minutebooks 17 Oct. 1903, 26 Jan. 1906, 21 July 1908, 25 May 1909, 5 Jan. 1910

27 Tariff Enquiry and Commission 1896–97, NAC, RG 36 8, vol. 1, 298, 308, 315–16

28 Canadian Manufacturers' Association, Nov. 1906, 13 Feb. 1907, NAC, MG 28 I 230, vol. 50

29 W.B. Rogers, 301, George McLagan, NAC, RG 36 8, vol. 1, 306. I find the arguments concerning supply-side constraints compelling as explanations for the structure of the industry. For a different view emphasizing the demand side see Forster, 'Finding the Right Size,' 164.

30 *Census of Canada, 1911*, vol. 2, 216; Peter Stalker and Clarence Helwig, HIHP, who were fourth generation, growing up in Hanover in the 1920s, described themselves as part of the first generation whose first language was English. See similarly Dankert, 'Autobiography'; *Hanover Post* 1 March 1900, 27 Dec. 1900.

31 Jean McCallum, 'The Town That Was Never Intended But Is,' typescript, Hanover Public Library; *Hanover Post*, 21 Oct. 1897, 19 Jan. 1899, 13 Jan. 1921

32 Dankert, 'Autobiography,' 9; *Hanover Post*, 1 March 1900, 28 Feb. 1918, visit of Rev Wm Kuhn, Philadelphia, General Missionary Secretary, German Baptist Churches of North America. Correspondence in German between Daniel Knechtel and missionaries of the German Baptist church of North America, QUA, KP 5

33 Kalbfleisch *History*, 34, 74
34 See similarly, Grant, 'Patterns,' 91–2; on patriotic celebrations see *Hanover Post*, 20 April 1899, 1 March 1900.
35 A.F. Duguid, *Official History of the Canadian Forces in the Great War, 1914–1919, I: Appendices and Maps* (Ottawa 1938), 165; Joseph Amedée Boudreau, 'The Enemy Alien Problem in Canada, 1914–1921,' doctoral dissertation, University of California Los Angeles, 1965, 30–1; Robert Craig Brown and Ramsey Cook, *Canada 1896–1921* (Toronto 1974), 225
36 *Census of Canada, 1911*, vol. 2, 216–17: 34 per cent of South Grey residents of German origin lived in towns and villages; 80 per cent of British residents lived in rural areas. Hahn, *Home*, 204–5
37 *Canadian Annual Review, 1914* (Toronto 1915), 281; both Desmond Morton, 'Sir William Otter,' 36, and Boudreau, 'Enemy Alien Problem,' 32, follow Hopkins in misidentifying Miller as the MP for Grey and in highlighting the acknowledgment of possible disloyalty. *Globe*, 1 and 5 Nov. 1914
38 Dankert, 'Autobiography,' 21, 40
39 *Hanover Post*, exemptions, 11 April, 9 and 23 May 1918; suicide, 31 Jan. 1918; draftees at train station, 24 Jan. 1918
40 *Hanover Post*, 6 June 1918, 28 Nov. 1918
41 *Globe*, 12 Sept. 1918; *Mail and Empire*, 11 Sept. 1918; *Sun* (Owen Sound), 13 Sept. 1918; *Advertiser* (Owen Sound), 16 Sept. 1918; *Hanover Post*, 19 Sept. 1918; Brown and Cook, *Canada*, 226; Southgate, 'Examination,' 50, 66, 75
42 On PC 2721 see Wilson ed. *Ontario*, lxxi, 75–7, and Duguid, *Official History*, app. I, 166–7; *Hanover Post*, 19 and 26 Sept. and 14 Nov. 1918; *Globe*, 17 Sept. 1918; *Sun* (Owen Sound) and *Advertiser* (Owen Sound), 19 Sept. 1918; Hahn, *Home*, 248–9; on the roles of Bluhm and Miltz in the community see, for example, *Hanover Post*, 24 July and 11 Sept. 1919.
43 *Hanover Post*, 25 Aug. 1932, 30 April 1936, 25 Nov. 1937; Thomas Schaus, Clayton Planz, Peter Gateman, Thomas Reis, HIHP .

CHAPTER SEVEN Manliness, craftsmanship, and scientific management

1 *Hanover Post*, 23 Jan. 1936
2 *Hanover Post*, 26 Dec. 1901; on work and the virtuous anabaptist man see Kakar, *Frederick Taylor*, 76–85.
3 *Hanover Post*, 2 June 1932; 3 Nov. 1898; 11 April 1907
4 Daniel Knechtel personified the patterns of personal power and authority that Richard Edwards described as characteristic of competitive capitalism

in *Contested Terrain*, chap. 2. *Hanover Post*, 2 Nov. 1899, 26 Dec. 1901; Minutebooks, 20 Jan. 1902, QUA, KP

5 *Hanover Post*, 8 Aug. and 30 May 1901
6 Board of Commerce, Condition of the Canadian Furniture Industry 1918 NAC RG 36 6 56; Furniture Manufacturers' Association file 110, Clarkson, Gordon, Dilworth survey of the furniture industry 20 Sept. 1918, QUA, KP 27; 'Memorandum Submitted by Furniture Manufacturers,' *Furniture Journal*, Dec. 1920. On depreciation allowances see Minutebooks, Directors' Meeting 27 Jan. 1917, QUA, KP.
7 *Furniture Journal*, Aug. 1919, 47; *Canadian Furniture World*, Aug. 1919; *Hanover Post*, 7 Aug. 1919
8 *Hanover Post*, 2 Feb. 1921; *CWFM*, Feb. 1924, James Ferguson reporting at a meeting of the Furniture Manufacturers' Association
9 *CWFM*, April 1921, 75; April 1926, 39; Forest Products Engineering (Chicago), 'Trade extension plan for Knechtel Furniture Company, 15 Dec. 1922,' QUA, KP; *Hanover Post*, 2 Sept. 1920
10 Knechtel reply to Clarkson Gordon, 1918, QUA, KP 27
11 Canadian Manufacturers' Association, vol. 50, Minutes of the Furniture Manufacturers' Association, 6 Nov. 1906, 24 Sept. 1907, 12 May 1911, NAC, MG 28 I, 230
12 CMA, vol. 50, FMA 27 Dec. 1907 NAC, MG 28 I, 230; Clarkson, Gordon, Dilworth survey, 20 Sept. 1918 QUA, KP 27. *CWFM* Oct. 1920, 63; Feb. 1920, 70. *Canadian Furniture World*, March 1919; March 1920, 47. 'Systemizing Furniture Manufacturing Costs,' *Furniture Journal*, March 1920; 'Furniture Manufacturers Hold Annual Meeting,' ibid., March 1923, 39. The classic discussion of the meaning of this term is Michael Bliss, *Living Profit*.
13 *CWFM*, April 1926, 41; March 1928, 55
14 *Furniture Journal*, March 1923, 41; *CWFM*, Aug. 1921, 76–8; Feb. 1922, 105; Jan. 1925, 37; *Hanover Post*, 22 Feb. 1923; see similarly H.L. Gantt, 'The Relation Between Production and Costs,' American Society of Mechanical Engineers, *Transactions* (1915), 113.
15 Hounshell, 'American System,' 126; Thomas D. Perry, 'The Engineer and the Woodworking Industry,' *Mechanical Engineering* 42 (1920), 448–50; B.A. Parks, 'Engineering in Furniture Factories,' ibid., 43 (1921), 85–90
16 Board of Tariff Commission 1920 London hearings, 29 Sept. 1920, testimony of Wm McCulloch, Stratford furniture worker, NAC, RG 36 8, vol. 8, 414
17 Haber, *Efficiency*, 27, 65; Noble, *America by Design*, 260
18 The observation that furniture workers were underpaid by comparison

with other skilled workers was common in industry publications after the war. See the Furniture Manufacturers' Association observations, *Hanover Post*, 16 Dec. 1921, 4; *Furniture Journal*, March 1924, 33; *CWFM*, March 1920, 39, March 1921, 128; *Hanover Post*, citing reports in the *Globe*, 7 Aug. 1919; there is a detailed discussion of labour costs as a proportion of sales, based upon an industry questionnaire in FMA file 110, Clarkson, Gordon, Dilworth survey, 20 Sept. 1918, QUA, KP 27.

19 For example, Report of the National Council of Furniture Association meetings in Chicago, 11 Sept. 1919, and J.L. Harris, Corporations Auxiliary Company of Ohio to Labor Committee of Furniture Manufacturers' Association, 24 March 1920, QUA, KP 27

20 *CWFM*, Oct. 1919, 33; Feb. 1920, 96; American Society of Mechanical Engineers, 'What May We Expect of Profit Sharing in Industry?' *Transactions* (1919), 811–12

21 *Furniture Journal*, April 1919, 29

22 Minutebooks, 6 Feb. 1912 and 28 Feb. 1919, QUA, KP; see similarly Spiesz Furniture Minutebooks, 28 Feb. 1919, QUA, KP 7, 20.

23 Flyer dated 28 Feb. 1919, QUA KP 27

24 Minutebooks, 1 June 1919, QUA KP; *Hanover Post*, 10 April 1919; *Canadian Furniture World*, June 1919

25 These meetings were covered in the *Hanover Post*, 25 Sept. and 14 Oct. 1919. No information concerning Hanover organizing was found in the union records which are part of the NAC Canadian Labour Congress collection. George Mitchell, the editor of the *Post*, was a member of the Knechtel board of directors. He frequently reprinted anti-labour polemics from *Saturday Night*; see, for example, *Hanover Post*, 26 June 1919.

26 Galenson, *Brotherhood*, 182, 196; Nadworthy, *Scientific Management*, 115–22

27 *Hanover Post*, 14 Oct. 1919; 11 March 1920; similarly from Patrick Green, organizer from the Carpenters and Joiners Union, *Hanover Post* 16 March 1922: 'When you men asked your wife to marry you, you promised her as good, or better a home than she was leaving – are you giving it to her?' Martha May discusses a similar pattern in the post-First-World-War United States, 'Bread Before Roses,' 10–13.

28 *Hanover Post*, 25 Sept. 1919

29 Wm Weigel to Knechtel, 27 Oct. 1919; reply 30 Oct. 1919; manufacturers' joint letter to furniture workers, 8 Nov. 1919, QUA, KP 27

30 W.D. Patchell, chairman of the investigation committee, to J.S. Knechtel, 20 Dec. 1919, ibid.

31 J.S. Knechtel to his employees, 20 Dec. 1919 and 22 Dec. 1919, ibid.

32 The petition is in QUA KP 27. There are no payrolls for 1919 but the 134

signatories probably were a third to a half of all the men in the plant. No union officeholders signed, but many men later active in union struggles did. The characterization of the profit-sharing system as a bribe is in *Hanover Post*, 22 Feb. 1923.

33 *Hanover Post*, 1 July, and 25 Nov. 1920, 1 March 1923, 16 Dec. 1920; the quote comes from the HIHP interview with Thomas Schaus; on industry conditions at this time, *Furniture Journal*, Dec. 1920, 49

34 T.W. Acheson has studied this generational change in 'Social Origins,' and in 'Changing Origins of the Canadian Industrial Elite, 1880–1910,' in G. Porter and R.D. Cuff, eds, *Enterprise and National Development* (Toronto 1973), 77–9.

35 *Hanover Post*, 10 Feb. 1938; Leonard A. Therrien to J.S. Knechtel 30 Jan. 1936, QUA, KP 5

36 *Hanover Post*, 18 Sept. and 2 Oct. 1919

37 *Hanover Post*, 9 Feb. 1922, 14 April 1921, 2 Feb. 1933, 17 March 1932, 22 June 1933, 29 May 1919, 2 June 1921. On salary see Minutebooks, 26 Jan. 1920, JSK salary 1920 $600 per month, QUA KP. Average earnings among production workers, including bonus, in 1923 was $581.

38 *Hanover Post*, 10 Feb. and 17 Feb. 1938; *CWFM*, Feb. 1938; there is a study of J.S. Knechtel's patents in Trant, 'Victorian Furniture,' 81–3.

39 On Taylor's views of factory owners' proper role see Bendix, *Work and Authority*, 277–80; Edwards, *Contested Terrain* 26–9; and especially Haber, *Efficiency*, 5–16, 165.

40 *Hanover Post*, 26 Dec. 1901

41 The reference to 'hands and handbooks' is from Noble, *America by Design*, 260.

42 *CWFM*, Aug. 1925, 42; Oct. 1927, 64

43 For a modern parallel to this dilemma in gender ambiguity see Gray, 'Sharing the Shop Floor,' 388–90 and Gagnon, 'Physical Strength.'

44 Forest Products Industries, QUA, KP 27; there are $9,484 in billings from six different FPI engineers between Dec. 1922 and March 1923. These were in addition to the original negotiated sum.

45 Forest Products Industries file, Wm Snaith 'Predetermining Furniture Manufacturing Costs,' QUA, KP 27; see FPI employees' articles in *CWFM*, Nov. 1921, 59–60; Feb. 1922, 105–6; Sept. 1921, 62–3; Nov. 1922, 61–3; Oct. 1922, 54–5. On Taylor's schemes see Haber, *Efficiency*, x; Braverman, *Labor*, 118–20; Bendix, *Work and Authority*, 274–7; Noble, *America by Design*, 260–76.

46 McLeod Young Weir, history of the Knechtel company, undated, signed by J.S. Knechtel 3 pp, QUA, KP 1; Knechtel's attendance at directors'

meetings was sporadic through 1922 and 1923; he was described as severely ill during the strike of Feb. 1923, Knechtel Minutebooks, 12 Feb.
1923. *Hanover Post*, 29 March and 8 July 1923; by the post-war period,
Forster's characterization of J.S. Knechtel's leadership as 'systematic
and dynamic' would not apply. Forster, 'Finding the Right Size,' 162

47 Petition of June 1922 and covering letter signed by Dressler and Fleet on
behalf of the men, QUA, KP 27. The outcome of the June petition is
described by Robert Hodder of Local 2013 of the UBCJ in his report to the
Department of Labour concerning the February 1923 strike, NAC, RG 27
330 23(9). Thomas Schaus, HIHP

48 Age data come from the municipal assessment rolls; records of the bonus
were kept separately in the payrolls; the department in which men
worked was inferred from their employee number on the payroll after
cross-checking with information from the interviews and newspapers,
and from the lists prepared in the 1930s under the Industrial Standards Act
and in the 1940s for wartime manpower registration. QUA, KP 3, 4. Of
the 226 employees at the Knechtel main plant in 1923 for whom age is
known, forty-four were aged fifty or over. Thirty-one of these earned
no bonus in that year. Eighty-three of the 140 employees aged thirty-nine
or under received no benefit from the system. Both bonus earnings and
department can be inferred for 210 of Knechtel 1923 employees. 60.47 per
cent of the eighty-six cabinet-makers earned no bonuses. Six of the ten
men in the rubbing room made over $125 extra during the year. Fifteen of
the twenty-six finishers collected bonuses. The sixty-seven men in the
machine room were equally divided; thirty-two made nothing from the
scheme; thirty-two made $125 or less.

49 Thomas Schaus, HIHP; Dietz left Hanover in May 1923 after a year in town,
Hanover Post, 10 May 1923. For reports by workers of Dietz's actions, to
Dan Knechtel and Max Armstrong during the negotiations to end the
strike, *Hanover Post*, 22 Feb. 1923

50 Galenson, *United Brotherhood*, 182–96; Nadsworthy, *Scientific Management*,
116, 151

51 *London Free Press*, 22 Feb. 1923

52 QUA, KP 27. The letter is dated in another hand, 'about Feb. 9/23.'

53 *Globe*, 19 Feb. 1923, in QUA KP 27; this file includes two protest letters and
refusal to work declarations from the desk and main plants of 10 and 15
Feb. 1923.

54 *London Free Press*, 22 Feb. 1923

55 All the quotes concerning the furniture workers' critique of scientific management are from *Hanover Post*, 22 Feb. 1923.

56 Payrolls 1923, QUA, KP 4

57 'The Place of the Engineer in the Woodworking Industries,' *Mechanical Engineering* 49:3 (1927), 259–61; on the goal of scientific managers to remove questioning and deliberation from the craftsman's work see Hoxie, *Scientific Management*.

58 The clearest statement against incentive wage systems is from John Houser of the Chesley Chair Company, in a village near Hanover: *CWFM*, Nov. 1931, 39; reservations, however, began to be expressed in *CWFM*, Sept. 1919, 40, May 1925, 67–8, Jan. 1926, 69–70. Four men interviewed in Hanover remembered working under the bonus system; see Thomas Schuas, Edward Wilson, Serph Gingrich, Thomas Reis, HIHP.

CHAPTER EIGHT For men and girls

1 John Richards, *Arrangement, Care and Operation of Woodworking Factories and Machinery* (New York 1885), xi

2 McIntyre, 'From Workshop,' 34; Koltun, *Cabinetmaker's Art*, 172

3 The poem 'The Woodworker' by Douglas Malloch was published in *CWFM*, Aug. 1925, 41. On beauty and usefulness see Kadar, *Frederick Taylor*, 68–9. On hand work see Ettema, 'Technological Innovation,' 197–224; Kenneth L. Ames, 'Grand Rapids Furniture at the Time of the Centennial,' *Winterthur Portfolio* (1975), 43; Hounshell, *American System*, 151; Peter Stalker, HIHP.

4 Richards, *Arrangement*, xii

5 On fathers and sons, Clayton Planz, HIHP; *Hanover Post*, 30 June 1898; *CWFM*, Sept. 1919, 37, 38, and March 1928, 71

6 Paul Willis, 'Shop Floor Culture, Masculinity and the Wage Form,' in J. Clarke, C. Critcher, and R. Johnson, eds, *Working-Class Culture: Studies in History and Theory* (New York 1979), 196; Gray, 'Sharing the Shop Floor'; Gagnon, 'Physical Strength'

7 *CWFM*, Feb. 1921, 67; Dankert, 'Autobiography,' 35–6; Peter Gateman, Henry Gateman, Clayton Planz, and Karl Ruhl, HIHP. The quote is from Planz.

8 Henry Gateman, Karl Ruhl, HIHP. See similarly Cockburn, *Brothers*, 43–6, on male kinship and craft hierarchy in the printing trades.

9 Gordon Peck, Peter Gateman, HIHP

10 *CWFM*, Jan. 1919; May 1919, 46. The earnings data are from QUA, KP, payrolls. I have most often used 1938 as the reference year because there is a detailed occupational listing available. Other payrolls can be disaggregated only to the departmental level. The personal data, here

and subsequently, are from the Hanover assessment rolls, Hanover town hall.

11 Wilf Cooper, Karl Ruhl, Henry Gateman, HIHP

12 *CWFM*, April 1925, 52; Jacob Krueger, HIHP

13 Wilf Cooper, Clarence Helwig, Ed Fischer, Peter Gateman, Gordon Peck, HIHP. In 1938 Knechtel's lead tenoner, William Ford, a leader in the union, earned $1,048 for 2,223 hours' work. The second tenoner in the plant, John Huenermoeder, worked 2,207 hours and earned $929. QUA, KP 3

14 *CWFM*, Aug. 1921, 69; July 1933, 12; Oct. 1929, 59--60; Feb. 1934, 17; Ed Fischer, Henry Gateman, Clayton Planz, HIHP

15 'A Code of Safety Standards for Woodworking-Machine Guards,' American Society of Mechanical Engineers, *Transactions* (1917), 1191–1200; *CWFM*, Oct. 1929, 59–60; Sern Madsen, 'New Factors Influencing the Design of Woodworking Machinery,' *Mechanical Engineering* 45 (March 1923), 180; *CWFM*, Sept. 1934, 12–14; Feb. 1919, 38. Karl Ruhl, Henry Gateman, Clarence Helwig, Gordon Peck, HIHP. The quotation about the concentration demanded by the work is from Dankert, 'Autobiography,' 37; Richards, *Arrangement*, 63–71.

16 See similarly Willis, 'Shopfloor Culture,' 196.

17 Yearly earnings, machine room employees: 1928, mean = $660, standard deviation = 462; 1938, mean = $661, standard deviation = 312. Calculated from Knechtel wage books, QUA, KP 3, 4

18 C.L. Babcock, 'Refinements in woodworking-machinery design,' *Mechanical Engineering* 48 (1926), 415–22. *CWFM*, July 1921, 72–3; May 1923, 63; July 1928, 96; March 1930, 53; Nov. 1931, 31–3; April 1939, 15–16. Henry Gateman, Gordon Peck, HIHP

19 *CWFM*, April 1929, 45–6; March 1936, 10; April 1936, 12

20 The quote concerning school leaving and the description of the accident is from Henry Gateman, HIHP 3, 8. Mrs Peter Gateman was recounting her own years in the machine room. Peter Gateman, HIHP. The summation about danger and responsibility is from Clarence Helwig, HIHP. See the analysis by Cynthia Cockburn of the imperative of keeping work sites homogeneous by sex, *Brothers*, 151–3, 179.

21 Average age in the cabinet-making shop: 1923, mean = 40.7, s.d. 14.2; 1928, mean = 43, s.d. = 12.0; 1933, mean = 41, s.d. = 12.3; 1938, mean = 41, sd = 12.9

22 This difference between the machine room and the cabinet shop emerges clearly in a comparison of the dispersion around the means in earnings. Machine room: 1923, mean = 660, s.d. = 462; 1938, mean = 661, s.d. =

312; cabinet shop: 1923, mean = 655, s.d. = 373; 1938, mean = 740, s.d. = 247

23 Edward Wilson, Alan Lang, Thomas Schaus, HIHP

24 Edward Wilson, HIHP

25 Alan Lang, HIHP; *CWFM*, Jan. 1926, 70

26 Richards, *Arrangement*, 147

27 Frank Edward Ransome, *The City Built on Wood: A History of the Furniture Industry in Grand Rapids, Michigan* (Ann Arbor 1955), 61; M. Silverstein, 'The Technology of Wood Finishes and Their Application,' *Mechanical Engineering* 48 (1926), 423–6

28 *CWFM*, June 1920, 82; F.L. Browne 'Wood Finishing – a Glance Ahead,' *Mechanical Engineering* 48 (Nov. 1926), 1286–8

29 *Hanover Post*, 2 Dec. 1897, 3 Feb. and 7 April 1898, 7 June and 5 July 1900

30 *Hanover Post*, ads for domestic servants: 13 June 1901, 9 Aug. 1900, 7 Dec. 1899, 7 Sept. 1899; for hotel workers, 29 June 1920, 13 June 1901

31 *Hanover Post*, Barltorp, 25 Aug. 1898; 25 Oct. 1900; ads from general merchants concerning the milliners they employed, 5 Oct. 1899, 16 Sept. 1897, 1 March 1900, 8 March 1900, 8 Sept. 1898, 9 March 1899

32 *Hanover Post*, Miss Bricker, 11 Nov. 1897; other dressmakers in rented rooms above general merchants 11 May 1899, 31 March 1898; businesses run from home 15 April 1920; 22 Feb. 1900

33 *Hanover Post*, 1 Feb. 1900 concerning the hiring of Jessie Graham as stenographer at Knechtel. Graham moved to Hanover from London and later became secretary-treasurer of the firm. 23 Nov. 1899, hiring of Miss Mary Gaskell of Owen Sound, as chemist for the cement company. 31 July 1919, retirement summary of the career of Mrs Patchell at the Bell Telephone Office

34 Populations of Hanover and Paris, 1901 and 1911

	Total population	Women	Men
1901			
Hanover	1392	732	690
Paris	3229	1830	1399
1911			
Hanover	2342	1178	1164
Paris	4098	2274	1824

SOURCE: *Census of Canada 1901*, vol. 1, 56, 62; *1911*, vol. 1, 73, 76

35 Hahn, *Home*, 196; *Hanover Post*, 17 March 1937, 25 July 1918, 3 April 1919, 4 Sept. 1919, 11 April 1918, 29 Sept. 1918, 7 Sept. 1922

36 *Hanover Post*, 1 April 1920, 29 April 1920, 4 May 1922, 16 Nov. 1922, 11 March 1926, 30 Sept. 1926, 13 June 1929; Hahn, *Home*, 197; *Hanover Post*, 7 Jan. 1932, 26 Dec. 1935, 7 Jan. 1937

37 *Hanover Post*, 16 Nov. 1922, 8 March 1923, 30 Sept. 1926, 13 June 1929; 21 Jan. 1932

38 Ibid., 22 April 1920, 14 July 1921, 12 April 1923

39 Peter Stalker, Clarence Helwig, Alan Lang, HIHP; *Hanover Post*, 27 May and 14 Oct. 1920, 12 April 1923, 23 Feb., 1 Mar., and 5 July 1928, 28 Feb. 1929, 22 Sept. 1938

CHAPTER NINE Single fellows and family men

1 *Hanover Post*, 4 Nov. 1920, 9 Dec. 1920; 16 Sept. 1937, 7 Oct. 1937; the quote describing Fischer as 'a good worker and a family man' is from Gordon Peck, HIHP.

2 Clayton Planz, HIHP

3 House ownership among Knechtel woodworkers

		1923	1928	1933	1938
All wage earners	%	56	57	64	56
	n	83/149	70/123	77/120	93/166
Married	%	69	67	72	67
Wage earners	n	75/109	64/95	71/99	83/124

SOURCE: Knechtel payrolls for these years are linked with the municipal assessment rolls.

4 Peter Stalker, HIHP. William McCulloch, a Stratford furniture worker, made the same point about how important it was for a workman, 'to know he can with security make his permanent home among our industries' in his testimony before the Tariff Commission, London hearings, 29 Sept. 1920, NAC, RG 36 8, vol. 8, 4113; Pilgrim Trust, *Men without Work* (London 1938), 188–93.

5 See similarly Davidoff, 'Separation of Home and Work? Landladies and Lodgers in Nineteenth and Twentieth Century England,' in Sandra Burman, *Fit Work for Women* (London 1979), 66–7; Pahl, 'Employment,' 4–5; and Gershuny et al., *Social Innovation*, 155; *Hanover Post*, 20 March 1919.

6 Clayton Planz, Thomas Reis, Edward Wilson, HIHP. *Hanover Post*, 8 April 1937
7 Modell and Hareven, 'Urbanization'
8 Clarence Helwig, Alan Lang, Henry Gateman, HIHP
9 Peter Gateman, Henry Gateman, Serph Gingrich, HIHP; *Hanover Post*, 4 Aug. 1932, 11 Aug. 1932, 13 April 1933, 10 Aug. 1933
10 Dankert, 'Autobiography,' 6, 50; Sam Howell, PIHP
11 *Hanover Post*, 8 July 1920, 15 July 1920, 5 Aug. 1920, 19 Aug. 1920, 26 Aug. 1920, 6 Jan. 1938, 27 Jan. 1938
12 Dankert, 'Autobiography,' passim; Johnson, *Carl Schaefer*; *Hanover Post*, 16 March 1933; Thomas Schaus, Karl Ruhl, Henry Gateman, Edward Wilson, Alan Lang, HIHP
13 Gershuny, *Social Innovation*, 188; Pahl, 'Employment,' 12–13; Gittins, *Fair Sex*, 129, 133, 140; Lummis, 'Historical Dimension'
14 Land, 'Family Wage,' 55, 64
15 Thomas Schaus, Serph Gingrich, Clarence Helwig, HIHP
16 Gordon Peck, Alan Lang, Clarence Helwig, Serph Gingrich, Henry Gateman, Thomas Schaus, Edward Fischer, Edward Wilson, HIHP; Dankert, 'Autobiography'

Number of children in households of Knechtel
employees, by age of employee

Age	1923	1928	1933	1938
20–29	1.7	1.6	1.4	0.95
30–39	2.7	3.2	2.5	2.28

17 Thomas Reis, Peter Stalker, Clarence Helwig, HIHP
18 Cohen, *Women's Work* 8, 43–4, 154–5
19 Alan Lang, Peter Gateman, Henry Gateman, Thomas Reis, HIHP; Jameson, 'Imperfect Unions,' 172–3
20 Thomas Schaus, Alan Lang, Jacob Krueger, Thomas Reis, Clarence Helwig, HIHP
21 Komarovsky, *Unemployed Man*, 1, 2, 60, 70. The results of the 1930s social science investigations are well summarized in Wandersee, *Women's Work*, 107–12; see also Elder, *Children*, 84–5.
22 Demos, 'Changing Faces,' 444
23 Connell, 'Crisis Tendencies,' 45–6
24 Proportion of single men on the Knechtel payrolls, 1923: 24 per cent; 1928: 18 per cent; 1933: 14 per cent; 1938: 19 per cent; average household size, Knechtel employees, 1928: 3.03; 1933: 4.7; 1928: 4.2; proportion of Knechtel

employees aged twenty to twenty-nine living in their parental home, 1923: 46.6; 1928: 47.6; 1933: 17.6; 1938: 33.3. Alan Lang, Gordon Peck, HIHP. Proportion of Knechtel employees aged twenty to twenty-nine who were married, 1923: 46 per cent; 1928: 50 per cent; 1933: 42 per cent; 1938: 50 per cent

25 *Hanover Post*, 25 Feb. 1932

26 Ibid., 10 Sept. 1931, 7 July 1932, 13 Oct. 1932

27 Stouffer and Lazarfield, *Research Memorandum*, 89; Komarovsky, *Unemployed Man*, 81; for similar observations based on more recent times see Johnson, *Unemployed Fathers*, chap. 3; *Hanover Post*, 21 March 1935, 4 April 1935.

28 *Hanover Post*, 5 May 1932, 14 Dec. 1933, 20 Sept. 1934, 7 Feb. 1935, 7 March 1935

CHAPTER TEN Union men

1 *CWFM*, Jan. 1933, 9–11 and May 1938, 12–13; Statement by the Furniture Manufacturers' Association, 4 April 1941, QUA, KP 5

2 Canada, Price Spreads, *Report*, 102, 104, 4297

3 *CWFM*, Feb. 1931, 29; 'Ontario's Furniture Industry Must Not Be Driven to Quebec,' *Beacon Herald* (Stratford) 26 Sept. 1933; James Malcolm to John R. Anderson, 21 November 1932, Malcolm Papers, NAC, MG 27 III B6, vol. 1; Canada, Price Spreads, 'Report,' 104, testimony by John Ross Shaw, 4297–9 and of C.V. Fessenden, an industrial engineer whose practice focused on the furniture industry, 4258–63

4 'Minutes of the meeting of the case goods section of the Furniture Manufacturers' Association, Walper House, Kitchener, 4 August 1933,' appended to a copy of the United States National Association of Furniture Manufacturers September 1933 Code of Fair Competition, in Office of the Deputy Minister, 'Low Wages and the Industrial Standards Act' AO RG 7 II-1, vol. 1

5 Humphries, 'Women,' 112–13; E.H. Lane to Karl D. Knechtel, 7 Dec. 1938, QUA, KP 30. *CWFM*, March 1933, 8–9; April 1933, 9–10, 18–9; June 1934, 18–20. The quote from Harry Cassidy is in *Hanover Post*, 15 March 1934.

6 *CWFM*, Nov. 1934, 9–10; Nov. 1935, 8; May 1936, 7–8; *Hanover Post*, 16 Jan. 1936, 12 March 1936, 8 April 1937; G.E. Gibbard, Napanee to David Croll, Minister of Labour, Ontario, 10 Feb. 1936, 'Minister ISA Furniture,' AO RG 7 I-2, vol. 3

7 The figures on the health of the firm are abstracted from Knechtel, 'Statement of particulars under the excess profits act,' December 1941, QUA,

KP, and from the year-end summaries in the same collection. Details on the changing management and salary schedules of the firm are found in Knechtel, Board of Directors, Minutebooks, 31 Dec. 1930, 20 May 1932, 11 Aug. 1932, 26 Aug. 1936. The Bank of Montreal interventions are described in these minutebooks, 3 June 1935, and in a letter from J.S. Knechtel to A.F. Bowman, 7 Feb. 1935. Daniel Knechtel's letter to Leyoldt, 22 Dec. 1932, was returned to J.S. on 1 Feb. 1936 and is in the envelope of correspondence surrounding Daniel's death, found in QUA, KP 5. The financial reorganization of 1939 is minuted in the directors' meeting of 4 Dec. 1939.

8 Gordon Peck, HIHP

9 Morton with Copp, *Working People*, 144

10 Hallman to Dowd, 21 May 1940, Canadian Labour Congress, NAC MG 28 I 103, vol. 63

11 Thomas Reis, Clarence Helwig, Alan Lang, Peter Stalker, HIHP; Hall et al., *Like a Family*, 218

12 *Hanover Post*, 21 Sept. 1933

13 *Hanover Post*, 28 Sept. 1933, 5 Oct. 1933; *Owen Sound Sun Times* and *Stratford Beacon-Herald*, 23 Sept. 1933

14 *Hanover Post*, 17 Jan. 1924, 18 Feb. 1932, 30 Nov. 1933; payroll 1933, QUA KP 3

15 *Hanover Post*, 5 March 1925, 2 April 1925, 16 July 1925, 28 July 1932; payrolls 1933, QUA, KP 3; assessment rolls 1933, Hanover Town Hall

16 The first description of Fischer is by the president of the local woodworkers in the 1940s. Gordon Peck, HIHP; the Oliver letter is Oliver to Roebuck, 3 Aug. 1934 in Deputy Minister, General Subject Files, Department of Labour, AO RG 7 II-1, vol. 12.

17 Oliver to Roebuck, 3 Aug. 1934 cited in previous note. *Hanover Post*, 15 March 1934, 5 Aug. 1934, 9 Aug. 1934, 16 Aug. 1934; Thomas Reis, Gordon Peck, HIHP; Knechtel shop committee to Arthur Roebuck, 10 Aug. 1934, Deputy Minister, Department of Labour, General Subject Files, AO RG 7 II-1

18 *Hanover Post*, 28 Feb. 1935

19 Morton with Copp, *Working People*, 150; Stuart Jamieson, *Industrial Relations in Canada* (Toronto 1957), 43; Abella, *Nationalism*, 112; Lembcke and Tattam, *One Union in Wood*, 42–3

20 Even after he left the Carpenters, Marsh retained a close interest in their affairs and a strong aspersion towards industrial unions. Their organizing progress can be charted through his Department of Labour correspondence, Deputy Minister, General Subject files – Unions, 1934. Note his response to an inquiry from Lorne Dreier, a Kincardine furniture worker,

22 Sept. 1934, addressed to Marsh in his capacity as deputy minister. Dreier asked about unions generally. Marsh replied that he had best write to Cooper. See similarly Marsh to James Wall, Listowel local of International Union of Furniture Workers [sic], 5 April 1935, 'Low wages and the ISA,' AO, RG 7 II-4, vol. 1.

21 *Hanover Post*, 9 Aug. 1934

22 Thomas Reis, HIHP; *Hanover Post*, 2 May 1935. The delay of the Hanover furniture workers in moving from the Furniture Workers' Industrial Union to the Carpenters and Joiners is clear in the early ISA conference minutes. William Fischer attended a meeting on 11 June 1935, but as deliberations proceeded through July, August, and September with increasing numbers of Carpenters' locals represented from former Furniture Workers' Industrial Union constituencies, no employee representatives from Hanover were present.

23 *Hanover Post*, 16 May 1935, 12 Sept. 1935, 19 Sept. 1935, 12 March 1936; Department of Labour, Strikes and Lockouts files, NAC, RG 27 371 35(141)

24 Bora Laskin, *Report of the Committee of Inquiry into the Industrial Standards Act*, vol. 1, July 1963, AO, RG 7, 1–12, Box 1

25 Cox, 'Limits of Reform,' 563–6

26 'Notes of meeting of furniture manufactures, received ... on December 12, 1934 by Hon. J.A. Roebuck,' AO, RG 7 VIII-1, Box 28. This pressure began in the spring of 1934. See John Ross Shaw's testimony before the Price Spreads Commission concerning the need for NRA-modelled codes, Canada, Price Spreads, *Report*, 4305. The Furniture Manufacturers' Association had petitioned H.H. Stevens in March 1934 for a code with 'soundly defined' limits, subject to enforcement by the courts. *Hanover Post*, 15 March 1934. Before the election that brought the Hepburn administration into power, Deputy Minister of Labour W.A. Crawford had reported to his minister, J.M. Robb, that he had been receiving pressure from furniture manufacturers to eliminate unfair wage competition in their sector. Crawford to Robb, 26 Feb. 1934, AO, RG 7 I-1, 55/2

27 See reports of Roebuck's speech, *Toronto Star*, 15 June 1934, 23, and a restatement of the same principle by Marsh, *Hanover Post*, 25 Oct. 1934.

28 Laskin, 'Industrial Standards Act' (1963)

29 *Hanover Post*, 8 Nov. 1934, 20 Dec. 1934; 'Notes of meeting of furniture manufacturers ... 12 December 1934' AO, RG 7 VIII-1, Box 28

30 Transcripts of meeting with advisory boards through the summer of 1935, Minister, ISA, General Subject Files AO, RG 7 I-1, vol. 11; Cox, 'Limits of Reform,' 569

31 Case files of Industrial Standards Officers, Furniture-First Agreement, AO, RG 7 VIII-1, vol. 31; Minutes of the meeting of 10 July 1935, Minister, ISA Furniture, AO, RG 7 I-2, vol. 3

32 Memo from Crawford to Croll, 25 June 1936, Minister, ISA, Furniture, AO, RG 7 I-2, vol. 3

33 Croll's speech before the legislature before the introduction of the 1936 admendments to the Industrial Standards Act, Minister, ISA, General Subject Files, AO, RG 7 I-1, vol. 11

34 'Statement of the Furniture Manufacturers of Ontario regarding the Industrial Standards Act, 18 June 1936,' Minister, ISA, Furniture, AO, RG 7 I-1, vol. 3

35 '9 Ontario furniture towns, March 1937,' Strikes and Lockouts File, NAC, RG 27 38 37(33); Stratford Beacon-Herald, 5 March 1937; Louis Fine to David Croll, 17 March 1937, 'Labour-Furniture,' AO RG 7 I-2, vol. 3

36 A.E. Lamb to Louis Fine, 15 Feb. 1937, 'Case Files of Industrial Standards Officers,' AO RG 7 VIII-1, vol. 31

37 See the scepticism of Fine concerning the agreement because of the lower level of employer representation in 1937 than in 1935, Fine to Croll, 31 March 1937, AO, RG 7 VIII-1, vol. 31, case file of Industrial Standards Officers; Hanover Post, 4 and 11 March 1937; '9 Ontario Furniture Towns, March 1937,' Strikes and Lockouts, NAC, RG 27 381 37(33).

38 O.C. Jennette to James Marsh, 12 March 1937, AO, RG 7 V-1, vol. 1; O.C. Jennette to Marsh, 13 April 1937, AO, RG 7 VIII-1, vol. 31, case files of Industrial Standards Officers; 'Hanover-Spiesz,' Strikes and Lockouts, NAC, RG 27 385 37(72)

39 Hanover Post, 14 Oct. 1937, 4 Nov. 1937; 'Hanover-Spiesz October 1937,' Strikes and Lockouts, NAC, RG 27 392 37(307)

40 'Hanover, Peppler – April 1937' Strikes and Lockouts, NAC, RG 27 385 37(73); Fred Ehmke to Marsh, 24 April 1937, AO, RG 7 VIII-1, vol. 31, case files of Industrial Standards officers; Alan Lang, Gordon Peck, HIHP

41 'Hanover – Peppler Brothers, October 1938' Strikes and Lockouts, NAC, RG 27 399, 38–167; National Furniture Workers' Union, Canadian Labour Congress, NAC, MG 28 I 103, vol. 63; Hanover Post, 4 Nov. 1938

42 Manpower survey cards, 1940, QUA, KP 4

43 The records of the congress locals in the furniture industry are in Canadian Labour Congress, NAC, MG 28 I 103, vol. 63; the suggestion that the IWA organized the furniture industry in Ontario is in Radforth, Bushworkers and Bosses.

44 Manpower survey cards, 1940, QUA, KP 4

45 Lembcke and Tattam, One Union in Wood, chap. 5; Thomas Reis, HIHP; R.E.

Hallman to Mackenzie King, 21 June 1947 in IWA General, 1945–47, Canadian Labour Congress, NAC, MG 28 I 103 47
46 'Hanover 1947,' Department of Labour, NAC, RG 27, vol. 455, file 104; HP, 12 and 19 June 1947, 3, 10, 17, and 24 July 1947, 14 Aug. 1947; Karl Ruhl, Edward Wilson, Jacob Krueger, Ed Fischer, Clarence Helwig, HIHP

CONCLUSION

1 Allen, *New Minorities*, 29; Morokvasic, 'Why women emigrate?' 133; Ewen, *Immigrant Women*, chap. 3
2 Macdonald, 'Ellen Silk,' 82–5; Lindstron-Best, '"I Won't Be a Slave,"' 36, 44–50; Barber, 'Sunny Ontario,'; Phizacklea, noting the work of Mirjana Morokvasic in her introduction to *One Way Ticket*, 7
3 Charlotte Macdonald in 'Ellen Silk,' 81, argues for closer study of communities characterized by sex imbalances. Burke, 'Cornish Diaspora,' 57–75, describes such communities.
4 See, for example, Lenie Brouwer and Marijke Priester, 'Living in Between: Turkish Women in Their Homeland and the Netherlands,' in Phizacklea, *One Way Ticket*.
5 This phrase, the title of a book by Arthur Copping (London 1911), was frequently used by Penmans emigrants remembering their encounters with recruiters.
6 Catherine Hakim, *Occupational Segregation: A Comparative Study of the Degree and Pattern of Differentiation between Men's and Women's Work in Britain, the United States and Other Countries*, Research Paper no. 9 (London 1979); Armstrong and Armstrong, *Double Ghetto*; Pat Armstrong, *Labour Pains* (Toronto 1985). There is an extended critique of the theoretical literature on the sexual division of labour, based upon the comparison between Paris and the English east midlands in Parr, 'Disaggregating the Sexual Division.'
7 An exception to this pattern is Valerie Kincade Oppenheimer, 'Sex-Labelling of Jobs.' Community and industry variations in access to skilled occupations are clear in Aldrich and Albelda, 'Determinants,' 332–5. Alison M. Scott makes this same point about the ways in which aggregation disguises the 'full extent and function of gender segregation' in her 'Industrialization,' 157.
8 Mary Stephenson, 'Women's Wages and Job Segregation,' in Richard Edwards, Michael Reich, and David Gordon, eds, *Labor Market Segmentation* (Lexington, Mass., 1973) 245–6. Ruth Milkman has made such distinc-

tions in her longitudinal study of male unionists and sex segregation in the u.s. case, 'Organising the Sexual Division of Labor.'

9 See Meg Luxton, *More Than a Labour of Love*, 27.

10 Peter Doeringer and Michael Piore, *Internal Labor Markets and Manpower Analysis* (Lexington, Mass. 1971); Barron and Norris, 'Sexual Divisions'

11 *Hanover Post*, 4, 18, and 25 April and 2 May 1901; Elizabeth Bloomfield, 'City-Building Processes in Berlin/Kitchener and Waterloo, 1870–1930,' doctoral dissertation, University of Guelph, 1981; Bloomfield, 'Municipal Bonusing of Industry: The Legislative Framework in Ontario to 1930,' *Urban History Review* 9:3 (Feb. 1981)

12 Rathbone, *Family Allowances*, 9. Stearns, *Be a Man!* 77; McIntosh, 'The Welfare State,' 157; Barrett and McIntosh, 'Family Wage,' 57; Grevet, *Besoins populaires*; Stacey, 'Gender and Stratification,' 224

13 See Gershuny's argument concerning the 'great transformation' in *Social Innovation*, 38–41, and 34 and 121 on the differing qualities of household and non-household; similarly Pahl, 'Employment,' 4–6, 16. On the tendency to analyse all production, including domestic work, in terms of and through its relationship to market production see Connell, 'Crisis Tendencies,' 35–7.

14 Connell, 'Crisis Tendencies,' 36 (emphasis in original)

15 Crompton and Mann, eds, *Gender and Stratification*, especially their 'Introduction,' 5, and the contribution by Stacey, 'Gender and Stratification,' 222; see also Connell, 'Crisis Tendencies,' 48.

16 Fox, ed., *Hidden in the Household*

17 The quote is offered in an ironic voice by McIntosh in 'State and the Oppression of Women,' 284.

18 Davidoff, 'Separation of Home and Work?' 66, and Delphy and Leonard, 'Class Analysis,' 66

19 Jane Humphries, 'Class Struggle and the Persistence of the Working Class Family,' *Cambridge Journal of Economics* (Sept. 1977) and 'Protective Legislation, the Capitalist State and Working Class Men: The Case of the 1842 Mines Regulation Act,' *Feminist Review* 7 (Spring 1981)

20 Abella, *Nationalism*; Morton and Copp, *Working People*

■ Picture credits

Paris Historical Society, Paris, Ontario: Seamers (19), Immigrant women (28), English mill families (31), Penmans mill, 1912 (37), Strikers, 1907 (49), Male knitters (68), Young girl and supervisor (79), Workers in the back garden (82)

Queen's University Archives, Kingston, Ontario: Examples of Knechtel furniture (130), Knechtel main plant, 1901 (132), Hanover Band (138), Three generations of Knechtels (143), A finisher (181), Lane cedar chest (210)

Brantford Expositor, Brantford, Ontario: Higgins and Williams (107), Picket line along Willow Street (112), Morrison (115), Burtch (116)

Archives of Ontario: Penmarvian ACC 9868 Env B-1 (38), Postcard view of Paris ACC 9869 Env B-7 (41), Penmans mills, 1949 ACC 9508-11708-3 (93)

Canadian Museum of Civilization: Knechtel employees outside the plant 74-17940 (151), Men and boys from the machine room 74-17937 (167), Spindle carvers 74-17938 (174)

Canadian Woodworker and Furniture Manufacturer: 'Life's Little Jests,' July 1926 issue, p. 39 (156), Operating a shaper, October 1937 issue, p. 12 (171), Running a planer, August 1925 issue, p. 21 (175)

National Film Board *Strike in Town*, stock footage: A router operator (173), Cabinet-makers (178)

National Archives of Canada: A stockinger NAC 74600 (61)

Fraser's Canadian Textile, Apparel and Fur Trade Directory, 1950–1, p. 21: Hand-powered circular knitting machine (63)

Nottingham Local Studies Library: Female knitters (65)

Edmonton Art Gallery, Edmonton, Alberta: 'Summer Evening in Town, Hanover,' Version V, 20 July 1942 (192)

■ Select bibliography

Abella, Irving *Nationalism, Communism and Canadian Labour* Toronto 1973

Acheson, T.W. 'The Social Origins of Canadian Industrialism: A Study of the Structure of Entrepreneurship,' PH D diss., University of Toronto 1971

Adamson, Nancy, Linda Briskin, and Margaret McPhail *Feminist Organizing for Change* Toronto 1988

Aldrich Mark and Randy Albelda, 'Determinants of Working Women's Wages during the Progressive Era,' *Explorations in Economic History* 17 (Oct. 1980) 323–41

Alexander, Sally *Women's Work in Nineteenth Century London* London 1983

Allen, Sheila *New Minorities, Old Conflicts* New York 1971

American Society of Mechanical Engineers *Transactions*

Armstrong, Pat and Hugh Armstrong *The Double Ghetto* Toronto 1975

Armstrong, Peter 'If It's Only Women It Doesn't Matter So Much.' In Jackie West, ed. *Work, Women and the Labour Market* London 1982

Baker, Elizabeth Faulkner *Technology and Women's Work* New York 1964

Barber, Marilyn 'Sunny Ontario for British Girls.' In Burnet *Looking Into My Sister's Eyes*

Barrett, Michele and Mary McIntosh 'The "Family Wage": Some Problems for Socialists and Feminists,' *Capital and Class* 11 (1980) 51–72

Barron, R.D. and G.M. Norris, 'Sexual Divisions and the Dual Labour Market.' In Diana Barker and Sheila Allen, eds, *Dependence and Exploitation in Work and Marriage* London 1976

Bassler, Gerhard P. 'The "Inundation" of British North America with "the Refuse of Foreign Pauperism": Assisted Emigration from Southern Germany in the Mid-19th Century,' *German-Canadian Yearbook* 4 (1978) 93–113

Beatty, Bess 'Textile Labor in the North Carolina Piedmont: Mill Owner Images and Mill Worker Response, 1830–1900,' *Labor History* 25 (Fall 1984) 485–503

Becker, Gary *The Economics of Discrimination* Chicago 1971

Bendix, Rienhard *Work and Authority in Industry* Berkeley 1974

Benson, John *The Working-Class in England 1875–1914* London 1985

Bird, Michael 'Cabinetmaker and Weaver: Friedrich Ploether,' *Canadian Collector* 15 (May/June 1980) 28–32

– 'When Furniture Becomes Folk Art: Neustadt Cabinetmaker John P. Klempp 1857–1914,' *Canadian Collector* 17 (Sept./Oct. 1982) 47–50

Bliss, Michael *A Living Profit: Studies in the Social History of Canadian Business* Toronto 1974

Bradley, Harriet 'Technological Change, Management Strategies, and the Development of Gender-Based Job Segregation in the Labour Process.' In D. Knights and H. Willmott, eds, *Gender and the Labour Process* Aldershot 1986

Braun, Rudolf 'The Impact of Cottage Industry on an Agricultural Population.' In David Landes, ed. *The Rise of Capitalism* New York Macmillan 1966

Braverman, Harry *Labor and Monopoly Capital* New York 1974

Brown, R.K., J.M. Kirby, and K.F. Taylor, 'The Employment of Married Women and the Supervisory Role,' *British Journal of Industrial Relations* 2 (1964) 23–41

Burke, Gill 'The Cornish Diaspora of the Nineteenth Century.' In Marks and Richardson *International Labour Migration*

Burnet, Jean, ed. *Looking Into My Sister's Eyes: An Exploration in Women's History* Toronto 1986

Cameron, Ardis 'Bread and Roses Revisited: Women's Culture and Working-Class Activism in the Lawrence Strike of 1912.' In Milkman *Women, Work and Protest*

Canada, Royal Commission on Price Spreads *Report* 1935

Canada, Royal Commission on the Textile Industry *Report* 1938

Canadian Furniture World

Canadian Textile Journal

Canadian Woodworker and Furniture Manufacturer

Chandler, Alfred *The Visible Hand: The Managerial Revolution in American Business* Cambridge, Mass. 1977

Christie, Robert C. 'The Development of the Furniture Industry in the Southwestern Ontario Furniture Manufacturing Region,' MA thesis, University of Western Ontario 1964

Church, Roy A. *Economic and Social Change in a Midland Town: Nottingham 1815–1900* London 1966

Cockburn, Cynthia *Brothers* London 1983

Cohen, Marjorie Griffin *Women's Work, Markets and Economic Development in Nineteenth-Century Ontario* Toronto 1988

Connell, R.W. 'Crisis Tendencies in Patriarchy and Capitalism.' In *Which Way Is Up?* Sydney 1983

– *Gender and Power: Society, the Person and Sexual Politics* Oxford 1987

Connelly, Patricia and Martha MacDonald 'Women's Work: Domestic and Wage Labour in a Nova Scotia Community,' *Studies in Political Economy* 10 (Winter 1983) 45–72

Cookingham, Mary 'Working after Child-Bearing in Modern America,' *Journal of Interdisciplinary History* 14 (Spring 1984) 773–92

Cooper, R.T. 'The Growth and Development of the Furniture Industry in Ontario,' *Ontario Economic Review* 2:12 (1965) 3–6

Corrigan, Philip 'Feudal Relics or Capitalist Monuments? Notes on the Sociology of Unfree Labour,' *Sociology* 11 (1977) 435–63

Costello, Cynthia 'Working Women's Consciousness: Traditional or Oppositional?' In Groneman and Norton, eds, *'To Toil'*

Cox, Mark 'The Limits of Reform: Industrial Regulation and Management Rights in Ontario, 1930–7,' *Canadian Historical Review* 68 (Dec. 1987) 552–75

Crompton, Rosemary and Michael Mann, eds. *Gender and Stratification* Cambridge 1986

Cuthbert-Brandt, Gail ' "Weaving It Together": Life Cycle and the Industrial Experience of Female Cotton Workers in Quebec, 1910–1950,' *Labour / Le Travail* 7 (Spring 1981) 113–26

Dankert, Clyde 'Autobiography,' typescript, Dartmouth College Library

Davidson, T. Arthur *New History of the County of Grey* Owen Sound 1972

Delphy, Christine and Diana Leonard 'Class Analysis, Gender Analysis and the Family.' In Crompton and Mann, eds. *Gender and Stratification*

Demos, John 'The Changing Faces of Fatherhood: A New Exploration in American Family History.' In Stanley Cath et al. *Father and Child: Developmental and Clinical Perspectives* Boston 1982

Diefendorf, Jeffry M. *Businessmen and Politics in the Rhineland 1789–1834* Princeton 1980

Dublin, Thomas *Women at Work: The Transformation of Work and Community* New York 1979

Earl, Polly Anne 'Craftsmen and Machines: The Nineteenth Century Furniture Industry.' In Ian M.G. Quimby and Polly Anne Earl, eds. *Technical Innovation and the Decorative Arts* Charlottesville 1974

Edgeworth, F.Y. 'Equal Pay to Men and Women for Equal Work,' *Economic Journal* 128:32 (Dec. 1922) 431–457

Edwards, Richard *Contested Terrain: The Transformation of the Workplace in the Twentieth Century* New York 1979

Eisenstein, Sarah *Give Us Bread, but Give Us Roses* London and New York 1983

Elder, Glen *Children of the Great Depression* Chicago 1974

English, John and Kenneth McLaughlin *Kitchener: An Illustrated History* Waterloo 1983

Epp, Frank H. *Mennonites in Canada 1786–1920* Toronto 1974

Erickson, Charlotte *British Industrialists: Steel and Hosiery 1850–1950* Cambridge 1959

- 'Why Did Contract Labour Not Work in the Nineteenth Century United States?' In Marks and Richardson, *International Labour Migration*

Ettema, Michael J. 'Technological Innovation and Design Economics in Furniture Manufacture,' *Winterthur Portfolio* 16: 2/3 (Summer/Autumn 1981) 197–224

Ewen, Elizabeth *Immigrant Women in the Land of Dollars* New York 1985

Fawcett, Millicent 'Equal Pay for Equal Work,' *Economic Journal* 28:109 (March 1918) 1–6

Felkin, William *History of Machine Wrought Hosiery and Lace Manufactures* London [1867] 1967

Forster, Ben 'Finding the Right Size: Markets and Competition in Mid and Late Nineteenth Century Ontario.' In Roger Hall et al., eds. *Patterns of the Past* Toronto 1988

Fox, Bonnie 'Conceptualizing "Patriarchy,"' *Canadian Review of Sociology and Anthropology* 25 (May 1988) 163–82

- ed. *Hidden in the Household* Toronto 1980

Frankel, Linda 'Southern Textile Women: Generations of Survival and Struggle.' In Karen Brodkin Sacks and Dorothy Remy, eds. *My Troubles Are Going To Have Trouble With Me*. New Brunswick, NJ 1984

Fraundorf, Martha N. 'The Labor Force Participation of Turn-of-the Century Married Women,' *Journal of Economic History* 39 (June 1979) 401–17

Furniture Journal

Gagnon, John H. 'Physical Strength, Once of Significance.' In Joseph H. Pleck and Jack Sawyer, eds. *Men and Masculinity* Englewood Cliffs, NJ 1974

Galenson, Walter *The United Brotherhood of Carpenters* Cambridge, Mass. 1983

Game, Ann and Rosemary Pringle *Gender at Work* London 1984

Gershuny, Jonathon et al. *Social Innovation and the Division of Labour* Oxford 1983

Gittins, Diana *Fair Sex: Family Size and Structure, 1900–1939* London 1982

- 'Inside and Outside Marriage,' *Feminist Review* 14 (1983) 22–34

- 'Marital Status, Work and Kinship, 1850–1930.' In Jane Lewis, ed. *Labour and Love* Oxford 1986

Goldin, Claudia 'The Work and Wages of Single Women, 1870–1920,' *Journal of Economic History* 40 (March 1980) 81–8

Grant, Christine 'Patterns of Growth and Change in the Furniture Industry in Ontario, 1850–1881,' MA thesis, Carleton University 1988

Gray, Stan 'Sharing the Shop Floor.' In Greta Hofmann Nemiroff, ed. *Women and Men* Toronto 1987

Grevet, Patrice *Besoins populaires et financement public* Paris 1976

Grieco, Margaret and Richard Whipp, 'Women and the Workplace: Gender and Control in the Labour Process.' In David Knights and Hugh Willmott, eds. *Gender and the Labour Process* Aldershot 1986

Groneman, Carol and Mary Beth Norton, eds. *'To Toil the Livelong Day': America's Women at Work, 1780–1980* Ithaca 1987

Gulvin, Clifford *The Scottish Hosiery and Knitwear Industry 1680–1980* Edinburgh 1984

Gurnham, Richard *A History of the Trade Union Movement in the Hosiery and Knitwear Industry, 1776–1976* Leicester 1976

Haber, Samuel *Efficiency and Uplift* Chicago 1964

Hahn, Josephine *Home of My Youth, Hanover* Hanover 1947

Hall, Jacquelyn Dowd 'Disorderly Women,' *Journal of American History* 73 (Sept. 1986) 354–82

Hall, Jacquelyn Dowd et al. *Like a Family: The Making of a Southern Cotton Mill World* Chapel Hill 1987

Hallock, James Lindsey 'Woodworking Machinery in Nineteenth Century America,' MA thesis, University of Delaware 1978

Hanover Post

Hartmann, Heidi 'Capitalism, Patriarchy and Job Segregation by Sex.' In Zillah R. Eisenstein, ed. *Capitalist Patriarchy and the Case for Socialist Feminism* New York 1979

Hounshell, David A. *From the American System to Mass Production 1880–1932* Baltimore, 1984

Hosiery Trade Journal

Hoxie, Robert Franklin *Scientific Management and Labor* New York 1915

Humphries, Jane 'Women: Scapegoats and Safety Valves in the Great Depression,' *Review of Radical Political Economy* 8:1 (1976)

Inoki, Takenori 'Aspects of German Peasant Emigration to the United States 1815–1914,' PHD dissertation Massachusetts Institute of Technology 1974

Jameson, Elizabeth 'Imperfect Unions: Class and Gender in Cripple Creek, 1894–1904.' In Milton Cantor and Bruce Laurie, eds. *Class, Sex and the Woman Worker* Westport, Conn. 1977

Johnson, George *Carl Schaefer*. Toronto 1986

Johnson, Laura *Unemployed Fathers: Parenting in a Changing Labour Market.* Toronto 1985

Jones, Beverly W. 'Race, Sex and Class: Black Female Tobacco Workers in Durham, North Carolina, 1920–40, and the Development of Consciousness,' *Feminist Studies* 10 (Fall 1984) 441–51

Joyce, Patrick 'Labour, Capital and Compromise: A Response to Richard Price,' *Social History* 9 (Jan. 1984) 70–1

Kakar, Sudhir *Frederick Taylor: A Study in Personality and Innovation* Cambridge, Mass. 1970

Kalbfleisch, Herbert Karl *The History of the Pioneer German Language Press in Ontario, 1835–1918* Toronto 1968

Kessler-Harris, Alice 'Problems of Coalition-Building: Women and Trade Unions in the 1920s.' In Milkman, *Women, Work and Protest*

– 'Independence and Virtue in the Lives of Wage-Earning Women: the United States, 1870–1930.' In Judith Friedlander et al., eds. *Women in Culture and Politics* Bloomington 1986

Klaczynska, Barbara 'Why Women Work,' *Labor History* 17 (Winter 1976) 73–87

Knowles, Margaret Anne 'Beyond Domesticity: A Study of Female Factory Employment in Paris Ontario, 1881–1891,' MA thesis, Queen's University 1987

Koltun, L.A. *The Cabinetmaker's Art in Ontario c 1850–1900* Ottawa 1979

Komarovsky, Mirra *The Unemployed Man and His Family* New York 1940

Land, Hilary 'The Family Wage,' *Feminist Review* 6 (1980) 55–77

Lazonick, William 'Industrial Relations and Technological Change: The Case of the Self-Acting Mule,' *Cambridge Journal of Economics* 3 (Sept. 1979) 231–62

Lehmann, Heinz *The German Canadians 1750–1937* (trsl. Gerhard P. Bassler) St John's 1986

Leibbrandt, Gottlieb *Little Paradise: The Saga of the German Canadians of Waterloo County, Ontario 1880–1975* Kitchener 1980

Lembcke, Jerry and William M. Tattam, *One Union in Wood* Madiera, BC 1984

Liddington, Jill 'Working-Class Women in the North West,' pt 2 *Oral History* 5 (Autumn 1977) 31–45

Lindstrom-Best, Varpu '"I Won't Be A Slave."' In Burnet, ed. *Looking into My Sister's Eyes*

Lown, Judy 'Not So Much a Factory, More a Form of Patriarchy: Gender and Class during Industrialisation.' In Eva Gamarniko et al. *Class Gender and Work* London 1983

– 'Gender and Class During Industrialisation,' PH D dissertation, University of Essex 1983

Lummis, Trevor 'The Historical Dimension of Fatherhood: A Case Study 1890–

1914.' In Lorna McKee and Margaret O'Brien, eds. *The Father Figure* London 1982

Luxton, Meg *More Than a Labour of Love* Toronto 1980

Macdonald, Charlotte J. 'Ellen Silk and Her Sisters: Female Emigration to the New World.' In London Feminist History Group *The Sexual Dynamics of History* London 1983

McHugh, Cathy Louise 'The Family Labor System in the Southern Cotton Textile Industry, 1880–1915,' PHD dissertation, Stanford University 1981

McIntosh, Mary 'The State and the Oppression of Women.' In A. Kuhn and A. Wolpe *Feminism and Materialism* London 1978

– 'The Welfare State and the Needs of the Dependent Family.' In Sandra Burman *Fit Work for Women* London 1979

McIntyre, W. John 'Arms across the Border: Trade in Chairs and Chair Parts between the United States and Upper Canada.' In Kenneth Ames, ed. *Victorian Furniture* Philadelphia 1983

– 'From Workshop to Factory: The Furnituremaker,' *Material History Bulletin* 19 (1984) 25–35

Mahon, Riane *The Politics of Industrial Restructuring* Toronto 1984

Marks, Shula and Peter Richardson *International Labour Migration Historical Perspectives* London 1984

May, Martha 'Bread Before Roses: American Workingmen, Labour Unions and the Family Wage.' In Milkman, ed. *Women, Work and Protest Mechanical Engineering*

Milkman, Ruth 'Organising the Sexual Division of Labor: Historical Perspectives on 'Women's Work' and the American Labor Movement,' *Socialist Register* 10, 1, no. 49 (1980) 95–150

– *Women, Work and Protest: A Century of Women's Labor History* Boston 1985

Modell, John and Tamara K. Hareven 'Urbanization and the Malleable Household: An Examination of Boarding and Lodging in American Families.' In Tamara K. Hareven, ed. *Family and Kin in Urban Communities, 1700–1930* New York 1977

Morokvasic, Mirjana 'Why Women Emigrate? Towards Understanding of the Sex-Selectivity of the Migratory Movements of Labour,' *Studi Emigrazione* 20 (June 1983) 132–40

Morton, Desmond 'Sir William Otter and Internment Operations in Canada during the First World War,' *Canadian Historical Review* 55 (March 1974) 32–58

Morton, Desmond with Terry Copp, *Working People* Ottawa 1980

Nash, June 'Resistance as Protest: Women in the Struggle of Bolivian Tin-Mining Communities.' In Ruby Rohrlich-Leavitt, ed. *Women Cross-Culturally* The Hague 1975

Nadworthy, Milton J. *Scientific Management and the Unions 1900–1932* Cambridge, Mass. 1955

Newbury, Colin 'The Imperial Workplace: Competitive and Coerced Labour Systems in New Zealand, Northern Nigeria and Australian New Guinea.' In Marks and Richardson, eds. *International Labour Migration*

Noble, David *America by Design: Science, Technology and the Rise of Corporate Capitalism* New York 1977

Oliver, J.L. *The Development and Structure of the Furniture Industry* Oxford 1966

Oppenheimer, Valerie Kincade 'The Sex Labelling of Jobs,' *Industrial Relations* 7 (May 1968) 214–34

Osterud, Nancy Grey 'Gender Divisions and the Organisation of Work in the Leicester Hosiery Industry.' In Angela V. John, ed. *Unequal Opportunity* Oxford 1986

Pahl, R.E. 'Employment, Work and the Domestic Division of Labour,' *International Journal of Urban and Regional Research* 4:1 (March 1980) 1–19

Parr, Joy 'Hired Men: Ontario Agricultural Wage Labour in Historical Perspective,' *Labour / Le Travail* 15 (Spring 1985) 91–103

– 'Disaggregating the Sexual Division of Labour: A Transatlantic Case Study,' *Comparative Studies in Society and History* 30 (July 1988) 511–33

Paris (Ont.) Star

Penmans Limited *What Penmans Offer You* Paris 1923

Perrot, Michelle 'The Three Ages of Industrial Discipline in Nineteenth-Century France,' In John Merriman, ed. *Consciousness and Class Experience in Nineteenth-Century Europe* New York 1979

Phillips, William H. 'Southern Textile Mill Villages on the Eve of World War II: The Courtenay Mill of South Carolina,' *Journal of Economic History* 45:2 (1985) 269–75

Phizacklea, Annie, ed. *One Way Ticket* London 1983

Poovey, Mary *Uneven Developments: The Ideological Work of Gender in Mid-Victorian England* Chicago 1988

– 'Feminism and Deconstruction,' *Feminist Studies* 14 (Spring 1988) 51–66

Pye, David *The Nature and Art of Workmanship* Cambridge 1968

Radforth, Ian *Bushworkers and Bosses* Toronto 1987

Rathbone, Eleanor *Family Allowances* London [1924] 1949

Reid, Donald 'Industrial Paternalism: Discourse and Practice in Nineteenth-Century French Mining and Metallurgy,' *Comparative Studies in Society and History* 27 (Oct. 1985) 579–607

Reville, Douglas *History of the County of Brant*, vol. II Brantford 1920

Richards, J. *A Treatise on the Construction and Operation of Wood-Working Machines* London 1872

Riley, Denise *'Am I That Name?' Feminism and the Category of 'Women' in History* Minneapolis 1988

Robertson, Norman *History of the County of Bruce* Toronto 1906

Rose, Sonya 'Gender Segregation in the Transition to the Factory: The English Hosiery Industry 1850–1910,' *Feminist Studies* 13 (Spring 1987) 163–84

Ross, Ellen ' "Not the Sort That Would Sit on the Doorstep": Respectability in Pre-World War I London Neighborhoods,' *International Labor and Working Class History* 27 (Spring 1985) 39–59

Ross, Ellen and Rayna Rapp 'Sex and Society: A Research Note from Social History and Anthropology.' In Ann Snitow, et al., eds. *Powers of Desire: The Politics of Sexuality* New York 1983

Rotella, Elyce J. 'Women's Labor Force Participation and the Decline of the Family Economy in the US,' *Explorations in Economic History* 17 (1980) 95–117

Rubery, Jill 'Structured Labour Markets, Worker Organisation and Low Pay.' In Alice Amusden, ed. *The Economics of Women and Work* Harmondsworth 1980

Santos, Michael W. 'Community and Communism: the 1928 New Bedford Textile Strike,' *Labor History* 26 (Spring 1985) 230–49

Saxonhouse, Gary R. 'Country Girls and Communication Among Competitors in the Japanese Cotton-Spinning Industry,' In Hugh Patrick, ed. *Japanese Industrialization and Social Consequences* Berkeley 1976

Saxonhouse, Gary and Gavin Wright 'Two Forms of Cheap Labor in Textile History,' *Research in Economic History*, Supp. 3 (1984) 3–31

Scott, Alison M. 'Industrialisation, gender segregation and stratification theory.' In Crompton and Mann, *Gender and Stratification*

Scott, Joan *Gender and the Politics of History* New York 1988

Scott, Joan W. 'Deconstructing Equality-versus-Difference: or, the Uses of Post-Structuralist Theory for Feminism,' *Feminist Studies* 14 (Spring 1988) 33–50

Smith, David M. *The Industrial Archaeology of the East Midlands* London 1966

Smith, Donald A. *At the Forks of the Grand*, vol. I Paris 1949

– 'The 1949 Strike against Penmans Ltd. of Paris,' typescript, Paris Public Library 1981

– *At The Forks of the Grand*, vol. II Paris 1982

Southgate, H. Jane 'An Examination of the Position of the Mennonites in Ontario Under the Jurisdiction of the Military Service Act, 1917,' MA thesis, Wilfrid Laurier University, 1976

Stacey, Margaret 'Gender and Stratification: One Central Issue or Two?' In Crompton and Mann *Gender and Stratification*

Stearns, Peter *Be a Man! Males in Modern Society* New York 1979

Stouffer, Samuel A. and Paul F. Lazarfield *Research Memorandum on the Family in the Depression* New York 1937

Strom, Sharon Hartman 'Challenging "Woman's Place": Feminism, the Left and Industrial Unionism in the 1930s,' *Feminist Studies* 9 (Summer 1983) 359–85

Talbott, Elizabeth Page 'The Philadelphia Furniture Industry 1850–1880,' PH D dissertation, University of Pennsylvania 1980

Taylor, G.W. *Significant Post-War Changes in the Full Fashioned Hosiery Industry* Philadelphia 1929

– *The Full Fashioned Hosiery Worker, His Changing Economic Status,* Wharton School, Industrial Relations Publication #13, Philadelphia 1939

Taylor, Sandra 'The Effect of Marriage on Job Possibilities for Women and the Ideology of the Home: Nottingham 1890–1930,' *Oral History* 5 (1977) 46–61

Thompson, Thea *Edwardian Childhoods* London 1981

Tilly, Louise 'Paths of Proletarianization: Organisation of Production, Sexual Division of Labor, and Women's Collective Action,' *Signs* 7 (Winter 1981) 400–17

Tsurumi, Patricia 'Female Textile Workers and the Failure of Early Trade Unionism in Japan,' *History Workshop Journal* 18 (Autumn 1984) 3–27

Turbin, Carole 'Beyond Conventional Wisdom: Women's Wage Work, Household Economic Contribution and Labor Activisim in a Mid-Nineteenth Century Working-Class Community.' In Groneman and Norton *'To Toil'*

United Kingdom, Royal Commission on Labour, 1892, c. 6795–VI, vol. XXXVI, pt 2, Second report of the minutes of evidence, group c, vol. II; c. 6795-III, pt 3

– Board of Trade, *Working Party on the Hosiery Report,* 1946

Walker, Mack *Germany and the Emigration 1816–1885* Cambridge, Mass. 1964

– *German Home Towns 1648–1871* Ithaca 1971

Wandersee, Winnifred *Women's Work and Family Values 1920–1940.* Cambridge, Mass. 1981

Wells, F.A. *The British Hosiery Trade* London 1935

– "Nottingham Industries.' In J.D. Chambers, ed. *A Century of Nottingham History* Nottingham 1952

– *The British Hosiery and Knitwear Industry* Newton Abbott 1972

Westwood, Sallie *All Day Every Day: Factory and Family in the Making of Women's Lives* London 1984

Williams, Glen *Not for Export: Toward a Political Economy of Canada's Arrested Industrialization* Toronto 1983

Wilson, Barbara ed. *Ontario and the First World War 1914–1918* Toronto 1977

Young, A.M. *The History of the County of Brant, Ontario* Toronto 1883

◼ Index